John White Chadwick

The Power of an Endless Life

And Other Sermons

John White Chadwick

The Power of an Endless Life
And Other Sermons

ISBN/EAN: 9783337033385

Printed in Europe, USA, Canada, Australia, Japan

Cover: Foto ©Lupo / pixelio.de

More available books at **www.hansebooks.com**

THE

POWER OF AN ENDLESS LIFE

AND OTHER SERMONS

BY

JOHN W. CHADWICK

AUTHOR OF "THE BIBLE OF TO-DAY," "THE FAITH OF REASON," "THE MAN
JESUS," "A BOOK OF POEMS," ETC., ETC.

FIFTEENTH AND SIXTEENTH SERIES.

BOSTON
GEO. H. ELLIS, 141 FRANKLIN STREET
1891

CONTENTS

Green Pastures and Still Waters.

THERE is no other portion of the Old Testament that has so much endeared itself to human hearts as the Twenty-third Psalm,—"The Lord is my shepherd." The dearest verse in this, no doubt, is that which runs, "Though I walk through the valley of the shadow of death, I will fear no evil"; but hardly less dear to many, tired and overborne with life's intolerable day, and to many others, however generally happy, in special moods of weariness and languor and disgust, the verse which reads, "He maketh me to lie down in green pastures: he leadeth me beside the still waters." The psalm in its entirety is one that sentiment has yielded, or will yield, to criticism very grudgingly. If sentiment could keep one word, one psalm, and but one, for the Shepherd King, it would be this, its tender words a reminiscence of the time his father's tinkling sheep were round about him in gray dawns and purple eves, and beneath the stars that gave to him another psalm, or when the noon lay broad and clear on the Judean hills. But the psalm loses nothing of its beauty when its Davidic authorship is successfully impeached. The freebooter David never could have written it; only a poet into whose heart had passed the beauty of the shepherd's life and grown into a symbol there of eternal guidance and almighty love and care.

The summer which is ending as we gather here to-day * has been such a summer of green pastures as few of us had ever seen before. No wonder that my neighbor's cows have straggled home with dripping udders from the luxurious feast. I went back to Marblehead, and the Lower Division,

* September 22, 1889, first Sunday after the Vacation.

of which I still know every nook and hollow better than I
know our city streets, and which often I have seen so
parched that hardly one green blade of grass was visible,
was like an emerald for greenness, high and low; while our
Chesterfield pastures kept till the September drouth, which
lately has been drowned, as fresh as when I saw them on my
arrival in the early summer.   One doesn't have to be a silly
sheep or munching cow to know what pasture-sweetness is.
A man may know as much.   The punishment of Nebuchad-
nezzar — who was turned out to grass, you will remember
— has always seemed to me a punishment that was as little
disagreeable as any could well be.   I count that man unfortunate who has never had a pasture-side to his experience in
boyhood, youth, or prime.   But there are pastures and pastures, as there are deacons and deacons, in the proverbial
phrase.   Those of my boyhood and my youth were, for the
most part, of the simplest elements, the thick, hard turf
almost unbroken save by the ledges cropping from it all
about, whose harvest of crinkled lichens I used to gather
with remorseless hands,— since bitterly accused,— for my
grandmother to steep into a golden dye.   But Salem Great
Pasture was another matter,— resinously sweet with savin
and with bay, with ground-pine tangle for our feet, and
blackberries, low and high, to teach me self-denial if I
would, robbing my mouth to heap the shining pail.   If I
should try to tell you of the beauty of our mountain pastures, I should want a language charactered with moss and
fern, with trees and shrubs more numerous than our common alphabet, with glorious outlooks on the hills beyond
the river.   They are beautiful with such rare and glorious
beauty that the poet or the painter who could put them
into picture or into song would do for them what the presence of Emerson (as Father Taylor said) would do for hell,
— I don't mean " change the temperature," but " cause the
emigration to set that way."

   If this has been a summer of green pastures, it has not
been a summer of still waters.   The floods have been abroad.

Even the streams, which generally are all peace and quietness, have had their sense of seasonable times confounded by the rush of many waters, as if the March or April torrents had come back. For once, our clearest stream, whose pure transparency no ordinary rain can mar, has worn a troubled look. The river into which it flows, whose general habit is so leisurely that it seems loath to leave our narrow valleys for the wider down below, has sometimes gone hurrying forward with a maddened rush, as if woe were unto it until it mixed itself with the embracing sea. There are who find a pleasure in this haste and tumult which the more quiet moods of brook and stream and river do not yield. Indeed, for almost every one there is a minimum of quietness beyond which the aspect does not please. There are those who have not thought so highly of the Concord River — the Musketaquit,— since they read that Hawthorne lived for several months upon its bank without discovering which way it was flowing. As between the Dead Branch of the Westfield, as its sluggish motion names it in rude farmers' poetry, and the East Branch, which is all hurry, ripple, laughter, flash, and gleam, I am sure all lovers of the brooks and streams would choose the latter for companionship and praise. Indeed, I should not wonder if the still waters that the Psalmist had in mind were not such as were glass or satin to the eye, but such as by their pleasant murmur made the silence audible. Such, at any rate, are the still waters that I love the best; and, in " a land of streams," with such I have had many an hour of gentle satisfaction as the summer wore away. Those that chatter loudest with their gleaming pebbles are not without their " cool dark pools and crinkling bends," to which " leaf-shade and sun-fleck lend their tremulous, sweet vicissitude." Stillness is a relative term. The noisiest of my mountain streams is generally still enough compared with rushing torrents and the roar of smiting seas.

The thing I greatly feared has come upon me. It was that I should clean forget the spiritual signification of my text in its suggestions of material things.   But, then, I dearly love material things.   They are a lovely manifestation of the Eternal God.   And they are the trellises on which Memory and Association climb, to which they cling, and fling out their fragrant blossoms, sometimes wet with tears.   Where one sees only water, trees, and stones, another sees the form and faces of long-lost or living friends, renews the rapture of moments long since added to the irrevocable past, and listens to unutterable words.   Nevertheless, I have not forgotten utterly the spiritual significance of the green pastures and still waters of my text.   They stand in men's imagination generally for the freshness and the quietness of life, and there-fore stand for that which many consciously desire, and many others sorely need.   They are no adequate symbols of the general tendency and aspiration of our modern life.   Fresh-ness and quietness are not the qualities of life which men so much desire as stir and noise, excitement, push, adventure, the fierce competitions of the forum and the market-place. Still waters!   No; but waters fretted by a thousand busy keels, on which the ocean steamers break each other's records, with much shifting satisfaction to their friends; waters that the mill-race captures in its snare and the great turbines tear to shreds and tatters; waters that convert in a few years the green pastures and the greener meadows of Holyoke and many a rival city into a huge aggregation of factories very wonderful to see.   Green pastures!   Yes; if they can fatten sheep and oxen for the shambles at a paying rate.   The arrival of his *Herald* is the brightest spot in many a summer tourist's day, the quotations of the Produce and the Stock Exchange more interesting than any sight of woods or waters.   The city *fauna* appeals to him as does not the country *flora*.   He likes the bulls and bears.   A major part of all who leave the city· for the seashore and the mountains in the summer go in search of some more keen excitement than their city life affords.   That they go for rest is a delusion by which no one is deluded for an hour.   If all this is not a railing accusation, if it is substantial truth and soberness, said I not truly that freshness and quietness are not the qualities of life that men desire? that the Psalmist's picture is no proper symbol of the things they crave and seek? Still waters, forsooth! Give them the foaming cataract, give them Niagara's headlong rush and thunderous roar.

Yes, you will say, perhaps; and it is the kind of people you have been describing that has kept the world alive and going. Of this kind was Columbus, the four hundredth anniversary of whose great discovery is now drawing near. Of this kind were the Cabots and Vespucci, and the other great discoverers of our coasts and inland waters. Of this kind were the colonists who followed in their wake, who made themselves homes and set up churches and school-houses and the town house and the State from Maine to Florida. Of this kind were the men who began shouting, "Westward Ho!" in the hill towns of Massachusetts almost before they had been fairly rescued from the wilderness, when the West was the Mohawk Valley one hundred years ago, and ten years later the Valley of the Ohio, and so on. Of this kind have been the men who have made America the wealthiest country in the world; who have set up their mills on every river and their manufactories in every town; who have covered the continent with a network of railroads from Maine to California, and from the St. Lawrence to the Gulf, with a finer network of telegraphic and telephonic wires. All this I hasten to admit, not grudgingly, but cordially, doubting a little, possibly, whether all our vast material successes and exploits are not sometimes a little overrated, whether life is as much happier as it is more complex and elaborate than formerly, whether a great majority of the people who go steaming about on our railways hadn't better stay at home, whether the sacrifice of a stable life and of a past of sweet and fair associations is made good by the colossal bigness and the infinite rawness of our Western civilization.

But let this civilization be construed as favorably as you please, as favorably, let us say, as Mr. Andrew Carnegie

has construed it in his "Triumphant Democracy," which
tears down our national eagle and puts a proud and jubilant
rooster in his place, and, when we have had our fill of admiration, the defects of our excellences will still remain. It
will still be true that we generally live a hot and restless life;
that in our character and in our literature there is less and
less of that meditative quality of which we find so much in
earlier times; that, like the camp-followers that straggle
on the skirts of an advancing army, there straggles on the
skirts of our Triumphant Democracy a host of brain dis-
eases, nervous ailments, and the like, in which young and
old are mingled in promiscuous incompetency and regret.
The hot and dusty ways of traffic, the struggle for position,
wealth, and power, the fierce and blinding competitions of the
market and exchange, make something of quiet and freshening necessary for our modern life. I speak of average things.
If there are not more people who rust out than wear out,
there are enough who do it even in these stirring times. A
life can be too quiet and recluse for mind or heart. The
country byways as well as the city highways have their own
insanities. They have also plenty of men who imagine they
have discovered some great thing in science or philosophy
or theology, which possibly and probably is the commonplace or the exploded nonsense of the universities and
schools and towns. That is an admirable phrase of Bacon
about our friends " tossing our thought for us," as if it were
a kind of hay that would mat down and spoil if it were not
well shaken up, so that it could have the sun and wind to
play through it and dry and sweeten it. A life unsocial
and recluse breeds infinite vagary, self-conceit, and whim.
Society is the maker of men : its most strenuous activities
are the makers of the best possible men ; but the more
strenuous the activities, the more the need of green pastures and still waters, of quiet and of freshening, to build
up the tissue worn and wasted by the stress and strain of
various toil and fret.

You will see at once that I have something more in mind

than any justification of my own summer idleness, or any plea for making general such a term. There are few of you the strain of whose habitual work is not much greater than my own, and who do not need more perfect annual or periodic rest from it than I from mine. But you dare not drop the reins so long. You are convinced that everything, as in Emerson's vision of Uriel, would slide to confusion if you did. Happy are they who are of a more easy disposition, who can deal less sternly with themselves, and find their wisdom and their courage justified by the event ; who can go riding off into the free without black care upon the crupper, ready and able to abandon themselves to the pure objectivity of natural sights and sounds. Green pastures and still waters in their most literal significance have wondrous healing in them for tired bodies and tired brains; if the still waters are alive with pretty speckled trout, perhaps so much the better.

> " We bring
> Our insect miseries to the rocks,
> And the whole flight, with folded wing,
> Vanish and end their murmuring,—
> Vanish beside these dedicated blocks
> Which who can tell what mason laid."

But what we really need, whatever we may have or miss of special opportunity for physical and mental rehabilitation, is a more restful habit in our average life. · Without such a habit, hardly can we avail ourselves of any special opportunity. The young man in the novel who described himself as "resting like fury" spoke that the thoughts of many hearts might be revealed. The resting oftentimes is just as restless, just as furious, as the work, and rests about as little. What we all need is what Ruskin says (quite incorrectly, I imagine) all rivers have,— a quiet, loitering side in our most busy ways, an element of quietness and freshening, something to which we can have habitual recourse, a refuge from the turmoil and the strife, some happy alternation of the struggle for existence with life's easy pleasantness and careless joy.

"Give me a thought," said Richter, "that I may refresh myself"; and in that memorable saying is a hint of one of the sure ways of quietness and freshening that is at the command of all, even the most humbly circumstanced. It was not always so. Time was when books were for the few; but the rise and progress of the art of printing have made them almost as common as the sunlight and the air. This is the most obvious contribution of practical science to the intellectual and moral life of man. What travels can we go upon by land or sea that give to us such new and wide horizons as do many books, as do the greatest most efficiently? In Keats's sonnet upon reading Chapman's "Homer," you have my thought transfigured and made perfect for all time : —

> "Much have I travelled in the realms of gold,
> And many goodly states and kingdoms seen;
> Round many western islands have I been
> Which bards in fealty to Apollo hold.
> Oft of one wide expanse had I been told
> That deep-browed Homer ruled as his demesne.
> Yet did I never breathe its pure serene
> Till I heard Chapman speak out loud and bold:
> Then felt I like some watcher of the skies
> When a new planet swims into his ken;
> Or like stout Cortes when with eagle eyes
> He stared at the Pacific — and all his men
> Looked at each other with a wild surmise —
> Silent, upon a peak in Darien."

It is always the great masters of literature who have for us the most of quiet and of freshening. They speak to us out of a great, deep calm ; and they imbue us with their spirit. It is not the newest books that are the freshest, or that have in them the most of freshening for us. Homer is fresher than the morning paper; Shakspere, than the latest novel. The intellectual vice of our immediate time, and one which is sometimes aggravated by our summer schools, Chautauqua circles, and similar appliances, in the exercise of their abundant good, is a mere touch and go acquaintance with a hundred different things, when what is needed for the steadiness and poise and calm of life is a close and intimate and deep acquaintance with a few things, it may be only one, whatever pleasant smattering there may be beside. One must snuggle down into the heart of Shakspere or Homer or Dante, like a bee into a flower, to get their utmost sweetness. And by this I do not mean that one must go to them in that microscopic fashion which is so common in our day, with the intention and resolve to find wonders everywhere and to magnify the grossest faults, as some have done with Browning, into excellences and virtues of the highest rank. There is healthy and unhealthy admiration. I have met this summer with a very rare and beautiful example of the healthy kind in Edward Fitzgerald, whose translation of Omar Khayyám is as likely to become a classic as any original poem of our time. No man ever allowed himself more freely the delights of admiration ; and yet with his most eager and abiding admirations there always went a certain noble energy of resistance and appeal. He always reserved the right to find fault, though it were with Æschylus or Sophocles or Shakspere ; and he exercised it with a manly freedom.

There could not be a greater fallacy than that all literature, as such, is freshening and quieting. It is written in George Eliot's " Spanish Gypsy," — I quote the thought, but not the phrase,—

> " There are winds that blow
> That set men's knives to stabbing, which else
> Were honest knives, cutting but garlic."

There are books which have a like disquieting effect. They blow upon our spirits like the mistral or sirocco, chilling us to the bone or parching lips and tongue with dusty heat. There are men of unquestionable power and genius, like Balzac, for example, who have this effect on us. But, happily, the men who quiet us and freshen us are not few or hard to find. Their name is legion. Scott is one of them, and Montaigne another, and Charles Lamb, forever blessed, is another. The poets of the century have been strong in this respect. What worlds of peace and quietness

there are in Wordsworth and in Matthew Arnold, father and
son after the spirit, for those who know them well! while of
Tennyson it might be said, as he has written of the Lotos-
eaters' land : —

> " There is sweet music here that softer falls
> Than petals from blown roses on the grass,
> Or night-dews on still waters between walls
> Of shadowy granite in a gleaming pass;
> Music that gentlier on the spirit lies
> Than tired eyelids upon tired eyes ;
> Music that brings sweet sleep down from the blissful skies."

We of America have been wonderfully fortunate in having
had upon the very threshold of our national literature a
band of poets who have had to a remarkable degree the gift
of freshening. They have all stirred us when we needed to
be stirred. Equally they have stilled us when we needed to
be stilled. I would place on Longfellow's monument, when
it is erected on the Cambridge meadows, the most precious
Latin words I know,— *Datur hora quieta,* "The hour of quiet
is given"; for I believe that he has given to the English-
speaking world of America and England and her islands of
the sea more sanely, sweetly, nobly quiet hours than any
other poet of our time.

If the literature of the immediate present is for the most
part disquieted in vain, there are oases in the desert. We
come upon one of them whenever we come upon one of
Sarah Orne Jewett's books or stories. We came upon one
this summer, called " Passe Rose." A very notable one was
Dr. Edward Emerson's book, called " Emerson in Concord."
Another was "The Story of William and Lucy Smith." Indeed, I do not know of any books that are more freshening
and quieting than the biographies of noble persons, especially of such as kept a heart of peace, like Lydia Maria
Child, without the least withdrawal from the time's all-press-
ing need, or of such as have been held steady and firm, as
Darwin was, by the life-long attraction of a great idea.

It goes almost without the saying that there is no garden
of refreshment like a well-ordered, beautiful, and happy home.

And a home may be all this without any great expenditure of money. You and I have known many that were all this in very narrow quarters, with the plainest clothes and fare. The faith that children are a blessing from the Lord is not yet wholly dead upon the earth; and there are fathers and mothers who from their children's faces, from their soft, dimpled flesh, from their tight-folding arms, get more of music, poetry, and art than others sometimes get from all the concerts, libraries, and galleries that minister to the æsthetic mind. At the same time, happy are they who can enhance the natural sweetness of domestic life by gifts of art and song. I often wonder if the members of a family in which there is a common love of music know what a bond of sympathy and mutual fidelity they have that others lack. Better, much better, than nothing was the old-time singing over of the Sunday hymns between the daylight and the dark. Old Milton's organ was a noble refuge from the sorrows and the disappointments of his life. One who can play the organ or at will can listen to the playing of a friend ought to be able to put his cares and worries underneath his feet more easily than other men.

That word, "a friend," suggests another source of quietness and freshening. Happy are they for whom these are incarnate in some man or woman whom they can call by this exalted name. It is not every friend, not every good and true and noble friend, who can dispense these gifts. And it is better so. Faithful are the wounds of a friend, the spurs that prick the sides of our intent when we are dull of sense and heart and will. Thank heaven for friends who rouse us, shake us, pull us to our feet, and drag us forth with them to do some task of human service greatly needing to be done! But these are not sufficient for our every need. There are times when we are hot and tired and overborne with many troubles and anxieties; and then happy are we, if we can go to those whose strength is to sit still, who have the gift of peace. The chances are they will be men and women who have had much care and trouble of their

own, but whose calamities at length are overpast, whom the
spirit has brought out into a large place, who have attained
to a serene and holy trust in God and in the good of life, and
who impart this trust to others, not in the shape of maxims
neatly turned, but as an influence which cannot be detected
or escaped.

"We live by admiration, hope, and love," as Wordsworth
said, no doubt, but by memory no less. There are no
greener pastures, there are no stiller waters, than those
which we call blessed memory and happy recollection. Especially, as we face the sunset and go down the western
slope of life, these things have more and more to do with
our peace, our satisfaction, and our joy. But the application
of this preaching is less to the old than to the young, to all
those who have it in their power to touch their own or others'
lives to finer issues. We are like those who plant in youth
trees under which they will sit down in age in the soft
shadows, or which shall shield their children from the glare
of noon. Alas that oftentimes the trees we plant are of
some Upas sort, whose exudations poison all the air of recollection with intolerable regret ! " Rejoice, O young man, in
thy youth, . . . and walk in the ways of thine heart, and in
the sight of thine eyes ; but know thou, that for all these
things God will bring thee into judgment." Not after death,
but in the solemn court of age, in which Memory brings the
accusation, and Conscience is the awful judge.

"Always young for Liberty," said Dr. Channing, when his
elation over the French Revolution of 1830 made his heart
leap up, to the astonishment of his more sober friends. The
implication of the story is that there is nothing better than
devotion to an ideal of character or work, than consecration
to some great and glorious end of truth or righteousness, to
keep alive the heart of youth, to breed perennial freshness
in the mind and heart. "Still nursing the unconquerable
hope, still clutching the inviolable shade with a free onward
impulse," — that is the history of thousands whose old age
has been or is more fresh and hale than the dull, sheepish,

or besotted years of some who still account themselves and are accounted young. Love, live for, work for, the undying truth and good,—that is the way to nourish an undying vigor of the heart; these are the waters of the Fountain of Eternal Youth.

"Give me a thought, that I may refresh myself." The words come back again, to give the benediction of the hour. There are thoughts of God, of Duty, of Immortality, of the wonder and the glory of the world as science has revealed it to our apprehension and imagination, that will calm and freshen every hour they visit with their beauty, grace, and power. They are the thoughts of God and Duty and Immortality, of the wonder and the glory of the world, which are less and less each day the possession of a few, or of a sect despised and feared. They are spreading far and wide. They are becoming vital and operative parts of the faith of Christianity in all its forms, and of religion under every name it wears. If life is meant for blessing, peace, and joy, then it would seem as if these thoughts must correspond to certain great realities; for the blessing, peace, and joy they give are quite unspeakable. There are no greener pastures, there are no stiller waters, no high, unutterable facts which these figures of speech but faintly body forth, more staying, strengthening, satisfying to the soul than these have been and are. And I am well persuaded that our deeper thought will only tend to give them a more adequate foundation, that they may lift a more complete and soaring beauty up from man to God.

There is a river the streams whereof make glad the City of God, the Holy Place of the Tabernacle of the Most High. So wrote the Psalmist almost thirty centuries ago. The words are different: the thought, for us, is much the same as that which a Psalmist of the modern world, one whom we knew and reverenced and loved, embodied in his sweetest song. Both words and thought came back to me one day this summer,—one of the most precious in the count of many happy days. It was the day I spent in Concord, preaching there in the old church which could ring out

such a history from its belfry tower if it could tell the half
that it has seen and known. And in the afternoon I went
to Sleepy Hollow, as they call it, where the dead are lying.
Hawthorne and Thoreau, Alcott and Emerson, are lying
there; and, hard by, Gerrish, my noble friend, our soldier
Barrett, too, and Ripley Bartlett, ever quaint and kind, and
little Laura Schaumberg, named on her low white monument by the pet name which love had given her when she
was all alive. And so the love of greatness and the greatness of love both spoke there to my heart, both spoke of immortality; and I was sure that what they said was true.
And at the quiet ending of the day I sat beside a friendly
door where I could see the river which gave Emerson the
form and symbol of his thought, just as he thought about
it when he wrote; for all its meadowy banks were overflowing with the "inundation sweet" of the great August rains.
And this is what he wrote,— a poem of that River of God
which flows for every man who lives, yet ever best for those
who have an eye to watch the motion of its never-ending
stream : —

> " Thy summer voice, Musketaquit,
>   Repeats the music of the rain;
> But sweeter rivers pulsing flit
>   Through thee, as thou through Concord Plain.

> " Thou in thy narrow banks art pent:
>   The stream I love unbounded goes
> Through flood and sea and firmament;
>   Through light, through life, it forward flows.

> " I see the inundation sweet,
>   I hear the spending of the stream,
> Through years, through men, through nature fleet,
>   Through love and thought, through power and dream.

> " Musketaquit, a goblin strong,
>   Of shard and flint makes jewels gay;
> They lose their grief who hear his song,
>   And where he winds is the day of day.

> " So forth and brighter fares my stream,—
>   Who drink it shall not thirst again;
> No darkness stains its equal gleam,
>   And ages drop in it like rain."

ENDURING HARDNESS.

FROM first to last, I doubt not, there have been many sermons written on the text which occurs in the second letter to Timothy, "Endure hardness as a good soldier." Especially in times that tried men's souls, when armies have been mustering and meeting in the shock of battle, not only the chaplain on the tented field or in the populous hospital, but almost equally the preacher who has remained behind with the men too old for service, the women and the children, must have found this venerable injunction dilating with a new significance, and fairly thrusting itself upon him as the only one entirely suitable to the exigencies of the hour. The text is one which, for its best interpretation, needs the flash of musketry, the blaze of burning villages, the light that shines in eyes that seek in vain for faces they will never see again. We should expect some soldier or some soldier's wife to write the best sermon ever written on this text. And, if we could collect and then collate all of the sermons ever preached upon it, I doubt not that the fact would be precisely what we should expect. Certainly, the best sermon I have ever seen upon it was written by a soldier's wife,— Mrs. Juliana Horatia Ewing. It is called "The Story of a Short Life." It isn't nominally a sermon, and, come to think of it, the text "Endure hardness as a good soldier" is not placed at its beginning and is nowhere quoted, if I recollect aright. No matter! The story is a sermon, and it is upon this text. This text is everywhere in and between the lines, as those of you who know it and love it as I do will bear me witness.

I am sure that many of you, and I trust the most of you, have read "The Story of a Short Life." Those of you who have done so will not, I trust, be sorry to recall its various charm for a few moments, while I indicate its character to the end that I may show what a pathetic and impressive sermon it is upon its silent text, " Endure hardness as a good soldier."

The short life was that of a little English boy whose stately home was very near the soldiers' camp at Aldershot, in which he took so great an interest that he was always wanting to go there and see what was going on. The barrackmaster was his uncle; and this fact, together with his father's local dignity, made him a lad of privilege with officers and men. He was not by any means a faultless child, but self-willed and obstinate; obstreperous, too, when crossed in any inclination. So, when there was to be some great parade of all the regiments in camp and others from elsewhere, he would take his dog with him in the carriage, and he would stand up on the seat to salute the soldiers, and he would hold the dog in his arms; and the dog didn't like the situation, nor did the horses; and they pranced, and Leonard fell, and from that day until his death he was a miserable little cripple, seldom without pain. But he wasn't made a perfect little saint at once by his misfortune. He was made more irritable than ever, and more impatient and exacting. Meantime, his interest in the soldiers had not abated in the least. Here was the mother's opportunity. She had wanted him to be a soldier, and was proud of his insistence that he would be one. Now this could never be; but was she willing that her son should be a coward because it was not the trumpet's sound that summoned him to fortitude? If she could not gird on his sword, might she not help him to carry his cross with martial courage? So she appealed to him to endure his hardness like a good soldier, with heroic patience, without complaint or murmuring. And the boy responded to her call. Henceforth, his aim was to translate his life, its pain and weariness and deprivation, into the terms of soldier-discipline and the vicissitudes of a soldier's life. His days in bed should be his days in hospital; his aching back should be a soldier's wound; when it was worst, a soldier's night upon the field of battle, wounded and faint, with sleepless eyes impatient for the break of day. And, though it didn't seem to him that anything that he could ever do or bear would merit a Victoria Cross, he did his best to keep from anger and complaint, until one day his soul went up to heaven from a narrow bed in the real barracks, cheered by a soldier's song that he had always loved to hear, but which this time he heard not to the end.

And now, perhaps, all of you are saying that the experience of this martial child was so peculiar and unique that really it does not afford a basis of experience for men and women generally, who are called upon to suffer and endure. It isn't every suffering child that has an Aldershot at hand to furnish his imagination with materials into which he can translate the pains and deprivations that are incidental to his marred and wasting life. It isn't every suffering child that has the stuff in him that vibrates to the music of the spirit-stirring drum, the ear-piercing fife, and all the various pride and pomp and circumstance of glorious war. Moreover, there was something childish in the boy's translation of his experience into the terms of camp and battle, wounds and hospital, which would be quite impossible for grown men and women, little given to sentiment or imagination, but with no immunity from the trials, calamities, and tragedies that enter so considerably into the majority of human lives. I have no desire to break, or even palliate, the force of these objections. Nevertheless, "The Story of a Short Life" is one which has significance for all men and women and for all boys and girls who have been "made subject to weakness," to deprivation, to dull or agonizing pain. Such cannot read it without sudden access of encouragement and strength. It is a story which all maimed and suffering folk might learn by heart with great advantage. It is a story which the most robust and fortunate of men, if they have any sensibility, cannot read without rebuke and inward shaming on account of their own fretfulness and impatience, simply because they have not everything they want.

Meantime, the only hardness in this world is not that of

physical pain and its concomitants of weariness and deprivation. It is only here and there, at rarest intervals, that we
meet a man or woman who appears to bear a charmed life.
And these do not invariably present an enviable appearance
to those who, measured by the usual standards, are miserable in comparison with them. There is something tiresome
in the sleekness of their dull complacency. It is like the
oily calm which sometimes settles on the sea, till we could
cry " Blow, winds, and crack your cheeks ! " Come anything
to break up this monotony ! Better the hurricane than this !

But there is little danger that the majority of men and
women will be afflicted by this " happiness of the greasy
kind," as John Morley aptly phrases it. " Man is born
to trouble as the sparks fly upward." The ancient text
is not discredited by the lapsing centuries. Even to hide
and sneak in cowardly avoidance of the burdens and anxieties that are incidental to the common life of men is no
security against them soon or late. But if one chooses
from the start to be a man among men, to do his part in the
world's work, to take his place in its wide ranks and march
with it to victory, then from the start he must make up his
mind to endure hardness like a good soldier, and that there
will be plenty of it for him to endure. Either to imagine
that there is very little hardness in the world, or that what
there is can be avoided by judicious management, is a profound mistake which the mistaken will discover soon or late.
The contingencies of business enterprise, of the professions
and the arts men freely choose for livelihood or in some
passion for ideal good, of political conscience followed in
despite of hostile taunts and friendliest admonitions, of
rational conviction openly confessed, let come what will, of
misunderstanding and misrepresentation on the part of those
whom we have loved and trusted most, of health that may be
broken, of labor that may change from a delight to utter
weariness, either because too long pursued or because cis-
terns that were full now gape at every stave, of love that asks
too little or too much, of death that makes a void where all

was pleasantness,— all these contingencies are natural and inevitable to the lives of men who are not only in the world, but of the world. And they are contingencies that involve hardness of an amount and bitterness which it is scarcely possible to overrate. Hardly a day goes by and we do not come upon some fresh example of the all-pervading tendency. What ruinous business losses and catastrophes overtaking men who seemed secure against all ruin or mishap, and whose honor was as stainless as the just fallen snow! What tragedies of physical suffering develop under the most genial superficial areas of apparent health! What seeds of later sorrow in the red rose of present happiness, whose breath intoxicates the heart! What cruelty of friendship which from a single act, mistaken or misunderstood, deduces an opinion counter to all the testimony of "a cloud of witnesses"! What bolts that sometimes fall out of the clearest sky to blast men's happiness! What dreadfulness of vacancy and silence where there has been dearest presence and voices that were sweeter than all music in our ears! Such are a few of the contingencies which life involves. Such is a little of the various and immeasurable hardness which in the natural course of personal and social evolution we are called on to endure.

And to endure it like good soldiers is the mark of our high calling. And how do good soldiers endure hardness? Much of the hardness that is incidental to a soldier's life they bear with genial merriment. They make a joke of it. "We'll buy out gloves *together!*" cry the cavalry riders who have lost each a hand in battle. Now, the great military memoirs of Grant and Sherman, and scores of regimental histories and volumes of personal reminiscence written by those who knew our soldiers well in camp and hospital, are studded thick with stories of this sort,— stories whose burden is the skill and genius that our soldiers had for finding something humorous and laughable in their discomforts and their deprivations, and even in their sufferings and wounds, as where the soldier whose cheek had been shot away, explain-

ing why he hadn't asked for what he wanted sooner, said
he "hadn't the face to do it." Goethe's mother said that,
when Wolfgang had a trouble, he made a song out of it, and
got over it. And so the good soldier of a hundred wars and
histories, when he has had a hardship, has made a joke out
of it; and, if he hasn't got *over* it, has got *under* it in such
a way that he can carry it without being bent or broken.
How many noxious swamps and barren wildernesses have
blossomed with this flower of noble gayety! And this soldier quality has often had abundant exercise under conditions outwardly very different from those of the camp, the
march, the hospital. True, there is hardness where it finds
no place. But there is much which can be taken far too
seriously and solemnly; and it often,— yes, it generally
is. Not only the hardness of life's small annoyances, which
are not few, but that of deprivations and discomforts which
are entailed by serious reverses of financial fortune, can be
so met that it will somewhat relax its frown if it does not
break into a laugh. The theme is stale. So many books
and chapters have been written about the capital good times
that people have who are in straitened circumstances that one
is sometimes tempted to believe that straitened circumstances
are the only ones to be desired. And, doubtless, there is
much exaggeration of the fact. There are straitened circumstances which are no such pretty play as those the novelists
report. The smile that they elicit must be very grim
indeed. But to extract sunshine from cucumbers is by no
means an impossible feat; and there are circumstances which
are as little promising which can be made to yield a bright-
ening gleam. The story-tellers have not in the least exaggerated (they could hardly do it if they tried) the pleasure
and the satisfaction that can be derived from conquering
difficulties, from making much out of a little. When things
were at their worst in the Crimea, a gentleman of my acquaintance visited the French and English camps. They
were equally bad off for food and comforts of all kinds.
But the Frenchmen had contrived to find a humorous point

of view. The *ménu* was elaborate, though every dish was fundamentally the same. A similar difference is continually reappearing in life's every-day affairs.

" Winds blow and waters roll
Strength to the brave and power and deity;
Yet in themselves are nothing."

How does a good soldier endure hardness? He endures it patiently and cheerfully. And then it often happens that some comrade or some fellow-soldier has been hurt more cruelly, or has been longer wasting on his narrow cot; and he asks himself, " Shall I not bear my suffering or waiting as sturdily, as uncomplainingly, as he is bearing his ? " And it often happens, in the circle of life's various experience, that, however sorely wounded we may be,— pierced through the heart, perhaps, but somehow living on,— or whatever grievous waiting we must do, we do not have to look far off to find some friend or fellow-mortal hurt more dreadfully than we, or caught in a more dreary calm, who, nevertheless, does not curse God, nor even wish to die, but bears his burden with a patient voice and heart, and is for us a high example and a holy invitation which we cannot choose but heed. Who of us has not known, at one time or another, some man or woman robbed of everything that makes life pleasant to one's soul, stripped of all comforts and delights, pent up, it may be, in some narrow room, year after year, and yet ever keeping up a brave and cheerful heart ? Who of us, by such soldierly endurance, has not many times been made ashamed of his own fretfulness and murmuring on account of hardness which, in comparison with this patient sufferer's, was not to be named or thought of — was an inappreciable speck ?

How does a good soldier endure hardness ? He endures it as a necessary and inevitable concomitant of his service as a soldier. It was what he expected when he accepted his commission as an officer or when he enlisted in the ranks. And so the man who in any sphere of life endures hardness as a good soldier endures it as a necessary and inevitable concomitant of his service as a man. Hardship is what such service always has entailed. By sneaks and cowards it may be avoided; but by a good man, who is a man good for something always, as little as by a good soldier can it be avoided. This is the very heart of what I have to say this morning: that the first prerequisite for enduring hardness as a good soldier endures it is to expect hardness as a good soldier expects it, and therefore, instead of always trying to avoid it, to meet it squarely when it comes. This was the gospel preached by Romola to Lillo, as he leaned his chin upon her knee, and she pushed his hair back from his brow: "There are so many things wrong and difficult in the world that no man can be great — he can hardly keep himself from wickedness — unless he gives up thinking much about pleasures or rewards, and gets strength to endure what is hard and painful." "And remember," she went on, "if you were to choose something lower, and make it the rule of your life to seek your own pleasure and escape from what is disagreeable, calamity might come just the same, and it would be calamity falling upon a base mind, which is the one form of sorrow which has no balm in it, and that may well make a man say, 'It would have been better for me if I had never been born.'

"I will tell you something," she continued. She had taken Lillo's cheeks between her hands and his young eyes were meeting hers. "There was a man to whom I was very near, so that I could see a great deal of his life, who made almost every one fond of him, for he was young and clever and beautiful, and his manners to all were gentle and kind. I believe, when I first knew him, he never thought of doing anything cruel or base. But because he tried to slip away from everything that was unpleasant, and cared for nothing so much as his own safety, he came at last to commit some of the basest deeds, such as make men infamous. He denied his father and left him to misery; he betrayed every trust that was reposed in him, that he might keep himself safe and get rich and prosperous. Yet calamity overtook

him." I have quoted this before, and I shall again without
apology; for in all literature I do not know of any other
passage that is for me so full and packed with ethical significance as this. Here is the lesson and here is the example.
It was her own husband Tito whom Romola described to
Lillo, his own child unlawfully. But there are Titos everywhere; we meet them every day. We should some of us
confess, if we were honest, that we are a little Tito-ish ourselves, and perhaps not a very little. We, too, like to avoid
hardness, to slip away from that which is disagreeable, and
we *know* that, so far as we have been subject to this disposition, it has unmanned us ; it has made us capable of mean and
selfish things ; it has prevented us from doing things which
we have known right well ought to have been done ; it has
betrayed us into doing things that we know equally well
ought not to have been done, till there is no health in us in
comparison with what there might have been if we had made
up our minds at first to endure hardness like good soldiers,
and had made good that high resolve by constant courage in
the face of various opposition.

It is to save ourselves from being Titos and from Tito's
fate — "calamity falling on a base mind," I mean, and not
his getting strangled on the river's bank, which was a matter
of comparatively small importance,— it is to save ourselves
from such intolerable things that we must be self-resolved to
endure hardness like good soldiers, and, to the end that we
may so endure it, to expect it, and a great deal of it, so that
when it comes we may not be surprised or found unguarded.
The disposition to avoid hardness, to slip away from everything that is disagreeable or unpleasant, is for the majority
such an active disposition, and its indulgence adds so to its
strength, that for its conquest and subordination it is necessary that there should be the clearest-eyed intelligence that
hardness is inevitable to the doing and the bearing of a
man's part in the world, and the steadiest resolve to meet it,
when it comes, fairly and squarely. But for a man to do this
in the first flush of his maturity, when for the first time he

recognizes himself as the master of his own actions, responsible for their quality of good or ill,— for him to see that hardness is inevitable, and resolve to grapple with it when it comes, is no such easy matter, if it is even possible, unless in childhood and in youth there has been some preparation for this attitude and spirit, some education of the will that shall have braced it for the choice of the right things, however hard, let the wrong things, however pleasant, plead as sweetly as they may.

But how often is the fostering and training of the child — the boy or girl, the youth or maid — of such a character in these last days that it affords this needful preparation, that it insures this education of the will ? Seldom, and almost never where there is any choice of means. Where strictest personal and domestic economies are enforced by straitened circumstances, there, given personal honesty, you will have self-denial, and you will have children told and taught that for them to gratify their every wish is quite impossible. And, when children are so told and taught, they have a preparation for the necessary hardness of their maturer years, they have an education of the will that may enable them to resist the allurements of things soft and and pleasant when things hard and painful are the things they manifestly ought to choose. But average the fostering and training of the children and the youth now growing up to shape the future of America, and consider what it has been for a quarter of a century, and the wonder is that the Titos are not much more numerous than they are ; the wonder is how many of the grown men next coming to the stage will be or can be anything but Titos, anything but selfish, pleasure-seeking men, slipping away from everything that is unpleasant, disagreeable, or hard. The poor vie with the rich in their unconscious tendency to impress their children with the idea that they must have everything they want, do everything they wish. The self-indulgence of men and women is only the inevitable corollary of the insane indulgence of them when they were children by their parents. Why should they not have everything they want, do everything they wish, when they always have had all they wanted, when they always have done everything that they have wished to do? The complicity with our peculators and defaulters does not stop short of the indulgence of the nursery and the home-life of children generally. The man must have all the yachts he wants, all the country-houses, all the fast horses, because as a child he had every plaything that he wanted, because as a boy his every wish was law. And so the wife who drives her husband into reckless speculation or dishonest practices, to keep up her splendor of attire, might often trace her shame and his back to a mother's fond indulgence of her every wish. Our educational methods often have a similar operation. Better the old curriculum forever than that the elective system in our colleges should mean that our young men should only study what they like. It is the studying and the mastering of what they do *not* like that gives them manly fibre and strengthens them for the resistances and struggles that no man can avoid without dishonor. What above all things we need and ought to teach our children is that to endure hardness is the inevitable concomitant of all decent manhood and all noble womanhood, and that, to endure it like good soldiers, they must begin betimes to give up many pleasant and agreeable things and to do many that are hard and painful. Moreover, let us teach them that it is not by any soft avoidance of the disagreeable and painful that they can attain to power and use or to the purest joy. Danger and difficulty have always been the nurses of men's higher faculties. The biographies worth reading are seldom those of pampered darlings, but they are those of bantlings who have been cast upon the rocks. "A thing of beauty is a joy forever," and how many things of beauty the architectural genius of Henry Hobson Richardson has left behind him in America, which are as certain as anything can be to inspire a multitude of others from the hands of men touched by his spirit! And the chances are that, but for the ruin of his paternal fortune, he would never have attained to self-possession, and we should never have had the joy in him which has delighted us. But his experience is only one of thousands where hardness that seemed absolutely ruinous has been as a celestial spear to force men back on their reserves of intellectual and moral power.

To avoid hardness without meanness, without pusillanimity and shame,— this, as the world goes, is hardly possible for any man or woman. The chances are that even those who cultivate a courageous expectation of things hard and painful will, as they go on, find their imagination far exceeded by the facts they will encounter in the way; for the hardness of physical pain may add to itself the hardness of broken fortunes, and these together may add unto themselves the hardness of death, making invisible for us our best beloved; and then the loss of love where life remains may add a bitterer pang, and then,— God help us ! but our hardest duty may be that which, if we do it, friends will hate us, or henceforth deny to us the fulness of their love. Let us expect these things, for they have come to many. And, if they come, let us endure them like good soldiers, as patiently and quietly, as cheerfully and sweetly as may be ; for it is by such courageous expectation and such brave endurance, and not by always being softly pleased, that we rise into the fulness of the spiritual stature and attain unto the regal carriage of the men and women who make it good for us to be alive, if haply we may be partakers of their spirit and partners of their glorious trust.

> " Ruby wine is drunk by knaves,
> Sugar spends to fatten slaves,
> Rose and vine-leaf deck buffoons ;
> Thunder-clouds are Jove's festoons,
> Dropping oft in wreaths of dread
> Lightning-knotted round his head.
> The hero is not fed on sweets :
> Daily, his own heart he eats ;
> Chambers of the great are jails,
> And head-winds right for royal sails."

THE BLESSED MOTHER.

THERE is one place in Florence which, to those who love the products and the history of art, must be forever dear. It is the Rucellai Chapel in the great Church of Santa Maria Novella. You reach it by a stairway ascending from the general level of the church to a deep recess made by the southern transept; and there, dim and remote, confronts you the Madonna of Cimabue. There it has been, so grave and calm and sweet, for six hundred and nine years. Upon what scenes, upon what men, it has looked down, through all these centuries! We may be sure that every one of the great painters of Florence has confronted it,— Michel Angelo and Raphael and Leonardo and Botticelli and Del Sarto and Fra Bartolomeo, and others,— coming from afar to see the wonder. We may be also sure that it has felt the waves of air vibrating to the stroke of Savonarola's mighty speech. Nor can we doubt that somewhere in the procession which brought the picture with flags and trumpets and acclaim from the painter's studio to the church, in 1280, there was a boy of fourteen summers, already brooding upon strange, mysterious things, whose name was Dante Alighieri. What gives this picture so much interest and importance is not, however, its great age, nor the high companionship it has enjoyed, but the fact that the historians of art have agreed to date from it the beginning of the modern art of painting. It was the first appreciable departure from the stiffness of the Byzantine school, its wooden lifelessness. I doubt if any of you would think it very beautiful. It is not so in comparison with many later works. To understand why it drove Florence wild with admiration, you must com-

pare it with the things that went before; and, even if it were
a hundred times less beautiful, as the beginning of a stream
that widened more and more till it was less a river than a
sea of glorious form and color, inundating Western Europe with its waves, it has a significance, a pathetic charm,
that may well draw you back time and again from lovelier
creations to join with the angelic company that encircle the
Madonna in doing tender homage at her feet.

But far away from Florence, and farther still from Rome,
where it was painted, there is another Madonna, which,
whether compared with what preceded or what followed it,
is equally satisfying to the spectator's mind and heart.
Nothing so beautiful had come before it. Nothing so beautiful was to come again. I need hardly tell you that I speak
of the Dresden Madonna, known as the " San Sisto," one of
the latest,* certainly the greatest work of Raphael. We
dallied with our joy. For an hour and more, two hours, we
passed from room to room of the great gallery of treasures,
feasting our eyes upon the mysteries of Rembrandt, the splendors of Titian, the tenderness of Murillo, and the beseech-
ing loveliness of Ribera's martyr saint, but studiously avoiding all the time what most we wishèd to see. We had waited
for this joy so long that we almost hated to transfer it from
the future to the past. But at length, the other wonders all
surveyed, we entered upon our inheritance. There is no
brother near the throne. The glorious picture has the room,
not large, entirely to itself. And in all my church-going in
Europe, and I was very diligent in this respect, I found
nothing so tender, reverent, and worshipful, as I found in
that presence-chamber of the Blessed Mother and her Child.
The people came .and went. They stole in with slow and
noiseless feet. They did not speak aloud. They seemed
to share the reverent silence of the saints upon the canvas
and the cherubic angels that look up in joyful awe. And
well they might. There are no words to signify the thoughts

* Painted in 1515.

and the emotions which that picture quickens in the mind and heart. It is so beautiful, it is so gentle and so pure, it is so noble and so grand, the mother's eyes dilate with such a sweet astonishment, as if they took in all the universal mystery without any doubt or fear.

Between that beginning of Cimabue and this culmination of Raphael, how many and how beautiful were the returns of art upon their common theme, the mother ever blessed ! In the churches and the galleries of Europe there are thousands of pictures of which she is the inspiration, and they are not so monotonous as an utter stranger to them might expect. The theme is one, but there are many variations. And these depend only in part upon the originality of the individual artist. Indeed, the originality of the artist was much circumscribed by the ecclesiastical tradition. But the ecclesiastical tradition was extremely rich and full. The legend of the Virgin had attained to a remarkable development. An astonishing ingenuity had added to the few texts concerning her in the New Testament a multitude of others from the New and Old. Every text that could be made to yield to her an attribute of tenderness or grace or power was forced into her service. Moreover, the apocryphal gospels of Mary and the Infancy, and so on, were as much material to serve the artist as the canonical books. We could ill afford to lose some of the Mary pictures, the subjects of which are drawn from sources wholly beyond the bounds of the New Testament; for example, Leonardo's charming picture of Mary sitting in her mother's lap. The legend had no meagre or contracted range, which, beginning with the marriage of her parents, Joachim and Anna, proceeded to her birth, to her presentation in the temple, to her marriage, to the annunciation, her relations with Elizabeth, the birth of Jesus, the coming of the Magi, the journey into Egypt and return, the journey to Jerusalem and the experience there, the crucifixion scenes and those that followed, her own death and assumption, and finally her coronation by her Son, who was at the same time her Father, and her Father who was at the same time her Son. Consider, too, that, in addition to this continuous historical legend, the artist had at his command an ideal expansion of the personality of the Blessed Mother that afforded him some of his most fertile themes. She was the *Madonna di Misericordia*, the Mother of Pity; she was the *Madonna Incoronata*, the crowned, the Queen of Heaven; she was the *Madonna Dolorosa*, the Mother full of Sorrow; she was the *Madonna Purissima*, the Immaculate Virgin, dearest of all to Spanish art as to Spanish theological imagination, attaining in Murillo to such entrancing beauty and perfection that hardly can your sternest rationalist find himself otherwise than glad that such a monstrous doctrine as that of the immaculate conception has been made an article of faith. And now, to the suggestions of the historical legend and those of the ideal personality, add the originality of the individual artist, which in the greatest masters could not be made wholly subservient to the ecclesiastical tradition, and you will see that there might be not only thousands of pictures of the Blessed Mother, but tens of thousands, as indeed there were, with little of monotony, with infinite variety of composition, character, and emotional appeal.

The great art period from the best of Cimabue to the best of Raphael was very far from being coextensive with the entire development of the legend and the dogma of the Blessed Mother. Apparently, the dogmatic development has had a longer course than the legendary. When the Council of Ephesus in 431 declared that Mary was *theotokos*, "the mother of God," it is evident that the dogma was already far advanced. But it has never ceased from growing. In the Piazza di Spagna in Rome there is an imposing column which commemorates the fact that the immaculate conception of the Virgin — *i.e.*, her absolute freedom from all taint of sin from the first moment of her existence — was made an article of faith Dec. 8, 1854. So recently! And still it may be that "the glories of Mary," as her faithful call them, have not yet come full circle. It may be that the results of the declaration of her eternal purity have not so justified the hopes of her enthusiasts as to permit them to feel that they have done enough for her. For the results expected from this declaration were magnificent. The bishop of Perpignan wrote to Pius IX., " We rely upon the hope that the most Blessed Mother, the Queen of Heaven and Mistress of the World, in return for the solemn declaration of her immaculate conception, will be pleased to dissipate all our sad and sorrowful vicissitudes and sharpest anguish, labors, and necessities, compassionating us with the most large affection of her motherly mind, as is her wont, by her most present and powerful patronage with God, and will quell and dissipate those most turbulent storms of ills wherewith the Church is tossed everywhere, and turn our sorrow into joy." The loss of his temporal sovereignty by the pope a few years after this was but a sorry realization of these liberal expectations, which were shared by all who assisted the pope in publishing the bull of 1854. It but remains to make the Virgin dogmatically what she is rhetorically and piously already,— the supreme object of worship. We are assured by one of the highest authorities of the Church that "the Mother of God herself embraces the human race with so much love and affection that, if the will of the Eternal Father were wanting, she would yet, of her own will, choose that her Son should die for men." Without pausing to remark upon the suggestion of a family difference carried by such words as these, let us go on to another illustration of the general tendency : " Since the Blessed Virgin is the Mother of God, and God is her Son, and every son is naturally inferior to his mother and her subject, and the mother is set over and superior to her son, it follows that the Blessed Virgin herself is superior to God, and God himself is her subject." These are not isolated expressions. There are many like unto them in modern Roman Catholic writings. What wonder that an ardent votary's zeal, outrunning his discretion, suggests, "Our Lady who art in heaven " instead of " Our Father," as the common form of prayer !

He is only a little in advance. The main body will come up to him before long.

If we could not have had the art representation of the Blessed Mother without the dogmatic development which has at length attained to such extravagant and monstrous exhibitions as we have seen in our own time, then those whose love of truth is dominant will say, " Better that never a Madonna picture had been painted!" But those in whom the passion for beauty is more powerful will say that *Un-wisdom is justified of her children*, that Mariolatry has done no harm that is not compensated by the satisfaction and delight which the Madonnas of Raphael and Titian and Bonifacio and Botticelli and Perugino and Murillo have secured for many generations. And more than satisfaction and delight for the æsthetic cravings of mankind has come from the most rare and beauteous creations of these artists and their glorious peers. All motherhood and all childhood have been endeared and sanctified by them. The ecclesiastical subject was the artist's opportunity for painting his ideal of womanhood, perhaps the woman that he loved, perhaps the wife and little one of his own home and heart. Only the love of little children could have inspired the painting of so many as the Italians painted, not as the Christ-child only, but as accessory in a hundred different ways. And these in turn inspired the love of children in the hearts of multitudes who came and looked on their perennial beauty. The dogmas of the miraculous birth of Jesus and of the perpetual virginity of Mary were an accusation of all ordinary marriage, an insinuation that the nunnery was more sacred than the home. "Ennobler of thy nature!" Dante hailed the Blessed Mother. But in her dogmatic aspect she degraded motherhood. The pictures of the painters were, however, stronger than the dogmas of the theologians. It was simple motherhood that the painters put into them. It was simple motherhood that youths and maidens found in them ; and many a youth, I doubt not, found in that vision of the beauty of motherhood and the loveliness of infancy a corrective for his tendencies to the monastic life. And many a maiden found in such a vision something more alluring than Saint Catharine of Siena's mystic marriage with the infant Christ.

But in having credited the exaltation of Mary, the mother of Jesus, with the most gracious aspect of the art of painting in the modern world,—and this aspect with the correction, in some measure, of the ascetic tendency, encouraged by the Marian dogma,—have we said all that can be said in justification of the legend and the dogma that have been so engrossing to the Roman Catholic consciousness for some fifteen centuries? I should hate to think that we had done so: it would speak so ill for human nature, for it to cherish for so long a legend and a dogma with so little in them of intrinsic or associative worth. And I think that we can find at least three elements of relative truth and excellence in that exaltation of the Blessed Mother which generally has been to Protestants the worst offence upon a list, which is not short, of Roman Catholic offences against man and God.

First: there had been in all the old religions some woman-goddess, men's worship of whom had been their joyful recognition of the generative force of nature, the fruitful world. This worship oftentimes assumed the grossest and most sensual forms. Nevertheless, it was entirely sound at heart. Men could not be too much impressed by the great natural miracle of birth and its attendant mysteries. They could not stand too much in awe of it. It was clearly a defect in Christianity that it made no allowance for this element. The early worship of the Virgin was a spontaneous effort to bring back under another name what had been lost. May we not owe to pagan influence the story of the mixed parentage of Jesus, so foreign to the Jewish mind, so perfectly in keeping with a hundred pagan myths of gods espousing daughters of the earth? Certain it is that the worship of Ceres glided into that of Mary by perceptible degrees, the attributes of the heathen goddess passing over to the Blessed Mother of the new religion.

Second: the defeat of Arius by Athanasius at the Council of Nicæa, which elevated Jesus to identity with God, destroyed his human quality, and made him infinitely remote from human sympathy. "Nearer, my God. to thee, nearer to thee!" is a song the hearts of men were singing for many centuries before Sarah Flower Adams put it into words. The place assigned to Mary in the Christian system after the deification of Jesus was the solution of this problem. The theologians had taken away from men their Lord, and they knew not where they had laid him,— somewhere in the abyss of uncreated being. But, if the Son was gone, the Mother was still left. They could go to her as to one touched with a feeling for their infirmities.

Third,—and here we have the most powerful influence that operated to exalt the Mother of Jesus to the place she has long occupied in the religious thought and feeling of the Roman Catholic communion,— Jesus, as time went on, was less and less the tender and compassionate person of the New Testament histories. He was more and more the awful judge, the stern avenger. As in the Protestant system Jesus stands between the sinner and the wrath of God, so in the Roman Catholic system Mary stands between the sinner and the wrath of Jesus. The situation was reflected very plainly in the art of the successive centuries. We have there at length the spectacle of a revengeful Jesus. With one hand, he points men to his wounded side, and with the other waves, "Depart from me, ye cursed, into everlasting hell." Life on such terms was insupportable. But the Mother was all tenderness and pity. She would make intercession with her Son. I cannot grudge the sad-eyed centuries the comfort yielded them by this device. I cannot but be glad that, when a pitiless Father and a pitiless Son confronted them, they fled for refuge to the Mother's warm embrace. Conceiving God and Jesus as they do, the Roman Catholics are amply justified in bringing all their highest admiration and their tenderest love to Mary's feet. The name is nothing. Though it be God, it cannot make injustice, cruelty, and implacable resentment worshipful. But love and tenderness and pity,—these are worshipful in Mary's name, or any other, though it were the devil's own.

To explain the origin of a worship, and to discover in it elements of truth and beauty, is not by any means to give in our adhesion to the legend which this worship has developed or the dogma which attempts its intellectual justification. Nor is it to affirm that for the truth and beauty associated with the worship we must go to that or miss them utterly. The legend of Mary, so meagre in the New Testament histories, is even there excessive of the bounds of critical belief; and beyond that it has not the slightest justification, while than the dogma nothing more utterly irrational and monstrous and absurd has ever been devised by men pretending to the rank of intellectual beings. The truth and beauty associated with her worship inhere more naturally and more abundantly in the Faith of Reason than in any creed or cult of Christianity still seeking supernatural support. For the Faith of Reason has brought back with scope and wonder multiplied a thousand-fold the sense of Nature's vast fecundity which enraptured men of old. It finds in this no play of manufactured energies, but the very life of God. And what one said two thousand years ago it every day makes good,—"The more thou searchest, the more thou shalt wonder." It has its solution for that problem of the "retreating god" which Christianity solved by interposing Mary between the deified Jesus and the yearning heart of man. Its solution of this problem is that not in Mary only, but in every blessed mother, the infinite God takes up his habitation; that not in Jesus only, but in every son of man, the Word becoming flesh is a divine reality.

> " He is the green in every blade,
> The health in every boy and maid;
> In yonder sunrise flag he blooms
> Above a nation's well earned tombs;
> That empty sleeve his arm contains ;

That blushing scar his life-blood drains ;
That bloodless cheek against the pane
Goes whitening all the murky street
Wi h God's own dread lest hunger gain
Upon his love's woe-burdened feet."

And here is, also, the satisfaction of rational religion for
that demand for a compassionating God which will be made
so long as man is man. The spontaneous heart of man is
wiser than the prying intellect. When the dying soldier,
lifted in the strong arms of his nurse, said, " Underneath
me are the everlasting arms," he went straight to the heart
of this whole matter. There is no human tenderness that
is not the tenderness of God. But the tenderness of God
is not exhausted by the tenderness of men and women.
For God is infinite, and all his attributes are infinite in him.

Quite other, then, the Blessed Mother of our faith from
her of the legend and the dogma of the Roman Catholic
Church. Not that we have no place of memory and praise
for her from whose deep heart Jesus of Nazareth must have
largely drawn the goodness of his own. Not that we do not
hail her blessed among women — still blessed, though the
sword that wounded him to death pierced through her own
heart also — in bearing and in rearing a man-child destined
by force of organism and environment and conscious will to
be the chief of men, to live such a life into the world that no
foolishness or baseness whatsoever of those who are accounted, by themselves, if not by all, the special guardians
of his name and fame, has been able to prevent its working
on the whole for human good. But the Blessed Mother of
our faith is not one mother out of all the mothers that have
borne and reared the saviors of the world, a countless multitude of thinkers, builders, painters, poets, ploughmen,
sailors, workers in wood and iron, with sword and trowel, in
field and mine, and anywhere and everywhere where there is
man's work and God's work to be done. Our blessed
mother,— she is every mother in the hushed and ordered
room, awe-stricken in that Real Presence of the Infinite

Word made flesh in the dear morsel at her side, the welcome child of health and mutual love. The Madonna picture has not yet been painted that is too nobly beautiful, too full of high suggestion, for the heart of any mother newly come into this peace. Is there more silent wonder in the Sistine Mother's face than in her heart? Is the Sistine Child more beautiful than hers to her? Are the saints on either hand more hushed and bowed than all should be before this mystery? Is the background, thick with angel faces, fairer than her happy dreams? Do those bright, winged creatures, from beneath, look up to her with purer passion of delight than swells her gentle breast? And, as the days and weeks and months and years go by, is she not still the blessed mother in that she can every day lay down a little of her life for the beloved child, that she can have a thousand little schemes all looking to some sweeter comfort or some greater happiness for him, that she can store his growing mind with gracious images, nourish his heart with tales of courage and devotion, quicken his conscience with examples of great duty bravely done? Thrice blessed she, if, as the years go by, the growing boy and girl prove themselves not unworthy of her patient love; if they elect the tasks and pleasures that are high and sweet; if they can trust her perfect will to do them only good, even when she denies them this or that on which their hearts are set; if they are quick to learn how they can ease the burden of her care and add some pleasure to her toilsome, if not anxious, days.

And it is here, if nowhere else, that my discourse turns clearly practical, and brings a word of earnest question home to every youthful heart. O children strong and bright, it fain would say to many where my voice can reach but few, O brave young men, O maidens pure and sweet, do you never think at night, when you cannot sleep at first for all the busy pleasures of the day,— do you never think of all the thought and care with which your mother has enshielded you from harm, has plotted for your good, has striven so to shape and to direct your life that it may be a blessing to yourself and to the world? And are you doing all that in you lies to make her noble expectation good, and all you can to cheer her anxious heart? and in all doubtful ventures do you go to her with frank confession? and do you keep for her especial joy some little portion of that store of nice consideration with which you are so lavish with your newest friends? The amount of blessed motherhood that there is in the world at any given time depends very much upon the self-asking of these simple questions, and the answers made to them in will and deed. Happy are they who ask and answer them aright before it is too late.

The blessed mother! The history of greatness knows her by a hundred and a thousand names: in the fifth century, as Monica, the mother of Augustine; in the eighteenth, as Susanna, the mother of Wesley; in the nineteenth, as Hannah, the mother of Parker. It has been Mary more than once since she of Nazareth was glad of heart. Once it was Mary Washington. The words of Parker have been made good in many instances more obviously than in that* of which he wrote: "When virtue leaps high in the public fountain, we look for the spring of nobleness, and find it far off in the dear breast of some mother who melted the snows of winter and condensed the summer's dew into fair, sweet humanity which now gladdens the face of man in all the city streets." But greatness is a rarity. Goodness is not so rare. And goodness, even more than greatness, comes from the mother's influence. So thought the ancient rabbis when they said, "Paradise is at the feet of mothers." The blessed mother! Blessed in that hers is the largest opportunity to shape the issues of the life that shapes the future of the planet in some glorious fashion.

But well I know that, as I have proceeded with my sermon, its recurring title-phrase has been more suggestive to your minds and hearts than anything that I have said. It is even possible that much that I have said has quite

* Daniel Webster.

escaped you, because you have been thinking nearly all the time of one blessed mother in particular, even your own, of whom I have not said a word. Well, I shall not regret such gravitation of your thoughts. They have been drawn thereby through larger circles than my thought has swept, where a more stainless ether beats on every side. The blessed mother! Across the busy years has come to you the vision of her bending face, the accents of her guiding voice, the memory of her thousand "little" — thank God! *not* wholly — "unremembered acts of kindness and of love." You have been asking yourselves if, while it was still yours, you knew the gift of God and prized it at its worth, and were not disobedient to the heavenly vision shining in her beloved face. And some of you have been rejoicing that she is not yet a memory only, but a living presence, and that some years, it may be many, still remain to you to make her life more blessed by your thought and care, and make it still more sure that at the parting of the ways you shall be haunted by no vain regrets for duties ill-performed and debts of love unpaid.

But for the mothers, also, there is a tonic word remaining in my mind. How often do they move about in worlds not realized! If they are not blessed, how often they have none to blame but their poor foolish selves, wasting upon a hundred frivolous aims the strength that might avail them for the building up of such a fair estate of womanhood as would not only be a blessing to themselves, but to all who came within the circle of their influence! Hail to the spirit that can find in humble tasks and narrow ways the stuff from which successful womanhood can be achieved! It is not in our stars, but in ourselves, that we are underlings. You know the story of the Venus of Melos, the noblest form of woman ever shaped in stone. The owner of "the little Melian farm," plying his humble task, came suddenly upon that wonder of the ancient world. So doubt I not that, under the hard and commonplace experience of many a wife and mother, and many a woman who is neither wife nor mother, is hidden an ideal, a possibility of womanhood, compared with which the Venus of Melos is not to be named. But the hard and commonplace experience must be worked in some high way to bring to birth this happy consummation. The Venus of Melos, her whom they once called "Love," they now call "Victory." But love is always victory when it is love and service of the best. And what she serves let every woman — mother, wife, beloved maid — demand in those who seek her love and bring to her their own, and human life will be transfigured in that hour.

> " Ah, wasteful woman, she that may
>   On her sweet self set her own price,
>   Knowing we cannot choose but pay,—
>   How has she cheapened Paradise!
>   How given for naught her priceless gift,
>   How spoiled the bread and spilled the wine,
>   Which, spent with due respective thrift,
>   Had made brutes men, and men divine!
>   High thoughts had shaped the foolish brow,
>   The coward had grasped the hero's sword,
>   The vilest had been great, hadst thou,
>   Just to thyself, been worth's reward.
>
> "Awake, O queen, to thy renown,
>   Require what 'tis our wealth to give,
>   And comprehend and wear the crown
>   Of thy divine prerogative!"

TWENTY-FIVE YEARS TOGETHER.

"Glory to God in the highest, and on earth peace, good will to men!"
LUKE ii. 14.

How CAN I hitch my anniversary wagon to this Christ mas star? Nothing is easier than to do it. Indeed, were it my custom to introduce my sermon with a text, I doubt if I could possibly have found from Genesis to Revelation one better suited to the time. For it expresses perfectly the two-fold character of the work that I have had in mind and heart these five-and-twenty years, which twofold work has corresponded to the twofold nature of religion. This was the subject of the first sermon that I preached to you after my ordination. It has been the specific subject of more than one sermon since. But that would be a little matter if the whole course of my ministry had not illustrated and enforced this twofold unity. I could almost say that every sermon I have preached has had for its subject "Glory to God in the highest" or "Peace on earth, good will to men," or it has blended into one these loving oppositions of the angel song, — the first corresponding to the God-side, the second to the man-side in religion; the first to worship, the second to morality. Of the 823 sermons I have written here from first to last, a very large proportion has been purely ethical. A different impression has frequently been got from the average character of the sermons I have printed in the successive series, the fifteenth of which is now well under way. But that is because for printing it has seemed good to choose more frequently than others sermons of a doctrinal or criti-cal or theological character. There has seemed to be more demand for these, as shown by the running out of the editions. I have sometimes smarted, just a little, under the suspicion of my critics and my friends that I was mainly theological and controversial. It would be strange if this suspicion were not soon effectually quelled, were not the effect of giving a dog a bad name proverbially known. For, of late, the character of my preaching has been almost entirely ethical. As between what you might call "life-sermons" and what you might call "thought-sermons," the former have for some time been getting more and more ascendency. Since I came back in September, I have not written a single theological or critical sermon, and those of last year were extremely few. It is, I think, because my theological and critical conceptions have now become so perfectly assimilated that I am almost as forgetful of them as of the sunlight and the air. "I can't tell you," said an orthodox clergyman to me,— he was picking at his shell, preparatory to a higher birth,— "how delightful it is to hear you speak of Jesus as if you had never thought of him as being anything but purely human." I am glad that it has come to that. But I recognize there is a danger here. For a long time yet there will be room and to spare for doctrinal, critical, and theological sermons; and every now and then, if one doesn't come naturally, I must pull myself together and write one with supreme deliberation.

This statement of the case must not be understood as an injurious reflection on the doctrinal and critical and theological sermons I have written. I am not ashamed of the gospel of rationality that I have preached. The ethical function is not the only function of a spiritual church such as we have been fain that ours should be. The spiritual is intellectual and emotional as well as moral. For a lofty worship and an intelligent morality alike, we must have intellectual clearness. The universe is the manifestation of God. The more complete our intellectual apprehension of the universe, the more wonderful it will appear to us, the deeper will be our awe, the more profound our reverence, the more serene our trust. And awe and reverence and trust are three in one, and that one is worship. We must have intellectual discrimination to exalt and purify our worship and to direct our ethical passion. Conscience cannot be separated from intellect any more than worship. There is much flouting of the intellect in popular preaching; but not many of the preachers are dangerously overloaded with this mental ballast. That I have apprehended my own function here too intellectually I have not the ghost of a suspicion. The church, I have imagined, stands for instruction, for education, as well as for moral instigation and emotional appeal. To reconceive the Bible, to reconceive the life and character of Jesus, to reconceive the universe and man and God, not with my own poor strength, but with the help of all the deepest, highest, noblest philosophical and critical and scientific thinking of the time,— these are the tasks that I have laid upon myself, and they have been worthy of my utmost consecration. The process has been intellectual; but it has had abundant ethical and emotional implications. A clearer vision of the world, a more awed and tender admiration of its mysterious beauty and perfection, a more resolute determination of the moral will to whatsoever things are right,— such are the ends and objects of a spiritual and working church. Such have I set before me always. Such have I endeavored to make real in your experience; and in this, I trust, I have not wholly failed.

Of all the phrases which, by frequent repetition, ossify the organs of intelligence, "mere negation," the favorite characterization of liberal thought with theological conservatives, is the most common and absurd. If I know anything about myself and what I have done, or tried to do, I have been no preacher of negations. A positive, conservative impulse has dominated me throughout. It has doubtless been a fault of my preaching that it has been too much directed to an imaginary audience, made up of those who have broken with the popular theology and reacted to a violent distrust of any reality whatsoever in religion. To this largely, but not wholly, imaginary audience, I have endeavored to make

clear that religion never was a more supreme reality than
it is now; that the God of reason and of science is a much
grander God than the God of theological tradition; that
man is a much greater piece of work than that tradition has
conceived; that the human Bible is a far more instructive
and suggestive and inspiring book than the Bible of the
supernaturalist; that the human Jesus is worthy of all honor,
reverence, and love, and has in him a power of help which
the superhuman Jesus never had; that, if the " dead certainty" of an immortal life is tending to decomposition, we
have a living hope, inspired by conscience and affection,
and not without such great encouragement of science as
makes all things possible.   But, however positive my general
purpose, not unadvisedly or carelessly have I set forth in
their true character, as it seemed to me, the things that are
not generally believed among us.   I have done this in the
interest of clear thinking.   " Preaching what you believe
and letting what you don't alone " is a device which has been
fruitful of no good results.   It is a device which has made
hundreds of hypocrites and equivocators in the past, and is
making thousands at the present time.   To distinguish
things that differ is the better way.

My earlier preaching was associated with the Transcendental system of philosophy.   That I could rest awhile in
this, when supernaturalism was no longer possible for me,
was a piece of fortune for which I have been always glad.
The Transcendental Philosophy — if I may be so bold with
one * of its most honored prophets close at hand — is itself
a modified supernaturalism.   It ascribes to every individual
soul a gift of supernatural revelation, assures it without
reasoning or experience of God and immortality and the
moral law.   How joyfully I accepted this in Theodore
Parker's way, so concrete and vital as compared with that
of his great leader, Kant !   To give it up was the most painful ordeal I have ever had to undergo.   To part with the
supernaturalism of my earlier manhood had not been half

* Samuel Longfellow.

so hard. Sometimes there came upon me a horror of great darkness, in which I feared that I could never preach again. This was in good part because I had not begun to realize the moral and religious implications of the experiential system. I was halting "between two worlds, one dead, the other waiting to be born." But the final outcome of my philosophical transformation was replete with confidence and joy. The light at length began to dawn, and it has been growing brighter and brighter ever since, until, sometimes, it seems as if I had attained unto the perfect day. But no : it is still far enough from that; and yet how good, how excellent it is ! Those great words, "God" and "duty," were the first of the immortal three to gather to themselves new meanings, higher and better than the old. I found an infinite element implied in every step of evolution ; back of the lowest a higher than the highest term of the ascending series, and so, by consequence, an Everlasting Better than our best of thought or hope ; and so, again, a moral universe building the moral life of man with its foundations in the seas of water and of fire. Not the materialization of mind, but the spiritualization of matter, "the divinity in the atoms," seemed to me the right interpretation of the result of science. The other great word, "immortality," was slower to assimilate the strength of the new doctrine. I rested in the greatness of my hope, and in my confidence that what was best for us the Eternal would provide. And I was happy so ; but happier when, at length, it was borne in upon my mind that this "better thing for us" — immortal life — is something without which the evolution doctrine cannot be made perfect. Never at any earlier stage of my experience did I have such a happy and rejoicing faith as I have now, and I cannot preach a sermon which is not infected more or less with its divine hilarity. You will bear me witness that, in these particulars, I am not drawing upon my imagination, but reporting the most obvious facts.

So much for the spiritual church. What has come of it of course I do not know. Time was when spiritual gains

were measurable,— so many professing Christians, so many
added to "the church." These standards are still satisfactory with many, but they are not available for me. I do not
know what I have done to make the beauty and the glory
of the world more vivid to your minds and more appealing
to your hearts. I do not know what I have done to make
the human excellence of the Bible and of Jesus clear to you,
and not only clear, but persuasive and exalting. I do not
know what I have done to make all human greatness more
inspiring to your minds, more energizing to your wills, to
increase your love for all high poetry and noble art, the
splendors of science and the grandeurs of social, political,
and personal ideals that shame the meanness and frivolity
of your habitual life. I have not been without assurances of
help received in all these ways, from you and many hundreds
whom I have never seen, and of strength and peace and
consolation in your times of sorest need. But, for the most
part, it is painfully uncertain whether I have accomplished
much or little. I am only saved by hope. The lawyer wins
his case; the merchant finds a market; the farmer reaps his
field; the mechanic has his building or machine to prove to
him that he has not worked in vain. How can the minister
but sometimes envy these? How can he help sometimes
crying in the silence of his heart; "Oh that I had some way
of finding out whether my work is helping men and women
to a life of higher thought and holier love!"

But here I am, talking away as if all these years I had
been merely working *for* you and not *with* you. It would
have been a miserable business if it had been so, and the
result would not have been appreciably large. It is of our
Twenty-five Years *Together* that I want to speak. This is
the beauty of it, the joy, peace, satisfaction, glory of it,—
that they have been YEARS TOGETHER, and this, too, in a very
real and vital way. I know how many who were with us
once have been received up out of our sight; but they, too,
are with us still, a cloud of witnesses, expectant of our best
of thought and will. Yet, when I count the vacant places,

or the dear names of those who filled them once, I sometimes wonder that we have any congregation left. I cannot
name them all, they are too large a company; and, in my
chance enumeration, you will miss many names of those you
never can forget. But I cannot forbear to name a few from
out the shining host. How I should like to linger on each
one, and to recall some salient charm of character and life!
They have no order or precedence as they swarm upon me
from the happy past: Gerrish and Clarke and Mills and
Seaver and Plimpton and Robbins and Stephen Noyes,
whom every day I miss; and Brigham and Barrett and Brown
and Merritt and Thallon and Manning and Whitney and
Fairbanks and Burleigh and Webster and Howe and Des-
mazes and Putnam and Maxwell and Newman and Phelps
and Bartlett and Booth,— all these and many more unnamed,
but not forgotten. And with these I gather up the names
of all those beautiful and true and gracious women who once
adorned and cheered our company,— Mrs. Hilliard and
Mrs. Putnam, Mrs. Daniell, Elizabeth Manning,— truly our
"Saint Elizabeth," and so much better than the sainted one
of old,— Lucretia Potts, Mrs. Volney Green, Mrs. Wood,
Mrs. Clarke, Mrs. Burleigh, Mrs. Hathaway, Mrs. Maxwell,
the mother, and the daughters of her home and heart; Mrs.
Stearns, that radiant presence; Mrs. McAllister, whose
heart had ever such a kindly beat; and Mrs. Olcott and
Mrs. Peckett and Mrs. Noyes, whose ministry of love has
never ceased on earth; and Mrs. Knowles, and Mrs. Camp-
bell, a most gentle lady, who this very day awaits her burial,
and many another worthy of mention as the best of these.
While all unnamed, but no less tenderly remembered, I
leave those younger folk, full of all generous possibilities of
worth and love, standing on the threshold of life's glorious
temple with uncovered heads and breathless listening, so
standing in our recollection evermore; and, in the background of all these, as in the Raphael "Madonna," a swarm
of angel faces, the little. children who never have grown old,
who never will. It is not the number of our dead that

impresses me most deeply with a sense of the vitality of
our common life. It is the quality of the men and women
I have named. These were individuals. These were men
of force and character, women of high intelligence and holy
will.

> "How strange it seems, with so much gone
> Of life and love, to still live on!"

And yet we have lived on, and in no sickly fashion. Certainly, the financial strength of our society is but a fraction
now of what it was in former times. But such is its moral
strength that every year, for the maintenance of the society,
and for our charitable and missionary work, we raise a great
deal more money than we used to in our palmiest days. If
some of the monthly collections are smaller than they used
to be, others are larger. If the music costs a good deal less,
the preaching costs a good deal more. The Union for Christian Work, our printing fund, our Friendly Guild, our collections for the Unitarian Association and the New York State
Conference, have required and got thousands of dollars of
your earnings to which there was nothing corresponding
twenty years ago. In 1872 the standing debt of the society
was paid,— $10,000,— and in 1876 a considerable floating
debt, the two amounts exceeding the original subscription for
the building of the church. Since then we have never been
in debt. And what boundless generosities to me and mine
these latter years have known, putting the world in our
hearts, storing our memories with a multitude of happy recollections and of gracious images of scenery and art, that will
outlast, I trust, the substance of our brains! The strength
of Galahad was as the strength of ten because his heart was
pure. The strength of many of you also has been as the
strength of ten because your hearts have been resolved that
what was here begun in faith should never suffer harm.

I have spoken of the preaching as if all that had been
work *for* you. But, indeed, it has been *with* you all the way
along. Your problems, your anxieties, your sorrows, and
your sins, as well as mine, have furnished me with many

themes. Then, too, the cordial praise has often helped, and not less the honest blame. I don't believe that any preacher ever had this last commodity dealt out to him more freely than I have had it dealt to me, or was ever troubled by it less. Now and then some super-sensitive or reactionary brother has emphasized his blame by taking himself off bodily to some other fold; but no one has ever for a moment sought to fetter or abridge the freedom of my thought and speech. One of the most delightful things about my ministry has been that these "fallings from us, vanishings," have never spoiled the pleasantness of my personal intercourse with my seceding friends. They have ended false relationships and been the signal for new and better understandings. The leave-takings have generally been solitary. Only once, in 1884, a little company went out, not because of anything I had preached,— for I had been perhaps too silent, only endeavoring to allay the passions of the hour,— but because it was conceived that in private speech and public action I had not been sufficiently careful of old comrades' sensibilities in a time of storm and stress. I cherish this interpretation as the immediate jewel of my soul. For, if there is any such principle as liberty of thought, it is a principle that does not stop with religion and the Church, but goes all the way through; and I should hate to think that any who had been for years a partner of our glorious hope could fail to apprehend our fundamental principle in all its applications. Would it have been better, possibly, to speak no word of this? But, then, I could not have expressed my gratefulness to those who, hit as hard as any, refused to let the real or imagined fault outweigh a score of busy, faithful years; still came and listened patiently, though it was long before the preacher could again give any pleasure to their souls. And in this connection I should surely say a word of those who have been compelled to leave us by the exigencies of their business life. My parish register reveals enough of these to constitute a large and vigorous society. None remaining with us have been

more completely *of* us than many of these have been and
are. They have often sent to me the yearnings of their
homesick hearts. They have been missionaries of our faith
wherever they have gone. I know that not a few•of them
are here to-day, although they occupy no space.

You have not only helped the sermons to a happy birth,
but you have started hundreds of them on a pilgrimage to
the most various parts of our own country and beyond the
sea. Your Publication Committee has published in books
and pamphlets about a hundred and fifty of my sermons,
while about a hundred more have been fully published
in the magazines and journals of the time. Making no account of this hundred, of the others about two hundred thousand have been cast abroad,— this at an expense which
would hardly keep our meetings here agoing for a year.
You are requested to admire the beautiful economy of this
expense. It costs no more to furnish two hundred thousand
readers with the good tidings than it does to furnish ten
thousand hearers. I think it safe to reckon a reader to each
printed sermon, because, if some fall by the wayside, and
others upon stony ground, and others among thorns, others
fall into good ground and multiply and increase. If some
are never read at all, others, I know, are read until they are
worn out. I must confess that this reading congregation
encourages me not a little. We are so few, comparatively
speaking, here, and so thoroughly indoctrinated in the faith
of reason, that, but for the larger reading congregation, I
might doubt the advisability of your spending so much
money for my maintenance and that of the society. But,
when hardly a day goes by without some word of gratitude
and blessing coming from near and far about these printed
sermons, I am disposed to be of better cheer. These letters
come to me from every corner of the civilized world. They
tell me of the reading of my sermons by individuals to little
companies in Germany and Russia and the farther East and
in many a corner of our own America. Many hundreds every
month are personally accounted for. I hear of them as be-

ing read for consolation over new-made graves, by swarthy laborers of the railroad and the factory and field; and I dare to say, as Channing said of similar echoes to his words, "This is a thousand times better than fame." I give to all of you the credit for this cheerful work, but that does not prevent my giving special thanks to those of you who have furnished the sinews of war; and you all know, or ought to know, that to one friend * as to no other we are indebted for the inception of the work and for its general success, though now, for two or three years, the pamphlet mission of our Women's Auxiliary Society has seconded his efforts in a very energetic and effective way.

Not all the agencies of our society have succeeded as we have wished they might. The Sunday-school has suffered from the ramification of the society into all parts of the city, a city of eight hundred thousand people and six hundred miles of streets. It has also suffered from the crypt-like character of the room in which it meets. It has still further suffered from the bric-à-brac development, which precludes the use of parlors for the children's romping fun. For the smallness of the Sunday-school I am consoled, only in part, by the bigness of our Ethical Association. This is, in fact, an offshoot of the Sunday-school,— a capital illustration of that evolutionary process which has engaged its study for two years. Beginning with Dr. Janes's Sunday morning class, it was next a week-day evening class, then met in the Sunday-school room, and now the church is frequently too small for the hundreds who attend its meetings, while its lectures of two seasons, handsomely published, have attained a large and useful circulation. More than for any other thing it stands for the religiousness of science. If in the freedom of discussion it ever wanders far away from this, Dr. Janes, my faithful coadjutor, always brings it back to it at last. To him all thanks and praise.

A year ago, in speaking of our works, by which our faith

---

* Mr. Monroe B. Bryant.

is proved, I said it seemed to me that all the available force of the society was already in the field, more than a score of our women being officially connected with different charitable organizations, many with more than one, and some with four or five, while twice as many more are unofficially at work in furtherance of charitable ends. At the same time, I expressed the wish that our society might establish a friendly guild in some vilest quarter of the city, in which the workers should not give their money, but themselves, to bridge the gulf between those who have many and those who have few or none of the good things of life. That hope has come to glad fruition. A beginning has been made in that direction, a good beginning,— so good that, if the means and men and women do not fail, it will accomplish much. Many of the workers here, as always happens in such things, are those who were the busiest before ; but many others who were saying, " No man hath hired us," have now enough to do, and "the wages of going on."

A hundred different aspects of our common life and work press for a word of mention in this discourse. But a page for every year is all that I allowed myself, and I have already gone a bit beyond. I have taken up one thing after another, as it has come uppermost, and very likely more important things have modestly remained behind. The very day of my ordination, Sherman's march to the sea had been crowned and glorified by the capture of Savannah. It was permitted us to begin our march together to the music of great events, and we have had that music all the way along. Our years together have been wonderful years in the science and the art and the inventive genius and the religion of the world. We have shared the perils and the triumphs of a scientific revolution which has given to us an entirely new conception of Man, the Universe, and God. For this once despised conception we have never had anything but generous expectation. But the religious transformation has been still more remarkable. Our heresies of twenty years ago are the commonplaces of the nominally orthodox to-day.

To have had such a development as this parallel with the development of our own thought and purpose has been a matter for profound congratulation. If it has thinned our Unitarian congregations, it has thickened the piety and the morality of a countless multitude of men and women,— an ample compensation for the seeming loss.

Mr. Longfellow writes to me, saying how short his seven years seem to my twenty-five. But to me my twenty-five seem shorter than his seven. I should like to be assured that they have been as fruitful of good thoughts and purposes ; that twenty-five years hence seeds of my planting will be bearing flowers and fruit, as seeds of his planting are to-day in many of your homes and hearts. But it does not seem long since I began. I have never got over the sense of starting in, of a new beginning. The church, too, has always been a church militant,— never a church triumphant ; and I have been glad of that. It has kept us young and growing. However it may seem to you, I have no consciousness of getting into ruts, save a few verbal ones that do not count. New aspects of thought never seemed to open out before so plentifully and pleasantly as they have done of late. What the future has in store for us I cannot even guess. Speech is silver, and silence is golden. Had you, last night, confined your sumptuous generosity to the one metal or the other, I might have had some clearest intimation of your judgment, whether I should go on with you or not. If you had come with silver only, that would have meant you were for further speech ; but, as you also came with gold,— symbol of silence,— I am thrown back upon my own appreciation of the case in hand. Nay, but I think your silver and your gold, your fruit and flowers, your pictures and your presence, and your kindly greetings, all had this meaning only,— that I should go on in the dear old way, doing as much better as I can. And that I mean to do, not without hope of openings here to larger things. I had only to look the possibility of a separation fairly in the face, a year ago, to know that I could never break away so long as you were glad to have me still remain. If we could have a church more centrally related than this dear and pleasant place to our sporadic congregation, unquestionably we might do more than by remaining here. So, too, we might do much more in many ways if, somehow, we could have parish quarters suitable to the exigencies of our various and growing work. If only I could see that Carcassonne of which I often dream, a study-parlor which should be yours as much as mine,— a great big room, in which, with books and pictures round about us, faces of saints and heroes looking down, we might have all our social gatherings, our study-classes, our Sunday-school! But that, I fear, can never, never be.

The past, at least, is secure. It has gone into our structure. It has gone into our lives, with all its sermons, hymns, and prayers, all its gatherings together, all its glad response to new and higher revelations of the infinite and eternal God. I must believe — no man shall rob me of this crown of my rejoicing — that it has wrought in you for righteousness and peace and joy. If it has not, then mine has been a miserably wasted life. If otherwise, then I will be as happy as I am. Words cannot tell how glad I am that I have been with you these five-and-twenty years,— with all of you, the whole family of earth and heaven,— nor how grateful I am for all your patience, kindness, tenderness, and thoughtful love. And yet I trust they hint a little of the truth which is the nearest to my heart this blessed day of days.

> " My song save this is little worth;
>   I lay the weary pen aside,
>   And wish you health and love and mirth,
>   As fits the solemn Christmas-tide.
>   As fits the holy Christmas birth,
>   Be this, good friends, our carol still,—
>   Be peace on earth, be peace on earth,
>   To men of gentle will."

The Anniversary Celebration.

INTRODUCTORY.

THE trustees * of my society have asked me to co-operate with them in publishing the proceedings of the celebration of the twenty-fifth anniversary of the beginning of my Brooklyn pastorate. They wish to furnish the society and myself with a memento of a happy time, and to share its happiness with those of my reading congregation who could not come to the celebration. A few of many letters are also published, with extracts from others, because they were evidently intended for my people quite as much as for myself; and none of them have heard them read. Should there seem a certain shamelessness in my consent to the publication of these letters, I would say that, while I am aware of their generous exaggeration of the value of my work, they seem to furnish me with some little justification for the unbounded kindness lavished on me by my people for so many years. It is no fault of theirs if in what follows the latest exhibition of their kindness has not been concealed.   J. W. C.

DECEMBER 21, 1889, was the exact anniversary of Mr. Chadwick's ordination and his installation as pastor of the Second Unitarian Church in Brooklyn, N.Y. At eight o'clock, the hour of the original exercises, Mr. and Mrs. Chadwick received their parishioners and friends at their residence, the society assuming all the cares of hospitality. Everywhere about the house there was a profusion of beautiful flowers, the gifts of many friends. For more than two

* The Committee of Arrangements for the Anniversary Festival, Saturday and Sunday, was the Standing Committee of the Society, Messrs. Sylvester Swain, George W. Banker, and Charles K. Ovington, assisted by Mr. Henry I. Faris, President of the Board of Trustees, and Mr. Her ey Brown, the Secretary of the Board.

hours there was an unbroken stream of visitors, not a few from other churches and denominations. Late in the afternoon there came a sumptuous case containing table silver, some seven dozen pieces, anticipating every use, and a gold watch to succeed one that was given to Mr. Chadwick by friends in the society in 1864, before his ordination. To these gifts from all the people, various personal gifts were added. There was no formal presentation, and there were no formal thanks. A congratulatory message was sent by the trustees to Mr. Chadwick's father and sister in Marblehead, Mass., regretting their unavoidable absence. The following poem, by Rev. Minot J. Savage, was read by Miss Ovington, Mr. Chadwick remarking, when the reading was concluded, that Mr. Savage was evidently the victim of an optical illusion,— he had seen his own image in his mental glass, and mistaken it for another man's : —

O preacher who art poet, too,
　Dare I attempt a song,
Nor fear a false note feebly struck
　Should do th' occasion wrong?
Crown preacher, poet, man, and friend
　With *triple* crown ?　No: see!
The pope's tiara's not enough :
　We bring thee *four*, *not three !*

A preacher frank and strong and bold,
　Whose only law is truth.
No voice uncertain thine has been,
　But fearless from thy youth!
The loud sensationalist bawls,
　The crowd sweeps past thy door,
But Wisdom's children know thy voice,
　And trust thee more and more.

A poet with the touch that tells
　Thine ear has caught the tone
The Muses love,— the secret speech
　That marks thee for their own.
And yet thy poet's breath has fanned
　No common, earthly fires :
It kindles altar flames, it lifts,
　It comforts and inspires!

Then, more than preacher, poet more,
  Thou'rt built upon a plan
As broad as earth, as high as heaven,
  A rounded, noble man!
Let human nature those revile
  Who at man's lot repine;
But thou art one of those who trust
  That human means divine!

A preacher, poet, man,—all these,
  Like rays that rainbows blend,
Thou weavest into one white light,—
  The halo of a friend.
And why thy church has loved thee so
  We partly understand,
When all thou art thou dost enclose
  In one warm grasp of hand!

A quarter-century of work!
  Hast thou earned thy release?
No! All thy past is but a bond
  That pledges work's increase.
So preach on, sing on! Man and friend
  Thou canst not help but be:
But preach, sing, till we celebrate
  Thy *half* a century!

SUNDAY MORNING, DECEMBER TWENTY-SECOND.

The church had been made as green as a woodland with
festoons of laurel and ivy and with palms of victory. After
the organ voluntary by Mr. Robert Thallon, who, in the
absence of Mr. King, conducted the music of the day, a
solo was sung by Miss Sessions, " Still, still with Thee when
purple morning breaketh." The Lord's prayer was repeated,
and then the congregation sang one of the many hymns by
which it keeps in constant touch with Mr. Longfellow, from
whose heart they came : —

O Life that maketh all things new,—
  The blooming earth, the thoughts of men!
Our pilgrim feet, wet with thy dew,
  In gladness hither turn again.

From hand to hand the greeting flows,
   From eye to eye the signals run,
From heart to heart the bright hope glows,
   The seekers of the Light are one,—

One in the freedom of the Truth,
   One in the joy of paths untrod,
One in the soul's perennial youth,
   One in the larger thought of God;

The freer step, the fuller breath,
   The wide horizon's grander view,
The sense of life that knows no death,—
   The Life that maketh all things new.

Then, after the Scripture reading from the vision of Saint John, and the prayer which gathered up the memories of the "Twenty-five Years Together," there was sung the following hymn, written by Mr. Chadwick for the day:—

TUNE,—" Federal Street."

O Thou whose perfect goodness crowns
   With peace and joy this sacred day,
Our hearts are glad for all the years
   Thy love has kept us in thy way.

Thy glorious truth has made us free
   From bounds of sect and bonds of creed;
Thy light has shone that we might see
   Our own in every brother's need.

For common tasks of help and cheer,
   For quiet hours of thought and prayer,
For moments when we seemed to feel
   The breath of a diviner air;

For mutual love and trust that keep
   Unchanged through all the changing time;
For friends within the veil who thrill
   Our spirits with a hope sublime,—

For this, and more than words can say,
   We praise and bless thy holy name.
Come life or death, enough to know
   That thou art evermore the same!

THE ANNIVERSARY DISCOURSE.

Silent Prayer.

After which, Mr. Chadwick repeated the verses written in 1876 for the twenty-fifth anniversary of the formation of the society : —

It singeth low in every heart,
　We hear it each and all,—
A song of those who answer not,
　However we may call.
They throng the silence of the breast;
　We see them as of yore,—
The kind, the brave, the true, the sweet,
　Who walk with us no more.

'Tis hard to take the burden up,
　When these have laid it down :
They brightened all the joy of life,
　They softened every frown.
But, oh ! 'tis good to think of them
　When we are troubled sore ;
Thanks be to God that such have been,
　Though they are here no more !

More homelike seems the vast unknown,
　Since they have entered there;
To follow them were not so hard,
　Wherever they may fare.
They cannot be where God is not,
　On any sea or shore ;
Whate'er betides, thy love abides,
　Our God forevermore !

ADDRESS BY REV. SAMUEL LONGFELLOW.

On an occasion like this, the first thought is of congratulation upon the continuance over the space of a quarter of a century of a ministry of religion,— a ministry which, amid all the changes which must occur in twenty-five years, has been unbroken in the respect and attachment on both sides. Such continuous ministry is rare in these restless days. Its cumulative force is precious, especially in our view, who regard the religious life mainly not as a conversion, but as an education.

Beside these twenty-five years, how does my ministry of seven seem to dwindle! Yet those were the first seven of this church's life; and they were shaping and establishing years. Whatever failed of accomplishment, I am sure that some principles of freedom were fixed; some deep spiritual impressions made; some minds helped forward from the old to the new; some of life's experiences made clearer; some living sense of God brought nearer. As I think of those years, I, too, see faces invisible, hear voices how clearly,— friendly faces, cordial voices,— coming so distinctly out of the past that one feels that there is no past, but that all lives in us. I name no names; but I cannot forget the generous sympathy with my thought and effort, the kindly criticism, the careful guarding of my freedom of speech, the patient bearing with my faults and shortcomings. And for these things I am truly and unforgettingly thankful to-day. And I am glad that your unforgetting kindness wished that I should come to join with you to-day, and say a few words to you, as of old.

Twenty-five years see many changes, "as the thoughts of men are widened." Lyell must rewrite his geology every ten years. I see upon the backs of books the new chemistry, the new astronomy; and among the most tightly creed-bound sects the new theology is freely spoken of. They are giving up many things which we combated and rejected many years ago; and things are freely said in Orthodox pulpits which the most liberal hardly whispered fifty years ago. The moorings are everywhere slipped, the anchors dragged, and the ship of the Church is fairly afloat. We long ago set sail, with God's sun and stars over us and his upholding sea beneath us, and within the trembling but trustworthy needle,— Hope at the prow, and Faith at the helm, and Freedom the inspiriting gale that fills our sail.

This freedom — thus guided, may I not say? — has not ended for you in wreck of any sort. You have neither foundered nor been dashed on any rock. And if, to any of you, it may have seemed at times that, in giving up some old beliefs for more rational views, there has been a temporary loss of devotional trusts that were sweet and consoling, and you for any moment feel a longing to get back to the unquestioning faiths of earlier years, remember that this is but the mark of a passing transition, and that the heart will gather again about the new and true tender trusts and associations even better than the old. When, in your garden, you find the trellis into which the delicate vine had twined itself and been upheld proves to be decayed, it must be taken away, and the delicate stems and tendrils will lie for a time torn and bleeding upon the ground. But, when you have built up the new and sounder props, the stems will lift themselves anew, and the tendrils gain again a firm clasp, and the buds will open toward the sunny skies and pour forth their fragrance on the summer air.

I remember that, at the beginning of my ministry with you, I defined a church to be a company of men, women, and children united by a religious spirit for a religious work. Do you ask what I mean by religious?

There are several new definitions of religion. We hear of the religion of humanity, whose animating spirit is the "enthusiasm of humanity," the desire to help the suffering, to lift up the fallen, and lift onward the struggling; to put forth in every way good will to man, the religion of doing good,— a consecration most generous and beautiful; worthy of all praise; worthy a man's or a woman's true devotion.

There is the religion of righteousness, the ethical religion, the religion of duty, inspired by that moral sentiment in man which a great philosopher declared filled him with awe like that with which he gazed upon the starry midnight skies,— a consecration able to give a noble elevation to a man's life.

There is the religion of piety, of devout and reverential

emotions, of hearts uplifted in yearning and humility and
trust toward the Unseen Power and Love; the ascent of
the human spirit to the Father's spirit; the laying hold
upon an immutable strength; the communing with a spirit
of eternal peace, and finding ourselves refreshed, cheered,
encouraged, and made strong to do and bear, our passions
stilled, our confusions ordered, our path made plain. It is
to this religion of the spiritual emotions that the name of religion is usually confined. Yet truly it is not so much religion as a part or phase of religion,— its proper name is *Piety*.
To those who experience it, it is most precious; and they
will cling to it in spite of any intellectual difficulties, since
its foundation is not in the understanding, but in the heart
and in the imagination. Its central word is God,— a word
not to be set aside. We gladly revert to it from all others
by which we try to indicate that unseen sanctity, because,
in its simplicity, it says so little and may mean so much.
With growing spirituality of mind, we divest it of all that
limits and belittles it, and make it to mean all that is least
defined, least tangible, but most powerfully borne in upon
us in our highest moods.

If I am asked which of these three forms or phases of
religion is the greatest and best, I can only say for myself
that the perfect religion will include them all,— Righteousness, Humanity, Piety.

To the teaching of a religion which includes them all, this
pulpit has from the beginning been devoted, with perhaps
varying emphasis. It has been always a satisfaction to me
that there has been this steady voice from the different lips
and in the varying tones of your preachers. May this religion continue to be taught and enforced here,— a religion
free, yet reverent; bold, yet not audacious; advancing, yet
not rash; earnest, deep, sincere, using no words of mere
use and custom; consoling, bracing, cheering,— a religion
separate from, yet at one with, all knowledge, all science, all
that is beautiful, true, generous, and helpful to man; which,
if it give new meanings to, also gives new emphasis to the

great words "God," "duty," "immortality"! Such a ministry the great Source of Truth, Holiness, and Goodness will gladly adopt, we may believe, as a channel for his good will to men.

After the singing of the following hymn, originally written by Mr. Longfellow for a meeting of the Anti-slavery Society, Mr. Longfellow pronounced the benediction : —

> Out of the dark the circling sphere
>   Is rounding onward to the light;
> We see not yet the full day here,
>   But we do see the paling night;
>
> And Hope, that lights her fadeless fires,
>   And Faith, that shines a heavenly will,
> And Love, that courage reinspires, —
>   These stars have been above us still.
>
> Look backward, how much has been won!
>   Look round, how much is yet to win!
> The watches of the night are done;
>   The watches of the day begin.
>
> O Thou whose mighty patience holds
>   The night and day alike in view,
> Thy will our dearest hopes enfolds;
>   Oh, keep us steadfast, patient, true!

THE EVENING SERVICE.

After an organ voluntary, the Rev. Merle St. Croix Wright, of the Harlem Society, New York, offered a prayer; and then the congregation sang the Rev. John C. Learned's hymn, the next best thing, said Mr. Chadwick, to having his elder brother of Divinity School days, and his friend ever since, visibly present.

> Great Spirit of renewing Truth,
>   Come shining through our darkened eyes,
> And make the tides of light roll in,
>   To cleanse from error and from lies.

If any falsehood of the past
  Round us has thrown its iron chain,
Burn through, and melt each fettering link
  And give us freedom once again.

Faith in the present we would have,
  Faith that God lives and works to-day,
That revelation never fails
  In souls that work and love and pray.

O Future, which we hold in trust,
  To build for thee a glowing way
Our hearts are pledged; no Past can bind;
  Before us lies the mighty day!

The Rev. H. Price Collier, of the First Unitarian Church in Brooklyn, read passages from the Bible ingeniously and seriously, and also humorously, adapted to "the hour and the man." The Rev. Stephen H. Camp, of Unity Church, Brooklyn, brought to the reördaining prayer a heart attuned to perfect sympathy by twenty years of fellow-service and his own recent celebration of those years. Mr. Chadwick then spoke as follows : —

At my ordination twenty-five years ago, I had very little to say; but I was a good listener, as sometimes I am not. (At least so I have heard it said.) I shall not say much to-night; but, as some of you were not here at my ordination, and those of you who were may not remember all about it, I am going to tell you something about the manner of it The new-fallen snow was lying heavy on the ground. Dr. Bellows was to have offered the introductory prayer; but Sanitary Commission work prevented his appearance on the scene, and Mr. Longfellow took his place. The Rev. Henry Blanchard, who was then a Universalist, has since been a Unitarian, and has now returned to his first love, read the Scriptural selection. In those days there was a real live poet in the congregation, William H. Burleigh, who looked, moreover, as a poet ought to look,— white-haired

and leonine; and he wrote the "Ordination Hymn," of
which the first stanza was:—

> Father, thy servant waits to do thy will!
>   Called to thy work, oh, clothe him with thy might,
> And with this threefold grace his spirit fill,—
>   Love, liberty, and light,—

a prayer which has been answered fairly well. As to the
light, I certainly have often wished for more. I have
never felt "the weight of too much liberty," but I have
always had enough. And, as for the love, I have had some
of the very best and sweetest that was ever given to mortal
man ; and, if any minister ever loved his people more than
I have loved mine,— well, I don't see how he could. Then
Robert Collyer preached the sermon which he is going to
preach again this evening (and I think he never preached
a better), and Mr. Frothingham offered the ordaining prayer
or poem,— it was both,— and Mr. Longfellow charged me
what I should and should not do in such a rousing fashion
that all the people said, "If we could only have him back!"
And Mr. Putnam — he wasn't Dr. then — gave me the right
hand of fellowship. Then we sang Mr. Frothingham's hymn
which he wrote in the Divinity School, and which was so
good that he would never write another. We will sing it
again a few minutes hence. After that, Dr. Osgood addressed the congregation. He alone of those who took
part in my ordination has learned what death reveals. The
rest are working still. But there is more to tell, although
perhaps it is too sacred to be told. That night, when it
was all over, and everybody else in the dear home where
I was staying had gone upstairs, and, as I thought, to bed,
I had a good, hard cry, I was so young and ignorant, and
the task which I had undertaken was so great. And a little
later, as I went stumbling to my room, my noble hostess met
me on the way, divining all, and kissed me as a mother
might, and said a few kind words; and those words and
that kiss have always seemed to me a part, and the best

part, of my ordination. I have now told you all about it; and we will sing together Mr. Frothingham's hymn, wishing we might see his face and hear the music of his voice : —

Thou Lord of hosts, whose guiding hand
Has brought us here before thy face,
Our spirits wait for thy command,
Our silent hearts implore thy peace.

And now with hymn and prayer we stand,
To give our strength to thee, great God!
We would redeem thy holy land,
That land which sin so long has trod.

Send us where'er thou wilt, O Lord!
Through rugged toil and wearying fight;
Thy conquering love shall be our sword,
And faith in thee our truest might.

Send down thy constant aid, we pray;
Be thy pure angels with us still;
Thy truth, be that our firmest stay;
Our sweetest rest, to do thy will.

The Rev. Robert Collyer, of New York City, then preached the sermon he had preached at Mr. Chadwick's ordination in 1864, from the text, "And Enoch walked with God," first giving some account of the way it came to him in his first days in Chicago, when his hands were not yet softened from the blacksmith's work. It was, he said, his Declaration of Independence. It is not printed here, because it can be found with others, almost as good, in his volume of sermons, "The Life that Now Is."

ADDRESS BY REV. THEODORE C. WILLIAMS OF ALL SOULS' CHURCH, NEW YORK.

I was not here at our brother's ordination, but he was at my installation a few years ago. This evening has been a time of reminiscences and personal anecdote, and perhaps

I can offer mine. I remember that Mr. Chadwick made the prayer, and some words which were addressed to Heaven I felt sure were intended by him to reach my ears on the way. Perhaps he thought I was not quite sound in the principles of liberty; and he prayed that I might never believe any time was holier than now, and more to the same effect.

When we go back over these twenty-five years of memory, I feel sure that none of those years was any more rich and complete in the feelings of friendly and pastoral affection between this minister and his people than this year that is just finished.

We have listened to-night to an antediluvian subject, but treated, as such subjects always are here, in the freshest way. It seems to me that, if one could sum up in a word the mission of your minister to you and to us all, it is that he has been the prophet of the religion of to-day, of this primitive faith of Enoch, the religion of the poet-prophet, the man of God who believes with his whole soul that no time is holier than now. Perhaps in my own preaching and ministry I am in the habit of feeling that other ages have been holier than this; but of this I am sure,— that, if we cannot see the divine light "in common things that round us lie," we shall not find it in the pages of our Bible or in the reminiscences of any holy man. If we cannot see the light of God in the faces of our brothers and sisters with whom we live, we shall not find it in the face of Christ or any prophet dead. It is the present that interprets to us the inspirations of the past. And so I congratulate you that you have had with you so many years this man who has steadfastly stood for the divineness of the human, for the divineness of to-day.

If I may be permitted one more reminiscence, I shall draw my remarks to a close. I make the reminiscence because it illustrates in my own experience the kind of service that your minister is rendering to-day, and has rendered so long, not only to you, but to that larger congregation with which you furnish him in the distribution of his printed

word. Not twenty-five years ago, but about fifteen years
ago, I happened to come into this church. I remember
that I didn't believe much of anything at that time. I was
under a spell of Huxley and Spencer and the men who were
then in vogue, and I thought I hadn't much of any religion.
I don't remember in the least what the sermon was about,
not a word, not an idea; but I remember what the impression made upon me was. I remember that I went out with
this profound conviction: Here is a man who does not seem
to believe any more than I do, and yet he has a religion,
after all. That was the service which that one morning
rendered me. I followed it up with further readings of your
minister, and, I need not say, I found that he believed a
great deal; but the impression made upon me is what I
want to enforce. The man who is the prophet of to-day,
who has the poet-soul in him that can interpret the divine
as it passes by him, is the man who renders a great service
to a doubting generation such as that to which he has min-
istered.

Some years ago, a venerable divine, venerable from age,
resigned his pulpit in Boston, with some laments as to the
fashionableness of young clergymen and as to the fact that,
as ministers grew old, they were less esteemed. A New
York paper, commenting upon this remark, drew attention
to the fact that some of the most revered ministers of the
Unitarian body were men a good deal past threescore and
ten, and were still preaching with great vigor, and suggested
that there might be some secret by which a minister, like a
man in any other profession, might become somewhat independent of the flight of time, and continue to exercise his
ministry with full vigor as long as a man in any other profession.

Now, your minister seems to have that elixir of youth in
him. I think it is Sainte-Beuve, or some Frenchman, who
has said that every man carries in his heart a dead poet.
Well, when the poet in the man's heart is dead, there is not
much left of him; but the poet in John Chadwick is not

dying, and will not. There is some secret by which a man can keep himself freshly abreast of the needs and questions of his own time, by which a young man who stands by the principle and purpose that he will be the prophet and interpreter of those revelations which God shall send him day by day,—there is some secret by which such a man maintains his power unabated to the end. What that secret is I am going to ask your minister the next time I have the privilege of a private conversation.

Mr. CHADWICK.— Now we will again sing together our anniversary hymn ; but before we do it, in concluding our services, may I not say a word of gratitude to all those who have done anything to make these anniversary days, yesterday and to-day, pleasant and beautiful to my soul? I looked forward to them with some joyful anticipation, with some fear and trembling. They have been much more beautiful and tender and sweet to me than I dared believe they could be. And, with this general expression of gratitude, may I not blend a special word of gratefulness to Mr. Longfellow for coming from the mystic East to shed his benediction on the scene, and to Robert Collyer for preaching over again my ordination sermon? You will not wonder that I wished to hear it again ; for was it not, as the Devon man said of "Lorna Doone," "a'most as good as clotted cream," or quite? Every word of it was as familiar to me as if I had only heard it last night, and it seemed even better than it seemed the first time. I don't think it is out of date at all; and if that wish should come true,— which many of you in your kindly foolishness have expressed,— that I should remain here another twenty-five years, I hope that Robert Collyer will come over from New York and preach that sermon again, which is not at all beyond the range of possibility, because, even then, he wouldn't be quite as old, I think, as our friend, Dr. Farley, is now.*

* He would be a little older: Dr. Farley was born June 25, 1800; Robert Collyer Dec. 8, 1823.

And here I will say that Dr. Farley has been very tenderly
in all our hearts to-day, although not bodily with us.   And
I am very grateful to my friend Collier for his good Scripture,—which wouldn't have been so good, as the sermon
taught us, if the good hadn't been in him to find it,— to
Wright and Camp for their dear words of prayer, and to
Williams for his "rash, superfluous praise."   I use his own
expression, out of that song with which his speech broke
forth five years ago at my twentieth anniversary, when,
having gone on for some time, saying many such things as
you have heard from him to-night, and which I thought very
nice, he said, finally, they were not about me at all : he was
only hinting at the man that all of us should wish to be.*

And now, if I am not bettered in my heart and life by all
the kindness and tenderness of these days and what they
have brought to me, and by the recollections of the years
before, they have revived, it will be very strange and sad.

ANNIVERSARY HYMN.

The hymn was sung very grandly by the great congregation, and a benediction by the pastor ended the services
of the long and happy day.

> * " Dear brother, forgive, when the song is through,
>   Its rash, superfluous praise ;
>   And account, if you will, that the praise of you
>   Is for him of the future days,—
>   The man you foreshadow, whose luminous word
>   Shall lead out of Egypt the host of the Lord.
>
> " The man we long to be wholly,
>   The priest we attain but in part,
>   Who shall scourge the children of folly
>   And bear the whole world in his heart,—
>   He is not come!   But blessed are they
>   Who cry in the desert, ' Prepare ye the way ! ' "

From the Letters.

FROM the following letters, excuses and matters purely personal have generally been omitted. In addition to those given here completely or in part, there were cordial greetings from the Rev. Dr. Hedge, Rev. Dr. Bartol, Rev. Samuel May, Rev. Charles H. Eaton, Dr. Lyman Abbott, Rev. J. H. Crooker, Mr. Wendell P. Garrison, Rev. W. P. Tilden, Rev. John M. Marsters, Rev. J. H. Clifford, Rev. Charles A. Humphreys, Rev. F. B. Mott, Rev. J. V. Blake, Rev. Francis B. Hornbrooke, Rev. Joseph May, and many others.

[REV. FREDERICK A. FARLEY, D.D., BROOKLYN, N.Y.]

I'm sorry my verbal greeting did not reach you by my son-in-law last evening. He was greatly interested in the entire services, but was moved to come away on the instant they closed, as he wished to tell me of them, and knew that I would be waiting. So he did not speak to you; but he brought me your admirable anniversary hymn, and told me how justly you judged that, though absent in flesh, I was with you in spirit. Yes, that I had been, be sure; and these few words would have gone to you earlier this morning had I not been prevented by a succession of calls I could not put aside. I must, even at this late hour, ease my own heart, however, by sending my congratulations on your having, to the rich satisfaction of your people and your own joy, so successfully rounded your quarter of a century of service among them. For myself, I am glad to tell you that twenty-five years of our unbroken friendship is to me a treasure I lovingly cherish. Not many more can I hope for this side the River. To you and your dear wife go my warmest Christmas wishes, in which my wife and my daughter join.

[Rev. W. H. Furness, D.D., Philadelphia.]

My dear Boy, — I've received an invitation to your Commemoration. It would give me great pleasure to be with you then. My heart has gone out to you of late, having come across some lines of yours that went right into it, and which I have committed to the treasure-box of my memory. If good wishes could be materialized in angel shapes, you would be well-nigh suffocated in the crowd on the 21st. God bless you!

[Rev. Grindall Reynolds, Secretary of the American Unitarian Association.]

I can assure you that it is with the greatest regret I am obliged to deprive myself of the pleasure of participation in the celebration of your twenty-fifth anniversary of ordination; but I have so many engagements that I cannot possibly get away. I do not see how it is possible that a young man like you should have been settled twenty-five years in one place; if you have,— and I am bound to accept the testimony of your committee,— it is evident that preaching of the gospel has been productive of health of body and youthfulness both of face and of mind. I can only hope that you have used the smaller instalment of your preaching time; for it does seem that one who preaches his own mind so frankly and yet so agreeably even to those who do not altogether accept his positions ought to live and preach forever. Anyhow, my own personal congratulations I have to put on paper; but they are just as real and living as they could be if I met you face to face.

[Rev. John R. Effinger, Secretary of the Western Unitarian Conference, Chicago.]

I send you greeting from the W. U. C. headquarters on the twenty-fifth anniversary of your ministry and of your pastorate at Brooklyn. Not many of us in these days round up a quarter of a century in one spot. But the years have gone

by like a dream, and have left you so young and fresh in spirit
that it seems almost incredible that it is a quarter of a century
since the hands of the elders were laid on your head, and you
were set apart to the ministry of a religion of freedom and
hope and courage.

Though rooted in one place all these years, your parish
has been widely extended, so that your voice is heard in
many a Western hamlet and farm-house on the verge of civilization; and its liberating message finds many a prepared
soul even within the enclosures of the prevailing faith. We
of the Western Conference are much indebted to you, not
only for the sermons which have been such welcome tools in
the work of the Post-office Mission (and so generously
supplied by your people), but for the steady support and
noble reinforcement you have given us in our hours of deepest depression. When some of us have felt as lonesome as
Elijah under the juniper tree, your note of jubilant faith has
helped us to feel the real security and the glory of the liberal
position, and you have cheered us on in the difficult way
which those must ever tread who step aside from the beaten
paths of religious thought and effort.

The time is now too short for me to send you officially the
greeting of our Board of Directors; but I am sure that I
voice the feeling of them all in sending to you and your
people this word of congratulation and greeting on this
happy anniversary, and their hearty wishes for your health
and prosperity and that of your society.

[Rev. Joseph II. Allen, Cambridge, Mass.]

Your coming anniversary marks a very interesting period.
You struck into public life just when the liberal movement
you have represented so gallantly was turning from its critical
and controversial stage to its constructive work. Twenty-
five years ago seems not very long to me who was then a
twenty years' veteran in the arena; but it brings back the
memory of an ardent pupil, whom Dr. Hedge encouraged and

loved, who "fleshed his maiden sword" in some matters of freshest attraction then, whose career since has been one of constant and warm interest to me.

[REV. WILLIAM C. GANNETT, ROCHESTER, N.Y.]

The hymn that didn't come was a very good one, indeed! I have been head and hands full,— though, as one writes hymns with the heart, I don't see why that should have dried the streams so.

So I must just tell you what you know full well,— how glad for you and glad with you we both are that you have rounded out the five and twenty years in the home you chose and that chose you so long ago. It seems so long — it seems so short a time! Only a thousand prayers away, only a thousand sermon-talks, only two thousand hymns away,— or have you sung three hymns a Sunday there? Where have they all gone to, John? Into heart-life somewhere; into thought-life; into character; that is the comfortable hope for us who so spend ourselves in words. I wonder if your boys and girls, now men and women dawning into gray, can trace many of them in themselves, or if the fathers and mothers can, who were young when they first listened, or if you can yourself trace many in your own life. The sermons do *us* good, anyway! And, more than most of us can hope, yours have done others good,— and how you must bless print! So I give you joy over your big family of silent sermons in the drawers, and of printed sermons that are travelling, and over the big family of souls that these have helped to make. For myself, I am very deeply glad that for the beginning of our friendship I have to think back even past the five and twenty years. Bless you, dear fellow, for the thousand welcomes in the home and in the letters all these years!

[HON. GEORGE WILLIAM CURTIS, STATEN ISLAND, N.Y.]

I have been so constantly away from home during the last three weeks that I am, as I feared I should be, unable from stress of occupation to come over on Sunday and say, God bless you! But I shall say it all the same in my heart, and add a private ejaculation for myself that he has blessed me by adding such a friend to a circle of friends so choice and beloved as mine. I rejoice in your happy anniversary, and in the completion of the quarter of a century which in itself is the proof of a strong and vital relation of reciprocal trust and affection between you and your people. For all that time you have the consciousness which ought to be very inspiring, that your church has been a power of spiritual independence and of religious sincerity, and therefore in the truest sense a Christian Church. Christ certainly taught no strange or mysterious doctrine. The common people heard him gladly, because he echoed the voices in their own hearts and consciences. The business of preaching now is to rescue his simple truth from the vast and splendid disfigurement of ecclesiastical tradition, and to show that that truth speaks to our condition in America to-day as to that of the little Syrian province in which long ago he lived and died.

Good-by! Remember on Sunday that, as with Uhland's traveller at the ferry, "invisibly to thee" many more than spirits twain will hover over you with benedictions.

[REV. O. B. FROTHINGHAM, BOSTON, MASS.]

It would give me real pleasure to accept your warm invitation to come to your anniversary, if I could. But in these days I must not go far from the "domestic hole in the floor." One of the best things I ever did was my God-speed to you twenty-five years ago. That prayer, at all events, has been answered. If liberalism has in any measure reconciled the utmost liberty of thought with spirituality of faith, it is largely due to you. You have a great many friends, and are cordially admired throughout our Unitarian community. It was lucky that you went to Brooklyn in my stead. Your society has my sincere congratulations, and from this distance I hail you as one of the leaders in the rational advance.

[REV. EDMUND B. WILLSON, SALEM, MASS.]

Gentlemen, — Your kind invitation to participate with the Second Unitarian Society of Brooklyn, in celebrating the twenty-fifth anniversary of the ordination of its minister, John White Chadwick, is hard to resist. I thank you for opening the door of welcome to me on an occasion of such rare interest to you; and which is one on many accounts of unusual interest to me also.

I have the happiness to think Mr. Chadwick my friend. His early home is next door to us in Salem. I have followed him in his career of notable success from its beginning. Not alone because his childhood's home is close at hand or his visits to our neighborhood have been frequent have we heard his voice and become familiar with his writings, but because his voice reaches far, and carries messages which the people have a mind to hear; because they like frank expression of honest thought, and are thankful when the earnest explorer gives them his best; because, too, they have a willing ear for the poet who sings well and speaks to their hearts in their deeper experiences. Entering into your joy and into that of my friend as I know well how to do from an experience of my own, I am faithfully yours.

[REV. CHARLES G. AMES, ROXBURY, MASS]

Happy years I am sure they have been, for you have loved your work; you have been bravely true; you have been steadily climbing; at each stage you have been cheered by widening prospects. Happy years, too, because, alike in your home and in the broader human environment, you have been keeping the company of angels *not* unawares; and even the pain of seeing some whom you have loved and trusted and who have loved and trusted you received up out of your sight has only seemed to lead you into the deeper peace.

I wonder if the quarter century which has flown by "on wings of air" since those December days when young John Chadwick made his advent to the Brooklyn Pulpit *can* seem

half so long or half so short as they do to one who was
ordained fifteen years before? Isn't it mournfully sweet to
be reckoned no longer as one of the younger men; to see
the shortening procession of your seniors and the lengthen-
ing procession of your juniors? We grizzlies are watching
our chances to taunt you, saying, " Art thou become as one of
us?" and I chuckle at the thought that when you are a
hundred years old I shall be only a hundred and eleven.

But we will not too much mind the years. Let 'em slip:
that's a way they have, and it's what they are made for.
Brave Browning, being dead, yet speaks: —

> " What's time?
> Leave *now* for dogs and apes;
> Man has forever."

But, for both of us, is all the past anything more than appren-
ticeship? Ought not the few last years or the second half of
any man's work to be by far the richest and ripest? So I
bid you hail and God-speed at the beginning of a new quarter-century, wishing you from a full heart all the blessings of
health, happiness, wisdom, and love.

[REV. WILLIAM J. POTTER, NEW BEDFORD, MASS.]

At this time of the week, I could not meet with you and
your friends; but my thoughts have often turned toward you,
and my heart has been with you. Your lines have been
cast in pleasant places indeed, and your ministry in the highest things has been a fine success. The fertility of your pen
in manifold ways amazes me; and, could I envy you in anything, it would be in your omnivorous ability to read and
digest all the good books with which the age teems.

In one respect, however, I keep ahead of you. By those
fateful five years with which I got the start, I rank you still.
Next Saturday finishes my thirty years; and that proud
superiority of years you can never wipe out.

I trust that the rumor which came to me a few months

ago that, after reaching your twenty-five years, you proposed
to retire from the pulpit, has no foundation in fact. It did
not seem to me credible, and I refused to believe it. You
are one who cannot be spared from the liberal pulpit. You
speak to too wide a circle to be easily released. I could
drop out of the ranks, and, except by the local group of my
New Bedford friends, not be missed. But you speak to a
denomination, and are one of the important agencies for
shaping the movements of the Unitarian body. With my
mental eyesight, I could not do otherwise than take and
hold to the isolated position which has been my ministerial
lot; yet I see, too, how good it is to have the larger opportunity and the closer elbow-touch which men like you and
Gannett and Savage could conscientiously keep. For years
yet may you continue your good work! At the fiftieth
annual mile-stone, perhaps, you may be released.

[Dr. Gustav Gottheil, Rabbi of Temple Emmanuel, New
York City.]

You know me sufficiently to make many words superfluous.
I am probably one of the latest friends you made in your
life. It was late in my own day when I learned to esteem
and love you. The common idea is that post-meridian
friendships do not sink deep into a man's nature. This may
be true; but there are exceptions to this rule, as to all
others. There are friendships that affect us like late-born
children: we feel more tenderly for them just because we
thought our time for such rewards of life had passed. I
rejoice in your happiness, and wish you a continuance of
vigor both of body and mind, that you may lead many more
to righteousness, and proclaim to old age that "the Lord is
good, and there is no wrong in him." I press your hand as
your sincere friend and brother.

[Rev. Edward H. Hall, Cambridge, Mass.]

I congratulate you heartily on your anniversary, and sincerely wish that I could be present and join in the festivities.

Few of our ministers deserve such an honor so well as you ; for few have stood so steadily and uncompromisingly for the highest thought, or borne such brave witness to the truth. Trusting that you have many years before you still for the same strong and earnest work, I am, etc.

[REV. CHARLES F. DOLE, JAMAICA PLAIN, MASS.]

I cannot be present except in the spirit; but I am very glad to be counted in among the friends who will bring their thanks and congratulations for a ministry that has not been for the Brooklyn church and city alone, but also, by the courage, truth, and music of its utterances, to many besides, more than you can know : sometimes lonely thinkers whose faith you have quickened, and often again sad hearts to whom in their trouble you have brought a message of hope. Please go on now preaching and singing for another twenty-five years !

[REV. F. L. HOSMER, CLEVELAND, OHIO.]

You may well be glad in the festival that is kept in recognition of these twenty-five years of service, and I rejoice in your joy and that of your people. That service has not been confined to the congregation that meets you from Sunday to Sunday, nor to your own city. It has reached through all our fellowship and far beyond on every side. To the words that will come to you, you must add many, many words of good that will find neither voice nor pen. Only a small part of those to whom you have spoken and sung through all these years can be named or known at your festival. In all these years, you, in a marked degree among us, have stood for that fellowship of the Spirit which there have been found some, even in our Unitarian company, to rim around with shibboleths of theological phrase. You have helped much to clearer thinking upon the great themes of religion, and to the holding of one's honest thought in that charity which is "greatest of all." We have all of us felt the helpfulness of your part in our common work. If the words of sincere praise and recognition on an occasion like this offend, forgive them me, and believe me, with joy in your deserved joy, and with the hope of your continued service yet many years, Yours, etc.

[Rev. Augustus Woodbury, Providence, R.I.]

I would be glad to congratulate the Society and Mr. Chadwick in person, and to express my cordial appreciation of your minister's service, well and faithfully rendered through a quarter of a century. As a native of Essex County in Massachusetts, and a fellow-alumnus of Exeter Academy and Cambridge Divinity School, I feel a certain pride in his good report and abundant success; and I would tender my best wishes for his continued happiness and your own in the mutual relationship which he and you are enjoying together.

[Rev. A. P. Putnam, D.D., Concord, Mass.]

I can hardly realize that it is a quarter of a century since you began your ministry and I gave you the right hand of fellowship. Why didn't you keep it, my lad? But, however you would insist upon distancing yourself from your old comrade, theologically or ecclesiastically, we have remained near to each other in ways beside; and so you will still count me among your fast friends, ever thankful for all the good words you speak or write, and all the beautiful hymns and poems you give to the world; and ever earnest in my wish and hope that blessings unnumbered may crown you and your family and people in the years to come.

[Rev. Richard S. Storrs, D.D., Brooklyn, N.Y.]

I heartily congratulate you on reaching so interesting and signal an anniversary in your life in Brooklyn. I wish that I might be one of the company who will offer their congratulations in person. But I have had to spend four days in

Boston this week, and the Sunday is too immediately before me. I can only say that I hope that you will live, love, and earnestly work until you are as orthodox as I am,— which will at least assure you another twenty-five years, and possibly more; and I hope they will all be years of usefulness, happiness, and ever-growing power for whatever the Lord gives you to do.

I have to write in haste with a pen as refractory as Quaker or Baptist ever was before the Pilgrims, but I am ever, with great regard, etc.

[Rev. Francis G. Peabody, D.D., Cambridge, Mass.]

I sincerely wish I could join your friends in celebration, and congratulate them in their good fortune of many years, little as I can believe that twenty-five years have thus flown away. The poets never grow old, and I must always think of you as among my younger brethren.

[Rev. Horatio Stebbins, D.D., San Francisco, Cal.]

I have just received your sermon "Enduring Hardness." Well, you are the hardest-headed and the tenderest-hearted man I ever knew or heard of ! A wonderful combination of pluck and gentleness, strength and sweetness, you are ! And when is this spider-life of spinning your thread from your own belly agoing to come to an end ? There does not seem to be the least reason that it should ever end. What is to become of us Liberals ? I think we can't come to a mean end, but shall always sustain about the same relation that we do now to the average Christian thought; that is, we shall represent humbly that spirit of truth which when it is fully come . . . [*sic*].

[Rev. Francis Tiffany, Cambridge, Mass.]

I wish I could have been at your twenty-fifth. Is it too late to send you my heartfelt congratulations? You have done a world of honest, steadfast, beautiful, and inspiring work in these now past days. I never read anything of yours without being helped mentally and spiritually by it. My idea of the millennium will be realized when you draw as large a crowd of eager listeners as Talmage, and he draws as small a one as you. So you see how insatiable and revolutionary my ideal is.

[REV. EDWARD A. HORTON, BOSTON, MASS.]

The music of the coming anniversary already sounds into New England. We wish all of us that we could be present, and, while giving our hearty congratulations, also receive the inspiration of the occasion. Poetry, theology, and philanthropy have had your valuable nurture during these twenty-five years, to say nothing of varied labors in other fields. It seems to me that your retrospect ought to be happy, the way the world goes and averages. A delightful home, a loyal church, a wide-read page, and a circle of friends,— all this, with accessories, means a great deal. Accept my hearty wish that all the exercises of the 21st and the 22d may be fulfilled in joyous spirit, and convey to the committee my regrets that I cannot accept the kind invitation to be present. Mrs. Chadwick is an important part of your jubilant doings, yes, a source in part, too, of the songs and sermons and services of your twenty-five years' work,— to her I send cordial greeting and congratulations.

[W. C. GANNETT, ROCHESTER, N.Y.]

Dear John,— It's Sunday night; bed-time. I hope you have had a very blessed day and yesterday,— you, Annie, and the people.

AN OLD TRANSLATION.

"ARE you afraid to do anything, do it." So Emerson has said or quoted, I have forgotten which. I am going to act upon that hint to-day. I am going to preach a sermon upon Robert Collyer's text,* "And Enoch walked with God." It will be so different that you can make no odious comparisons. The text goes on to say, "He was not, for God took him." And in the letter to the Hebrews we read that "Enoch was translated so that he should not see death." It is on the second part of the Old Testament text and on the related verse in the New Testament that I propose to build up my discourse. And now you see what I intended by the subject I announced, "An Old Translation"; namely, the translation of Enoch. And who was Enoch? Shall we say, A man who without any Bible, sacraments, or church, or Christ, managed, nevertheless, to walk with God, and in such a lordly fashion that you can say of him as Dante said of Beatrice,—

> "No quality of cold, nor yet of heat,
> Robbed us of *him* as it of others does,
> But *his* supreme benignity alone"?

That is the ordinary rendering, from which all the brave conclusions of Mr. Collyer's sermon followed, as naturally as the wind-flowers and the violets follow a spell of soft, warm April weather, but which is not necessary in the least degree to the establishment of those conclusions. But now come the scholars and the critics, and they say, with a great deal of unanimity, that there was never any such man as Enoch, that the brief mention of him in the Old Testament is the

* The previous Sunday, Dec. 22, 1889.

survival of some solar myth. They call our attention to the fact that he was 365 years old when he died, and these years, they assure us, represent the 365 days of the solar year. I do not feel entirely sure that they are right, though it is quite as likely that they are as that a man of the third generation on the earth, whose father was a murderer, should have been too good to live, and too good to die like other people, so that God took him, or, as the New Testament has it, he was translated.

Whatever be the merits of the question, I am very sure of this : that in the critical rendering of the text there is quite as much that is suggestive and inspiring as in the other. I am by no means sure that I can draw it out. The popular rendering had to wait two or three thousand years for Robert Collyer to come along and get the splendid meaning out of it that he got last Sunday night. When the critical rendering has waited as long, some Collyer of the future may bring to its interpretation so much poetry and genius, humor and pathos, and broad human strength and sympathy, that it will open in the same flower-like way that the old text did the other night, and let loose as rare a fragrance and disclose as sweet a mystery. However that may be, I can myself, if I am not mistaken, find certain meanings and suggestions in the critical rendering of the text which are not inappropriate to the ending year, and to your general condition, when, after our own special holiday and that in which all Christendom unites, you are disposed to take things quietly and to do as little serious thinking as may be.

"An Old Translation," I have said ; yet is it newer than the newest I have read of late,— one that Theodore Williams had just made, not from the Japanese, but from Goethe's "Prometheus." This year of God, 1889, has already been translated up to date as perfectly as any year that warmed or chilled the heart of man in the first generations of the world. The old mythologist blundered into a bit of real science. Matter is imperishable. Force is indestructible. There is never any real loss : what disappears on one side reappears upon the other. The vanished heat turns up as electricity or chemical or vital energy. What Longfellow wrote of the domestic side of things is true of every side, of universal life,—

" There is no death. What seems so is transition."

As it is with force and matter, so it is with time. We have not only "all there is": we have all that has ever been. We are heirs of all the ages ; and what a great inheritance is ours !

Where did the old years go to in the morning of the world ? When God took them after they had walked with him the measure of their days, what did he do with them ? He translated them. And into what language ? Into as many languages as there are forms of matter and of life : into the language of the sea, advanced a little here, withdrawn a little there ; into the language of the rocks, seamed by the frost, abraded by the rush of many waters ; into the language of the forests and the shrubs and grasses, ripening a million million fruits and seeds for plantings yet to be ; into the language of the birds and beasts, turning to songs in little quivering throats, to skill in tiny nests, to care of mothers' wings ; turning to the glorious strength of the lion and the tiger, hungering for their prey, to the beauty of their tawny coats, all sunshine or else flecked with sun and shade, to the fierce, innocent joy and rapture of their love and war. Into what language were the old years translated ? Into the language of the human, when at length the beast that had been prone stood with his port erect, his face towards heaven, and the endless cycles of man's life on earth began ; into man's widening knowledge, as the ordered world began to shape the order of his thought ; into domestic love, as more and more the child set in the midst necessitated common care ; into the beginnings of the State and Church ; into the beginnings of Science and of Art. And, as God took those far-off years and translated them so that they should not see death, so has he taken all the years that have been numbered by the sun's majestic round.

And it is very wonderful and beautiful to see how, in this labor of translation, man has been co-operant with God. We can believe that nothing of the old years really died; that all of men's old years lived on in the new order of their personal lives and in the social order of which they were a part. But we have to walk by faith, and not by sight, a great deal of the way; and so we are the more grateful for so much as we can touch and say, Here is something into which God translated the old years of men. And the "so much" is really not a little, even of times that are already three or four thousand years remote. Men did not wish the years to die. They had an instinct to preserve them, hardly less strong than the instinct of self-preservation; and so, in the ages before history and the ages before literature, they fell to singing stories of their tribes and clans, stories their fathers and their grandfathers had told to them, and so began that linking together of the generations which is *social experience*, which more than anything, perhaps, marks off the human from the animal world and makes social progress possible. Men were poets long before they were historians, and their songs lived in men's memories for many generations before they were written down. It is very likely that the Iliad and Odyssey had no other life than this for generations. In our own time the "Nibelungen Lied" and "Kalevala," the great epics of the Teutons and the Finns, have been for the first time materialized from the soft air. And, when men began to write their stories down, they wrote them all in poetry at first, not because they thought it more beautiful than prose, but because it was easier to remember. All of the oldest parts of the Old Testament are bits of song. No bit, but a great rounded whole, is the tremendous Song of Deborah in the Book of Judges, in whose bloody stream you are about as near as you can get to the fountain-head of Hebrew literature. But what a translation of the undying years of Hebrew history is the Old Testament in its totality, and how the shifting life of tents lives on for century after century in the metaphors and similes of the prophecies and psalms! And so the Bible in its turn has passed into the life of five-and-twenty centuries of Jewish, twenty centuries of Christian men. I was reading an article only a few days ago about the Bible in Tennyson. But it is not much more in Tennyson than it is in all the modern world. The author was trying to make out that Tennyson was specially Biblical. But I think that my old grandmother knew a dozen Scripture phrases where Tennyson knows one. We are talking Bible and Shakspere all the time, though quite unconsciously. What a man of peace was Garrison! yet such a reader and rememberer of his Bible, and especially of the Old Testament, that its metaphors of war and battle were continually upon his lips.

What is all language but a translation of the years of the immeasurable past? "These words are vascular; cut them, and they will bleed," said Emerson of Swedenborg's. Is it not true of words in general? Is not almost every one of them a history? Milton said we might as well kill a man as kill a book. To kill a word is hardly less a sin. And yet we have among us a new set of assassins, calling their scheme of wholesale murder phonetic reform, who would, if they could have their way, destroy the organic life of language, and make it a mere set of arbitrary symbols, with the poetry and history and humanity of years innumerable that have walked with God clean gone from it forever.

Into what language does God translate the years when he takes them, so that they may not see death? Into the language of history, using to that end such mighty penmen as Thucydides and Tacitus and Grote and Freeman and Carlyle and Green and Mommsen and Ranke. Be not deceived. Here is no epitaph of death for which there is no resurrection. Here is the life of the past, unwasting like the widow's cruse of oil, for prophets in the wilderness of every later time. Here are great personal examples to instruct and to inspire. Here are great laws of social and political life revealed for those who have the intelligence to penetrate to their essential good. But, if the life of the past lived only in its history for the present and the future time, its unending exodus would be very small and slight compared with what it actually is. It is translated into the unconscious and yet most veracious history of literature and laws and institutions, social, political, and ecclesiastical. Your personal autobiography is seldom to be wholly trusted. Every man is an idealist when dealing with the things of his own past. A good biography always brings us nearer to the truth. But the autobiography of races and of nations is the historian's best resource. He finds it written in their language and their literature, in their institutions and their laws. But, if there were no historians, the living past would still remain. God takes the years of strong will and endeavor and translates them into the life of men, into their organic social immortality.

The lesson of such immortality was the greatest lesson Herder and Lessing and Goethe had to teach the modern world. Baffled by his milkman's score, one of the *characters*, who were the comic almanac of my thoughtless youth, suggested, "Rub it all out, and begin again," suiting his action to the word. He was accounted foolish, but was not a whit more foolish than the social and political reformers who have a similar suggestion for the settlement of our political and social score. What Lessing, Herder, and Goethe taught, but what few of our reformers have ever learned, was that the past could not be rubbed out all at once, that there could be no absolutely new beginnings. The history of every great political or religious revolution proves how little can be done at once, how indestructible is the past, how vigorously it will assert itself when we think that it is dead. The French Revolution was a great example. The worst elements of the Revolution and the Terror were simply a revival, a resurrection, of the worst elements of the monarchy. The Revolutionary Tribunal was but the arbitrary procedure of the Capets back again. In Robespierre, the ecclesiastical spirit was incarnate. He had all the attributes of the religious persecutor, of the grand inquisitor. Was never a better illustration of the New Testament saying, "The life is the light of men," than that afforded by the establishment of our own National Constitution. Every part of it that proved workable was the product of experience, a reproduction of the methods of the mother country and the individual States. The new departures were failures almost without exception, the Electoral College the most pitiful of all. This is the lesson that our social and industrial reformers may well take to heart. Because the entire tradition of the past has been translated into the men and women of to-day, no social or industrial system can be conceived, however excellent, which would not be as a log in the rapids of Niagara in the rush of *human nature as it is,* which would not very shortly have all the old foes, however new their faces, on the scene.

But enough and too much of these sweeping generalizations. Look at an individual aspect here and there. Take the career of any good man who walks with God in justice and sincerity, and see how God takes him, translating him so that he may not see death, into the life of churches and communities and states, into the life of families, the happiness and tenderness of quiet homes, the sweetness and nobility of children's lives. This very day * that brings us here — I trust that few of you have failed to note the fact — is the birthday of that grand old man, William Ewart Gladstone. He has attained to fourscore years; and, if they are still labor, they are not yet sorrow, unless it be that he may die before his eyes have seen the great salvation. And see how the great God has taken his years, one by one, and translated them into the best life of the English people, into their commercial freedom, undoing centuries of cruel wrong, into their widening liberties, into their partial justice to the Irish nation and their hope, which shall not be denied, of a completer justice which shall carry a more perfect union in its heart. No! the old years do not die. God takes them and translates them every one. Our own Abraham

---

* December 29, 1889.

Lincoln would also have been eighty if he had lived till now. God took his years, with Garrison's and many another's, and translated them into the emancipation of the slave, but into more than that,— into the loving admiration of a hundred million hearts, which shall become a thousand million yet, and wherever it is quickened it shall make for the superiority of simple manhood to all the accidents of birth and education.   In the same year with Gladstone and Lincoln came also Darwin ; and God took his toilsome years and translated them into a new vision of the vegetable and animal worlds, a new vision of humanity and the eternal things.   They have not seen death, no one of all of them. They are still alive and working in the methods of a mighty company of botanists and biologists and anthropologists who have found the doctrine of Darwin fruitful of abundant truth, and his spirit guarding them from any disposition to make his doctrine a finality.   And in the same year with these was born Alfred Tennyson, and in the same month with him our own poet, Oliver Wendell Holmes.   To what heavens have their Enochs been translated, the years that they have walked with God in the cool gardens of delightful song !   Into the heavens of imperishable beauty and of stainless joy !   What rod or line can measure all that they have done to sweeten and ennoble life ?   How many thousands have found peace and comfort, or at least a sympathetic pain, in Tennyson's immortal elegy in memory of Arthur Hallam !   And how many thousands has one poem of our Autocrat, "The Chambered Nautilus," one stanza of that poem, summoned, and not in vain, to purer purpose and to more exalted aims ! —

> "Build thee more stately mansions, O my soul,
>   As the swift seasons roll !
>   Leave thy low-vaulted past !
> Let each new temple, nobler than the last,
> Shut thee from heaven with a dome more vast,
>   Till thou at length art free,
> Leaving thine outgrown shell by life's unresting sea."

I have named the members of an accidental group connected only by the circumstance of their birth in the same year, 1809. What is true of them is true of scores and hundreds of statesmen, scientists, and poets. They have never seen death. They are living still in the ampler justice of the world, in its wider knowledge, in its consciousness of beauty and of joy. And it is not as if only the great and famous ones enjoyed this conservation of their energy, or even those who ranked but next to them, like our good Oliver Johnson, who two days ago kept his birthday upon the other side, while we did not forget it here. And that same year came our own Richard Henry Manning, whose faithful years have been translated into grateful memory for all who knew him well, and inspiration for the best and honorablest things. There came another in that year who was more to me than any of all these, more than Gladstone or Lincoln or Darwin or Tennyson or Holmes or Oliver Johnson, or even Richard Henry Manning, though I enjoyed with him a friendship that made no account of difference of age. It is of my father that I speak, mainly that I may say that, if I have ever failed in gratitude to you for all your kindness to me here, he has never failed. He knows your names, and tells them over as if they were a rosary's sacred beads. Your health, your joy and sorrow, always touch his sympathetic heart. But this is by the way. He is one of many thousands who are so little to the noisy world, and so much to a few of their own blood and state who know their worth. And all the years of all these simple, quiet folk God takes, and, translating them so that they may never see death, makes them a perpetual and undying part of all the goodness and the sweetness of the world. Not one of them is lost or wasted any more than the great years of a Lincoln or a Darwin, a Gladstone or a Tennyson. Yea, saith the Spirit, my sheep hear my voice, and I know them, and they follow me, and I give unto them eternal life, and no one shall pluck them out of my hand.

Look at this matter from another point of view. Take

any little fact that enters into the composition of a passing
year, and look at it closely, and see how its undying quality
at once appears. What shall it be ? A bit of sunset glory ?
Very well.

> " Where did yesterday's sunset go,
> When it faded down the hills so slow,
> And the gold grew dim, and the purple light
> Like an army with banners passed from sight ?
> Will its flush go into the golden-rod,
> Its thrill to the purple aster's nod,
> Its crimson fleck the maple-bough,
> And the autumn-glory begin from now ?

> " Deeper than flower-fields sank the glow
> Of the silent pageant passing slow.

> " It flushed all night in many a dream,
> It thrilled in the folding hush of prayer,
> It glided into a poet's song,
> It is setting still in a picture rare;
> It changed by the miracle none can see
> To the shifting lights of a symphony;
> And in resurrections of faith and hope
> The glory died on the shining slope.

> " For it left its light on the hills and seas
> That rim a thousand memories."

Is it so with sunsets only, or is it so with every circumstance of beauty, strength, and grace that impinges on our
lives, and, not less, with every hideous and hurtful thing ?
Yea, more. " We are such stuff as dreams are made of,"—
our dreams of excellence, of beauty, of honorable success ;
of sordid pleasure, too, and low ambition, and things gross
and sensual. It is the story all the world over of Longfellow's song of the arrow and the song,— if we could only
have Lilian Henschel here to sing it now ! The word or
deed goes from us, and we know not whither it has gone.
But it has gone somewhere, besides returning on ourselves.
It is not lost. We must give account of every idle word
in the day of judgment, and that is every day ; and the
account is written in our blood and on the fleshly tablets of
our hearts.

Look at it from the other side. See how God takes the years of our friends' lives, and what he does with them ; how he translates them so that they may not see death,—translates them into memory and hope and good resolve. Into memory. How beautiful these daily resurrections are ! — the comings back to us of our friends in the quiet places of our minds and hearts, their words, their tones, their sweet forgiveness when we had done them wrong, their noble expectation that could not be discouraged by our fault, their tender blame, the great moments of our life with them, the dawn of love, the perfect recognition, the spoken vows, the wedding bells, the miracle of birth, the cradle-song, the anxious watchings over the restless or too quiet bed, the greetings morn and eve,— only such things, and yet enough to stir the deepest founts of gratitude and tears. Into hope : for not to hope for glad reunion with the friends whom we have lost,— that is impossible, except for those who never loved at all. George Eliot's insistence that our finest hope is finest memory has not another proof and illustration that is so good and sweet as this, though it is one she would not have allowed. And our finest memory is our finest hope. Our sweetest memory is our sweetest hope. Our noblest memory is our noblest hope. Let the memory be altogether fine and sweet and noble, and it will be very strange if the hope does not attain unto the greatness of that faith which is the substance of things hoped for, the evidence of things not seen. But God's translation of our beautiful past years into memory and hope is not the best that he can do, that he and we can do together. He can translate them, we can translate them, into good resolve. What would they have us do ? — our noble dead — we ask ourselves ; and straightway everything is plain. We see the way that we should go, and we are strengthened for the climb. And then it is that we attain to the beatitude of those who can be thankful for the things they miss.

It is not only the years of our friends' lives that are translated into the substance of our own. It is equally, nay, in fuller measure, our own lives. If they have been strong and brave, if they have been pure and true, if they have been kind and sweet, then have they a beautiful fatality for us, compelling us to more of strength and bravery, more of purity and truth, more of kindness and sweetness. If they have been quite the opposite of these virtuous things, then such fatality as they have is thrown upon the side of evil inclination, and sometimes with such force that it speaks and acts for us, while, as the poet of these things has said, we stand by and wonder at our baseness. But too much can easily be made of this fatality of an evil past. It is not as if it acted in a vacuum or with unrelated force. Its unconscious operation is qualified by our conscious memory of evil courses which makes them dreadful in our eyes, by the memory of heights of noble purpose and of valiant conquest which we have sometimes attained, and by the memory of those whose eyes, too pure to look upon uncleanness, regard us from the solemn stillness of the eternal years. It must be a monstrous and incalculable bulk of evil doings, organically assimilated in our lives, that can outweigh such energies for good as these which I have named.

> "No good is ever lost we once have seen,
> We always may be what we might have been,"

or something just as excellent and sweet and fair: it may be something better for the fault which we have put away. And now how naturally, to end the parable, and to end the year, the words of Emerson present themselves to heart and mind: "That which becomes us, embosomed in wonder and beauty as we are, is cheerfulness and courage and the endeavor to realize our aspirations. Shall not the heart which has received so much trust the power by which it lives? May it not quit other leadings, and listen to the Soul that has guided it so gently and taught it so much, secure that the future will be worthy of the past?"

THE UNKNOWN GOD.

RECENTLY I have had in hand a book which will, I trust, have a wide circulation; for it is calculated to do much good in a direction where there is need of help. Its title is the title of my sermon at this present time, "The Unknown God." Its author and compiler is Charles Loring Brace, who is best known to you as the efficient head of the Children's Aid Society in New York. But, while he is a man who lays upon himself, as Milton did, the lowliest duties, he is also one who has availed himself, as Milton did, of frequent opportunities for "beholding the bright countenance of truth in the quiet and still air of delightful studies." A few years ago, he published a book called "Gesta Christi," the works or deeds of Christ, which was an eloquent enlargement on the beneficence of the Christian centuries, and much too confidently, it seemed to me, claimed for Christianity the credit of all this beneficence. There was little or no allowance for the influence of nationality or race, and we were allowed to imagine that Christianity in India would have been the same as Christianity in Europe if it had been planted there. I doubt it very much. Noting the different shades that Christianity has taken on in Teutonic and in Latin Europe, and what a worthless matter it was for centuries in the Eastern Empire and is to-day in Armenia and Abyssinia, it does not seem improbable that a Hindu Christianity would have been very much like what Hindu Brahmanism is now, and that a European Brahmanism or Buddhism would have been very much what European Christianity has been and is. But Mr. Brace's "Unknown God" is a much more catholic performance than his former work. It is even

easy to believe he had set out to make some large atonement for the drift of that. At least, he has compiled a very
wonderful and beautiful anthology from various ancient
Scriptures,— Egyptian, Brahmanic, Buddhist, and Iranian,—
and from Greek and Roman writers, especially the Stoics,
whose writings are not generally classed as Scriptures, but
are as deserving of such classification as any of the rest, or
any that our own great Bible's spacious lids enfold. What
rebuke is here in these golden sentences of spiritual insight
and ethical provocation for the old-time classification of religions as true and false, the Jewish and Christian standing
alone in the former category, and all the others in the latter! What rebuke, as well, of the classification which puts
the Jewish and Christian religions by themselves as supernatural and all the others by themselves as natural! How
many are the sentences of calm and genial wisdom in those
others, of flaming indignation against wrong, and glorious
enthusiasm for the right, which we would gladly add to the
Old Testament or New, though giving twice or thrice their
number of the baser sort in fortunate exchange!

The defect of Mr. Brace's book is that he often speaks,
from force of habit it would seem, of the Hebrew and Christian religions as if they were different in kind as well as in
degree from the other great religions of the world. This is
the stranger, as he allows to these a supernatural inspiration, "perhaps not miraculous," he says. But he often
speaks of their revelation as being partial as compared with
that of Christianity, which is complete, though at the very
last his better genius triumphs, and he lifts up a prayer to
the *Agnostos Theos*, the Unknown God, as if the God of
Christianity were to be so considered equally with the gods
of Egypt and Chaldea and India and Iran and the profound
religious thinkers of the Greek and Roman world. That is
the only just and fair conclusion of the matter. "The
Unknown God" is a misnomer for the God whose awful
Oneness flamed forth alike from the polytheism of every
great religion of the elder world, unless that designation be

applied to the God of Christianity, whether viewed in his New Testament appearance or in his historical development. And in his last, best thought Mr. Brace makes the common application. So runs his prayer: "Thou Unknown God! . . . we thank thee that thou hast made thyself known in all ages, to all men, of every race and tribe. . . . They have only known thee in part; but who hath known thee wholly? They have given up thought and heart and life to what they conceived thy will. If they have erred, who of us is free from error? They have called thee by various names; but what are names to thee?" In simple truth, the famous text of the Athenian altar, "To an Unknown God," was not a happy one for Mr. Brace's book. It is not the God whom the religionists of olden time *ignorantly* worshipped whom he declares to be the true and only God. It is the God whom they *intelligently* worshipped, with the knowledge of their noblest prophets, saints, and seers. The whole drift of his discourse is that they *did* know God, the one true God. Why, then, "The Unknown God"? "Unknown, and yet well known," is the choral affirmation in which Hamite and Semite, Hindu and Iranian, Christian and Greek and Roman, join with consenting mind and heart and voice. Who can search out the Almighty to perfection? And yet we know him well enough for boundless adoration, trust, and love.

But, in choosing for my subject at the present time "The Unknown God," I did not mean to dwell so long as I have dwelt on Mr. Brace's book and on the line of thought which it suggests. Where he went for his title I would go for a suggestive hint. Upon his title-page there is a picture of an Athenian altar, with the inscription Ἀγνώστῳ θεῷ, to the, or to an, Unknown God. We are assured that there were in Athens many such altars, the inscription being generally "to the unknown gods." Here was no reflection upon the current polytheism of the time, only a confession of the incompleteness of the classified catalogue of deities in the crowded pantheon. Here was no suggestion of the One only God declared by Paul in that great sermon on Mars' Hill, with which a preacher who is not without honor in his own country, nor his own city, which is also ours, has lately entered into competition. The polytheism of Greece had in its best days been very different from that of Rome, as different as one of Shakspere's plays from the so-called Moralities of an earlier time. Here, in Rome, all abstractions, there, in Greece, all living personages of a drama full of human interests transported to the Olympian seats. But the Greek polytheism had become Romanized in the first century of our era; * and in Athens, as in the Eternal City, there were as many gods as there were aspects of human life. There was one for every season, one for every trade, one for every social aspect, every aspect of thought and feeling. It became the regular thing for the college of pontiffs to invent — or shall I say discover ? — new deities for new emergencies. For example, when they used copper money, they had a god of copper, Æsculanus ; and, when silver money was introduced, the pontiffs, "friendly to silver" like our "silver-tongued orators" from Nevada, introduced a god of silver, Argentinus. There came a time when gold was introduced, and really worshipped as it is worshipped now, but no god Aureumnus was invented, and this neglect was a sure sign that the religion had stopped growing and had begun to die.

Out of this disposition to deify all manner of abstractions and to set up a special deity for every virtue, every occupation, every emergency of life, came naturally enough, and frequently, a trying situation. It is so with every system of rules that aims at completeness and exhaustiveness. The amateur sportsman who had carefully studied up, when a bird came and lighted on the muzzle of his gun, unable to recall any instructions for such a situation, laid down his rifle to consult his manual, and lost his shot. When the Jewish rabbis had a separate niche for every special fault, they were in mortal terror lest, after all, the classification should be imperfect. Hence such a prayer as that in the 19th Psalm,— "Cleanse thou me from secret faults." The faults intended were not faults deliberately hidden, but faults

---

* As the Roman had become Hellenized.

of which there was no consciousness. A like temper was evinced by the Athenian altars to the unknown gods. There were emergencies where no one of all the many of the pantheon seemed exactly fit,— calamities and sorrows very special to the individual life. Yet for such also surely there must be a god. Then, too, there was a fear that some un-named, unhonored god might be defrauded of the rever-ence due to him. Here was another motive for the altars to the unknown gods.

But all this is so far and away that perhaps you wonder why I speak of it at all, unless possibly I am endeavoring by my talk of something merely curious and archaic to divert your minds from the cares, anxieties, and sorrows that press upon you with a too constant and too heavy hand. But no: 'tis skies and centuries, not hearts, that change. In your revised New Testaments you will find it does not read, "God hath made of one *blood* all nations of men," but simply, "God hath made of *one* all nations of men." Of one what? Of one humanity, however various the blood that quickens it. I am every day surprised anew by the freshness of the oldest literature. Not long ago I was reading certain letters of Synesius, a neo-Platonic Christian who died some fifteen centuries ago, and they read as if the ink were hardly dry. They were full of the same great hopes and fears and the same little worries and anxieties and the same loves and admirations that are new to us every morning and fresh every evening. Wherefore, it would be very strange if in those old Athenian altars to the unknown god or gods there were nothing coming home to us, nothing in the Athenian impulse to set up such altars corresponding to the impulses of our eager, passionate, or painful life.

It is quite otherwise than so. The one God of Christian-ity, or the three of the most blessed Trinity, or the four, if we count the devil in (as we surely ought to do as generally the "great king above all gods," in the theology which our Presbyterian friends are now revising, ten times, a hundred times, as strong for evil' as God or Jesus or the Holy Spirit

for any good, his hell as much more populous than their
heaven as Manhattan Island is than Nantucket) — this
Christian pantheon of one or more divinities has often been
as baffling, as unsatisfactory, to the Christian worshipper as
was their pantheon to the Athenians.   What but so many
altars to some unknown God, at least some god before unknown, unrecognized, unhonored, have been the sects and
schisms of the Church, the new movements in theology, the
heresies of powerful thinkers, the doubts of quiet, unobtrusive
men?   It is one of the most pungent sayings of Thoreau
that "atheism may be comparatively popular with God";
and it is full of truth, so often has men's deliberate atheism
had in it more reverence for beauty, truth, and goodness
than the conventional religion of the time.   As Emerson has
said, "God builds his temple in the heart upon the ruins of
the churches and religions."   Thoreau's saying was really
nothing more than a daring variation of Plutarch's, eighteen
centuries old: "I would rather men should say there is no
such person as Plutarch than that they should say he is
cruel and revengeful and malicious.   And so God (I repeat
his thought, but not his words) would rather have men deny
his existence than assail his character."   What but an altar —
to the unknown God, yea, a temple, a cathedral — such a
jumble theologically as never was old St. Paul's architect-
urally, built and patched with every style from the eleventh
to the seventeenth century — is the new Presbyterian revision of the Westminster Confession?   That Confession
aimed at a complete enumeration of the attributes of Deity,
as the Athenian scheme of worship aimed at an exhaustive
catalogue of deities.   But there were some serious omissions.
George Fox felt them, and raised his Quaker altar, — a contradictory metaphor, I am well aware.   Wesley felt them
keenly, and raised his Arminian altar to the omitted
powers.   Channing felt them, and raised his Unitarian altar
to the omitted Dignity of Human Nature and the Divine
Benignity; and Hosea Ballou felt them, and raised his altar
to the Everlasting Love.   And, for so doing, all these and

their followers have been esteemed heretics and infidels, and their place and portion have been assigned in the lake that burneth with fire and brimstone. But now hundreds of Presbyterians are discovering that there was a very great omission in the Westminster Confession,— even the same that old Dr. Ripley encountered in the pulpit hymn-book that was the worse for wear, so that he read anent the Prince of Peace, "'And justice, mercy, truth, and'— another word that is blotted out — 'adorn his princely dress.'" The blotted word was "love," the word that has been always blotted in the Calvinistic creed. To this unknown God, how many altars have been raised from time to time, and what curses have been rained upon the heads of those who laid their courses in fair colors and cherished their aspiring flame!

But those of you who have paid the best attention to my words have noticed that the analogy of my altar-building of the heretics and the come-outers with the Athenian altars to the unknown god or gods has not been quite exact. The new departures in theology and church-life have been recognitions of a god, a good, before unknown, but recognized at length with gladsome mind and heart. There is, however, something in the manifestation of our religious life that is exactly analogous to the Athenian altars. We build after their fashion whenever in our sorrow and perplexity all that we have ever read or heard of the eternal things, all of the theology, all of the science, and all of the philosophy are too little for our need; and yet we dare believe that there are higher, holier things than these have formulated with their utmost care.

> "A warmth within the breast would melt
> The freezing reason's colder part;
> And, like a man in wrath, the heart
> Stood up and answered, I have felt."

We say the heart; but, in truth, it is rather the whole man, and not merely the discursive intellect cut off from the imagination and the moral sense. It is the moralized imaginative intellect that dares believe that there is more than this when the last word of speculation has been said. And it has a right to dare, because it is impossible that we can think or hope or dream a better than the Best, from which we come, to which we tend, is able to bestow.

But the Athenian altars to the unknown god or gods were not more the resort of men's dissatisfaction with the accepted formulas of deity than they were an expression of their desire that no excellence of beauty, truth, or good deserving reverence should go unrevered. Given with us a like desire, and how many altars should we raise, if not in stone, fair-hewn and gleaming bright, in grave and earnest speech or silent memory and praise? What need we more amidst the noise and bustle of this work-day world than a fresh summons every day to honor and reverence for the unnamed, unclassified, untrumpeted divinity of human life? Are not our daily papers for the most part altars and monuments, not to the known or unknown gods of life, the things that are beautiful and reverend and sweet and pure, but to the known demonhood and devilhood of the time? It is probably as fair to measure the moral and spiritual attainment of the present time by our daily papers as it is to measure the period of the Italian Renaissance by the Memoirs of Benvenuto Cellini, or the period of the early empire by the Satires of Juvenal, or the sixth century B.C. in Palestine by the diatribes of Jeremiah. But what a picture of our time — making the page of Tacitus to blush for shame — would rise upon the vision of some future Bancroft, Fiske, or Freeman who should use the journals of our time as *mémoires pour servir*, who should draw from them the facts of our condition! They would think there was no health in us. What catalogues of murders every day; what horrible domestic complications; what broken faith in the commercial world; what miserable political intrigues; what legislation as monopolizing as the making over to their favorites by old kings and queens of exclusive rights of manufacture and of sale; what insane assumption in the national legislature of a partisan advantage, sure to invite reprisals when the outs are in again! Woe is unto us if we cannot build our altars to the unknown gods who struggle for the mastery with these devilish powers of selfishness and wrong; if we may not dare believe that evil things, though they are vaunted so, though they are so forward and obstreperous, are not in the majority or the ascendency; that in a thousand and ten thousand quiet, simple ways good things are being done, and spirits shaped to finest issues are giving nature freely of such thanks and use as she demands! If it were not so, the political and social order would not hold together for another day.

"One of the best things" in Bellamy's "Looking Backward," I was told the other day, is his elaborate metaphor of the stage-coach on which the rich ride joyously along in peace and comfort, high up from mud and dust, and watch their human fellows tugging in the traces, who, if ever faint with hunger they let go, are crushed beneath the wheels, and so forth and so on. You know the passage well enough. If you have gone no farther in the book, you have doubtless gone as far as this. If this is one of the best things in the book, the worst must be extremely bad. To me this seems the worst, the very worst, and bad as bad can be. The rest, for the most part, is a fanciful Utopia, which we could not realize if we would, and would not if we could. Better, infinitely better, the present as it is, with all its miserable imperfections, follies, crimes, than such a dull, lack-lustre level of mere hopeless mediocrity or worse as it offers to our admiration. But the stage-coach metaphor is an arraignment of our present industrial and social order; and, since Iago slandered Desdemona, a more false and wicked accusation never has been brought by any man against his fellow-men. Were not the man a jolly joker and no more,* he would here after cross no rich man's threshold lest he should be shown the door; and no poor man's either, lest suddenly he should find himself "looking backward" with astonishment at the projectile force of one of his coach-horses' hinder legs. For his coach metaphor is equally insulting and outrageous to the

* See his confession in *The Nationalist* and his later extravaganzas.

capitalist and to the wage-earning class. It must be remembered that he is treating of classes, and not of individuals. There may be individual rich men as selfish and contemptible as the lazy do-nothings on his coach's top. There may be individual poor men as abject as his starving creatures pulling at the rope. But that our rich men as a class are lazy, selfish do-nothings, beholding with indifference or wordy sympathy the struggles of their human cattle, only those believe whose rich men are evolved, like the German's camel, from their inner consciousness; while the most humble laborer who should recognize himself and his fellows in the fellows tugging at the Bellamy rope would well deserve to be so harnessed for a time. Lazy, good-for-nothing, selfish, brutal idlers are they,— the rich men, the capitalists of America, who have organized her gigantic industries, her great systems of transportation, her interstate and international trade? who have endowed her colleges, and built her hospitals, and founded her professorships and libraries, and blessed her towns and cities with ten thousand charities that soothe and heal and bless? "Toilers at the rope," starving, emaciated, bleeding, crushed, are they,— the millions of manual laborers who in the workshops and the fields of the United States are doing what they can, man-fashion, for the support of their families and to sustain the state of the world? What parity in such a metaphor with the joyousness of honest labor that is its almost universal attribute, with "the rigor of the game" that gives such zest, with poverty that turns continually to competence, and competence that turns to wealth, obedient to the stress of patience, courage, self-denial,— rewards much better worth the straining sinews of a man than any silly decoration on the breast! The preacher's sermon in Mr. Bellamy's book, you will remember, was a glorification of the new punch-card society. Its text might well have been, "All is vanity,"; for vanity is made the only motive to industrial endeavor, or to any social help, in Mr. Bellamy's intolerable world.

I dwell too long on this, but it is not as if the Bellamy-

coach accusation were an isolated or peculiar accusation of
our industrial and social order. It is a sample article of
stuff which is the stock in trade of all our socialist reformers.
Mr. Pentecost has it for wholesale in his sermons and for
retail in his Kilkenny journal every week. Mr. Henry
George has it in that huge block of rotten stone ("The rich
are growing richer, and the poor are growing poorer") which
he has made the corner-stone of his imposing temple built
upon the ruins of the eighth commandment, which is, "Thou
shalt not steal." The more men have, the more they want;
and though Kent says in "Lear," "Nothing but misery
almost sees miracles," it is true that the most prosperous
times have ever been the times when the Utopian imagination has been most riotous. It is a significant fact that the
strikers are generally the men who are best paid,— in my
native town the shoemakers, who earn as much a day as their
fathers could earn in a whole week twenty-five years ago.
So ever the good things lead on to better things and larger
hopes. God forbid that we should rest in any foolish acquiescence with the misery, the injustice, and the wrong our
present system carries along with its triumphant flood; but it
were base ingratitude to fail to recognize the enormous gain
that has been made, and utter foolishness to imagine that
evolution without revolution is not sufficient for the correction of every vested wrong and old abuse of privilege and
power. The builders of altars and temples to the known or
unknown devils of the industrial and social order have been
legion in these latter days, and they have brought to them
an exaggerated worship. They have sacrificed to them
truth and justice and sincerity. Let us have now and then
an altar to the unknown good,— the nameless excellence of
the industrial and social order that has been wrought out by
the consenting strength and skill of countless laborers with
head and hands, which has had, and which has, so many
brave fidelities, so many splendid generosities, so much god-
like patience and endurance, so much honorable and glorious
success.

"We take some things for granted," said Dr. Bartol, when it was suggested that a meeting of the Radical Club should be opened with prayer. We do, indeed; but do we always take for granted what we should? In social ways, it seems to me, we build our altars to the unknown ill much oftener than to the unknown good. It was a rule with old geographers to place chimeras in the regions of which they were entirely ignorant. We often follow their example. Where we are ignorant of motives, we impute bad motives; we infer that we are slighted, when the neglect that we have felt has been perhaps more painful to our friend than to ourselves. It has been unavoidable. We are too apt to forget that there are other people in the world besides ourselves, and that they have their claims; that they may be sick or sorrowful, and that our friend who seems to have forgotten us may have remembered them. Our minister, perhaps, has failed to satisfy us with the exercise of his parochial function: he has not been to see us for so long. And we imagine him as wrapped in Sybaritish ease, living a *dolce far niente* life, wandering hither and thither at his own sweet will among the books and pictures that he loves, when, if we could see the record of his morning, afternoon, and evening work from day to day, the countless axes and the little hatchets that he has to grind, it may be for those who have no claim on him but that of human brotherhood or sorrow or anxiety, not his parishioners at all in any narrow sense,— if we could see all this, we should judge him much more leniently. We take too little unknown good, too much of unknown ill and blame, for granted in all the relations of our social and our friendly life. Happy are those who are themselves so frequently remiss from absolute necessity that they can make allowance for the remissness of their acquaintances and friends! Friendship is hardly worth the name, much less the cherishing, that cannot go on trusting steadily in despite of silent weeks and months and years. Ever beautiful to me is that story of Emerson's regret when Dr. Furness broke the silence of many years,— it had been so sweet for each to trust the other's faithful heart without a word of witnessing. If we could all of us cultivate something more than we now have of that spirit, building in the silent places of the mind and heart beautiful altars to the unknown, but not untrusted faithfulness of others, life would be much more rarely sweet and fine than it is now, and much more noble and serene.

As we do not make enough allowance for the unknown fidelity and truth of some, so we do not make enough allowance for the unknown resistance of others to those temptations by which they are overborne. To put yourself in his place is not enough. The tempted man is not *you*, he is himself; and where you might easily resist the temptation that solicits him (as he might easily resist your besetting sin), he goes down before it into ignominious dust. If we could think of these things rightly, I am sure our pity would be increased an hundred-fold, and that our blame of over-tempted men would be proportionately less.

Thank Heaven that, in our apprehension of the material universe, our wonder and our adoration are not commensurate with our scientific knowledge!

> "Those earthly godfathers of heaven's lights
> That give a name to every fixéd star
> Have no more profit of their shining nights
> Than those that walk and wot not what they are."

Sometimes, great Shakspere, they have less, and sometimes they have vastly more. But, if we could individually appropriate the whole result of science, we should still be obliged to say, "Lo! these are a part of His ways, but how little is yet known of Him!" and from the yet unknown, the infinitely transcendent God, would come to us an invitation that would with irresistible compulsion force us to our knees in speechless adoration. To say this is to take nothing from the glory of Science. It is she herself who builds in every heart that knows her mysteries an altar to the unknown God, beyond the moving and receding confines of her

clear intelligence there stretch such huge immensities of un-
fathomed order, harmony, and law.

Let us build altars to the unknown divinity that hides
within our throbbing human hearts. *Nosce te ipsum,*—" Know
thyself." It is not an easy matter. The higher up or deeper
down we go, the vaster seem the regions which we have not
explored. And all that we *do* know convinces us that they
are regions that abound in wonderful and glorious possibilities of beauty, truth, and good. There comes from them an
air, a breath, fresh with an intimation that here upon this
bank and shoal of time we but begin a spiritual progress of
immeasurable scope.

> "Still glides the stream, and shall not cease to glide:
> . . . .
> We men who in the morn of youth defied
> The elements must vanish; be it so!
> Enough, if something from our hands have power
> To live, to act, and serve the future hour;
> And if, as toward the silent tomb we go,
> Through love, through hope, and faith's transcendent dower,
> We feel that we are greater than we know."

CREED REVISION: WHITHER?

In making "Creed Revision" the subject of my discourse this morning, and in repeating Dr. Briggs's question "Whither?" I make no apology, as if I were asking your attention for a matter in which you have little interest. If you have little interest in it, the fact is not to your credit but to your shame. You may not care for archæology, and this matter of Presbyterian creed revision may seem as archæological to you as the microscopic examination of the integuments of an Egyptian mummy. But that there was in the mummy once a human heart that beat with love and fear gives to his poor belongings a certain human interest. Moreover, if the examination of his integuments, or any scroll held in his crumbling hand, were to any body of men a matter of eager, painful interest, on their account you ought to feel the interest of the Roman Terence,— "I am a man, and nothing human is foreign to me." Now, the Presbyterian creed revision is a matter of eager, painful interest to hundreds and thousands of human beings who are earnestly desirous to know what is the truth and to do what is right. Their creed may be a mummy now, and undecipherable the scroll it clutches in its crumbling hand; but it was once as much alive as any living thing, and walked the earth as royally as any Pharaoh of old,— ay, broke the necks of proud and foolish kings.

When I resolved, some days ago, to preach a sermon on the Presbyterian commotion, I said to myself, "Go to now, get and read all that you can grub together bearing on the matter." My newspaper clippings went but a little way. They were too brief and fragmentary, and preserved the humors and the oddities more than the essential elements of the debate. Your average reporter is too apt to be "a snapper-up of unconsidered trifles," to the exclusion of more solid matter. So I got me Dr. Briggs's volume "Whither?" and Dr. Crosby's "Good and Evil of Calvinism," and Dr. Schaff's "Creed Revision in the Presbyterian Churches," and Dr. Warfield's Princeton book, "On the Revision of the Confession of Faith,"—a plea for its inviolable sanctity, lavishing upon it all manner of tender and endearing epithets, stirring its brimstone phrases round and round, as Mr. Squeers the watered milk, and crying out, "Here's richness!" I read them all; and, when I had finished, the very chairs and tables in the room looked strange to me. I could have pinched myself to get assurance of being actually alive, or have asked, "Can anybody tell me who I am?" so far away had I been taken from this actual warm and breathing human world by the most reactionary and apologetic of the authors I had read, and so little way had I been brought back to the living present even by the most manly protestants against the obsolete and monstrous phrases and ideas of the Westminster Confession. There is something infinitely pitiful in the unreality of the whole business. We are dealing not with what men think, nor even with what they think they think, but, possibly, with what they think they ought to think. I found myself wishing that you all and every Unitarian might read what I had read. It would give you and them a new sense of the gift of God we had in the clear voice of Channing, in his freedom from the scholastic curse of making the self-consistency of a scheme the measure of its truth, and from the fashion, which Schleiermacher did more to introduce than any other, of making the old theological phrases arbitrary symbols of ideas wholly foreign to their original contents. It would be an interesting study, why these Presbyterian reformers, nearly a century after Channing's early utterance, with the advantage of all that has been since accomplished, should be to him much what a London fog is to our days of

perfect clarity. It would seem that every Unitarian who
should read the literature of this Presbyterian controversy,
its most forward as well as its most backward looking,
would have a new sense of his debt to Channing and Dewey
and Parker, a new sense of his obligation to repay this debt
with loyal service to the cheerful faith which is his great
inheritance or glorious acquisition.

Yet, if we turn but for a moment from the doctrinal
aspects of Calvinism and the Westminster Confession to the
character of Calvinism as an historic faith, we shall not wonder that a faith which has such splendid personal and historical associations has a hold, not easy to be broken, on the
affectionate loyalty of men's beating hearts. No faith has
ever had a grander history, whether in the way of individual greatness or in the way of wide political significance.
It boasts such names as William the Silent, Coligny, Henry
of Navarre, each in turn first hero, and then martyr, dying
by a priest assassin's hand; such names as Maurice and
Barneveldt, and Cromwell and Milton, and Knox and Samuel Adams, and, in our own time, Thomas Carlyle, never
more Calvinistic than when his dear old mother thought he
did not read his Bible as he should, even in his rejection of
Calvinism Calvinistic still. Now take the wider view. If
the creed had worked logically, the outcome would have
been general moral laxity. If some were elect without any
reference to their moral character, and others were reprobate,
why should anybody strive for personal character or public
good? Why not say, "God mend all!" and leave it there?
So did not they, the Calvinists of the sixteenth and seventeenth centuries. Praised as the most logical of creeds,
Calvinism has ever been the most illogical; for it has insisted on human responsibility, while at the same time insist-
ing on human inability and divine election. I have read
hundreds of pages seeking to reconcile this contradiction,
and it has seemed, after all, as irreconcilable as at first. But
Coligny's Calvinists, and William the Silent's, and Cromwell's,
and John Robinson's, never doubted their responsibility; and,

if they generally thought themselves elect, not reprobate, they thought themselves elect to do great things. And they did them gloriously,— in Huguenot France; in the United Netherlands saving a country plucked already from the sea from Philip's and from Alva's iron hands, ready to give it to the sea again, if only so it could be saved from them; at Naseby and Worcester and Dunbar and Marston Moor breaking the arm of arbitrary power; and on our wild New England shore taming the wilderness, beating back the combined malignity of Indian and Jesuit enemies, establishing that local liberty which has made us everything we are, and which now our craze for centralization puts in constant jeopardy, even amid the recreancy of the churches furnishing that fibre to our national growth which broke the axes in their traitorous hands who would have laid us low. Can any think it strange that men with such traditions at their backs are proud of them and of the faith with which they are allied? Or even that a creed as cold and hard as frozen steel should, by the force of its association with such a glorious history, glow with reflected light, as if it held some warmth within itself, some fire of human excellence?

The Westminster Confession, which is now on its defence in Presbyterian churches, presbyteries, and assemblies, is to the average Presbyterian imagination as old as Christianity itself. In fact, it is not yet two and a half centuries old. The Westminster Assembly which formulated it sat in the Jerusalem Chamber at Westminster Abbey, while the Long Parliament sat in the great Westminster Hall close by, from 1643 to 1652. It was the creature of that Parliament, subordinate to the State and formulating that subordination in its creed. The Assembly set out to amend the Thirty-nine Articles of the Church of England; but, after spending a year or two upon this work, and getting no further than the fifteenth article, it made a new start, and proceeded to make a new Confession, which, however, resembles the Thirty-nine Articles at many points, and the Irish Articles of 1615 at many more. In the Westminster Confession there are only thirty-three articles, some of them containing several sections,— fifty-three in all. Taken as a whole, the Confession is unquestionably one of the most careful and conscientious pieces of work that have ever proceeded from the theological and ecclesiastical mind. But of late there has been a growing dissatisfaction with it in the Presbyterian Churches of Great Britain and the United States. The continental Calvinists of France and Switzerland and Holland long since abandoned those features of their creeds of Augsburg, Dort, and so on, similar to those which are the objective points of the American revisionists of the present time. A few years ago the impression was very general that the Scotch Presbyterians had remained wholly unaffected by the tremendous theological upheaval in the English Church, which found in Arthur Penrhyn Stanley — physically as slight as our own Channing, but of spacious mind and yet more spacious heart — its best representative. Suddenly there was in Scotland an outburst of impassioned protest against the traditional creed, in comparison with which that of the English Church appeared unimportant. It expressed itself in the admirable critical studies of Professor W. R. Smith, entirely sympathetic with the studies of such Dutch and German radicals as Kuenen, Reuss, and Wellhausen; in the broad-minded, generous utterances of Principal Tulloch; and in that famous volume of " Scotch Sermons " by several hands, which exploded like a ton of dynamite in the orthodox camp. The explosion shook the English Presbyterians from their heavy sleep, and they began to rub their eyes and look about them. Much has transpired since then. The Established Church of Scotland has broadened its terms of subscription, being unable to alter its Confession without act of Parliament. The Free Kirk has resolved upon revision. The United Presbyterians have adopted a declaratory resolution, denying their allegiance to certain articles of the Confession. The English Presbyterians have formulated a new Confession, which we should think a great improvement on the Westminster, while still thousands of miles away from our ideal of reasonable religion.

Here in America the Presbyterians were not the first, as they were not in Scotland and England, to feel the lift of the wide-heaving energy of emancipated thought. The Episcopalians had their Heber Newton and their Phillips Brooks, and many quietly, if not openly, sympathetic with their thought; the Congregationalists had their Abbott and Munger and Gladden, and a noble company of their spiritual kin; while still the Presbyterians gave no sign. We thought they were not even musing; but they were. And, while they were musing, the fire burned, and at length it burst out into a lively flame, which never will be quenched till it has burned away not only those parts of the Westminster Confession which are at present most obnoxious to the revisionists, but many others which are now objects, like the non-elect, of *preterition; i.e.*, they are *passed over*, not exactly reprobated yet, but sure to be erelong. For the present, it must be confessed that the American Presbyterians are far behind their Scotch and English brethren. The break of the would-be revisionists with the terms of the Confession is marked by no such fresh, invigorating, human quality as that of the "Scotch Sermons" of 1880. The scholastic spirit is still dominant with the former; while the latter have drawn deep breaths of Science's vital air, and their minds have the expansion that cannot come in any other way. Our American Presbyterians are so much subdued to what they have so long worked in — like the dyer's hand — that as yet they "see men like trees walking." Nothing is clear to them, or, if it is, they deliberately obfuscate it, putting their new wine into the old bottles, and making the new labels look as much like the old cobwebbed ones as they have skill to do it.

Of the thirty-three articles of the Westminster Confession,*

* Within my usual sermon limit I cannot consider the general character of the Confession, as I would like to do. Its most striking general aspect is its Gnosticism, its stupendously pretentious knowingness, its gross familiarity with every mystery of God's being, character, and operation. No geological specimen was ever described more completely; no flower or insect ever dissected with more absolute confidence. Compared with this presumptuous Gnosticism, the Agnosticism of our own time is reverent and even worshipful.

only two, the third and tenth, have excited any wide-spread feeling of dissatisfaction. The third is that concerning "God's Eternal Decree," and the most obnoxious clauses are the third, fourth, and seventh. The third reads, " By the decree of God, for the manifestation of his glory, some men and angels are predestinated unto everlasting life and others foreordained to everlasting death." The fourth reads, " These angels and men, thus predestinated and fore-ordained, are particularly and unchangeably designed ; and their number is so certain that it cannot be either increased or diminished." The seventh reads, " The rest of mankind [*i.e.*, the non-elect] God was pleased by the unsearchable counsel of his own will, whereby he extendeth or withhold-eth mercy as he pleaseth, for the glory of his sovereign power over his own creatures, to pass by, and to ordain them to dishonor and wrath for their sin, *to the praise of his glorious justice.*" * It is the expression in this clause, " to pass by," which has its Latinized correspondent in the term "preteri-tion," which has been used so much in this debate. It veils the horror of the idea from the multitude, and even from the scholarly divines who cannot look upon the face of it and live. The tenth article deals with effectual calling ; and the section which has given most offence is the third, which reads : " *Elect* infants dying in infancy are regenerated and saved by Christ through the Spirit. . . . So are all other *elect* persons, who are incapable of being outwardly called by the ministry of the word." The fourth section reads, " Others, not elected, although they may be called by the ministry of the word, and may have some common operations of the spirit, yet they can never truly come to Christ, and therefore cannot be saved, much less can men, not professing the Christian religion, be saved in any other way whatsoever, be they never so diligent to frame their lives according to the light of nature and the law of that religion they do profess ; and to assert and maintain that they do is very pernicious

* And yet the historian John Richard Green says that these men had no sense of humor.

and to be detested." The sixth section of the twenty-fifth article and the third of the twenty-fourth are also fit subjects for revision in the opinion of Drs. Briggs and Schaff and many others. The former reads, "The Pope of Rome . . . is that anti-christ, that man of sin and son of perdition that exalteth himself in the Church, against Christ and all that is called God." The latter forbids marriage "with infidels, papists, and other idolaters." The revisionists would have this read "infidels and idolaters," so that the marriage of your sons and daughters with the daughters and sons of good Presbyterians will remain abominable. That all Unitarians are "infidels" according to the general terms of the Confession there is not the slightest doubt; nor is any change proposed that would remove from them this ban. The proposition to exchange the words declaring that the pope is antichrist has great historical interest. For it may be safely said that, however ridiculously uncritical the identification of the pope with the anti-christ of the Apocalypse, no article of the Confession was more central to it and to Calvinism in its historical character than the article in which these words occur. Of nothing else was the sixteenth and seventeenth century Calvinist so certain as that the pope was anti-christ, and no other certainty so braced him to heroic action and sublime endurance.

But the articles that reflect upon the pope and papists so injuriously are not the standards around which the fight has raged most valiantly. These have been the third and tenth articles, the former setting forth what Calvin himself called "the horrible decree," although he sanctioned it with all the force of his inexorable will. "We assert," said Calvin, "that by an eternal and immutable counsel God has once for all determined both whom he would admit to salvation, and whom he would condemn to destruction. We affirm that this counsel so far as concerns the Elect is founded on his gratuitous mercy, *totally irrespective of human merit;* but that to those whom he devotes to condemnation the way of life is closed by his own just and without doubt irreprehensible but incomprehensible judgment." If anybody could save human responsibility upon these terms, John Calvin could have done it. He tried, and failed; and every trial since has ended in like failure. Our friend, Joseph Henry Allen, ventured a few years ago to say that no man living uses such terms at this day with any serious attempt to attach distinct meaning to them. But Dr. Warfield's attempt to do this in his eloquent plea against revision, or the need of it, is sufficiently serious. But his failure is as complete as every other to show that a decree of reprobation, conditional on no foreknowledge of sin, can be because of sin. If any man upon these terms would not take up with the advice of Luther to "sin and sin valiantly," it must be because he is better than the God of Reprobation.

The article affirming the damnation of non-elect infants has never — to the credit of human nature, be it spoken — been a popular one, either with Presbyterians or Congregationalists. It has been evaded with the most lively ingenuity. It is still so evaded, Dr. Warfield blandly assuring us that the antithesis is not with non-elect infants, but with elect adults! To get the force of this evasion, you must go directly to his book. It is a marvel in the way of theological trickery, where hardly anything is marvellous. The Rev. Michael Wigglesworth assigned to the damned babies "the easiest room in hell." Augustine, less remorseless than Calvin, assigned to them a state of privation rather than of positive suffering, and Bellarmine a limbo at some distance from the burning flames. A modern Roman Catholic has however published, with the censorial permission, a book in which his imagination revels in the tortures of the doomed babies and children in a manner that sends us for a cooling draught to Boston's "Fourfold State" or Jonathan Edwards's "Sinners in the Hands of an Angry God."

Dr. Schaff, perhaps the clearest, frankest, most straightforward of the revisionists, has said, "These doctrines are no longer believed by the majority of Presbyterians, nor preached by any Presbyterian minister, so far as I know."

Dr. Cuyler has asserted that "ninety-nine hundredths " of his sect do not believe the damnatory clauses. This is certainly encouraging; and so was the fact that, when Dr. Schaff requested any one who doubted the truth of his assertion to stand up, no one had the disposition or the courage to do so. Why, then, should there be any question of revision? It is evident there is a strenuous minority, in some presbyteries a majority, opposed to change for one reason or another. But how has it been possible for men who have not believed the damnatory clauses of the Confession to continue in the Presbyterian ministry? In this way: "It is well understood," says Dr. Schaff, "that ministers and elders are allowed, according to the 'Form of Government,' liberty of dissent in all those articles of the Confession which are not necessary or essential to the system of doctrine taught in the Holy Scripture." Well may Dr. Schaff confess that he does not like this mode of subscription. It is the mode of double dealing. It is the mode of jugglers who play fearlessly with serpents whose fangs have been extracted, while they fling serpents that retain their poisonous fangs into the curious crowd.* It is the method of Deuteronomy, where it is commanded, "Ye shall not eat of anything that dieth of itself, but thou mayest give it to the stranger that is within thy gates, that he may eat it; or thou mayest sell it unto a foreigner: for thou art an holy people unto the Lord thy God." Surely, such a clause as that asserting the general doctrine of election, or that asserting the damnation of non-elect infants, is a "thing that dieth of itself." If such tainted meat is not good enough for pastors and deacons, it ought not to be good enough for any stranger to their liberties, to any foreigner who has not been initiated in the Christian art of saying what you do not mean.

But it is not probable that many of those Presbyterians who are most strenuous for the keeping of the Confession undespoiled of any monstrous phrase would publish frankly

---

* This metaphor, not the words, was used by Dr. C. C. Everett at the Unitarian Berry Street Conference, 1889.

and persistently those parts of it which have aroused the indignant protestation of so many of their brethren, and among them many of the most highly honored. What they want is to save an appearance of infallibility and sanctity for the Confession by keeping it intact, the obnoxious clauses, like so many flies in amber, in innocuous desuetude. This has long been their state, and it has measured the amount and force of the belief in them. When doctrines are preached persistently, and with such uncompromising frankness as that of Jonathan Edwards's "Sinners in the Hands of an Angry God," it is safe to suppose that the belief in them is real and vital, or deadly, as the case may be. But fancy what would be the consternation if a modern Presbyterian preacher, at any time during the last half-century, had introduced into a sermon *as his own* the following passage from one of the most saintly of the Westminster divines: "Suppose we saw with our eyes," he says, "a great furnace of fire, of the quantity of the whole earth, and saw there Cain, Judas, Ahithophel, Saul, and all the damned as lumps of red fire, and they boiling and leaping for pain in a dungeon of everlasting brimstone, and the black and terrible devils, with long and sharp-toothed whips of scorpions, lashing out scourges on them ; and if we saw there our neighbors, brethren, sisters, yea and our dear children, wives, fathers, and mothers, swimming and sinking in that black lake, and heard the yelling, shouting, and crying of our young ones and fathers blaspheming the spotless justice of God,—if we saw all this while we are living here on earth, we should not dare offend the majesty of God." The consternation of any modern Presbyterian congregation at such a glowing picture would be hardly less than would be yours if I should preach such doctrine as my own. Not even Dr. Shedd, who gives three pages to Heaven, eighty-seven to Hell, in his "Dogmatic Theology," would care to preach such stuff as this, or even such as he has written. But, as Dr. Schaff has said, "What cannot be preached in the pulpit ought not to be taught in a Confession of Faith, either expressly or by fair logical inference."

Now, what are they going to do about it? That they will follow the advice of Dr. Warfield, and do nothing, neither relaxing the formula nor the subscription to it, is hardly possible. What then? Leaving the formula intact, will they still further relax the subscription? For so doing they would have the example of the Established Church of Scotland. But they would not have the excuse of that Church, which is that, being an established church, it cannot without act of Parliament revise its creed. Our own Presbyterians escaped from this dilemma through the Red Sea of the Revolutionary War, and in 1788 they adapted the Confession to the situation. Nothing could well be more demoralizing than a strict confession with an enabling act, permitting its subscribers to believe as much or little of it as they please. The Scotch Presbyterians will probably believe very little of the Westminster Confession at the century's end. Their actual belief and their confession will grow more incongruous from year to year. I will not believe that our American Presbyterians will choose this way of miserable equivocation.

A second is suggested by the course taken by the United Presbyterian Church of Scotland in 1879,— a declaratory statement to the effect that certain things in the Confession are incredible, and therefore not to be conceived as binding on the believer's faith. That is to let "I dare not" wait upon "I would," like the cat in the adage. That is to have two contradictory statements standing side by side, each l aughing at the other mournful laughter. A third method is that which is now being pursued by the Free Kirk of Scotland, the method of revision by omission and modification. Of the three Scotch Presbyterian Churches, the Free Kirk is that with which the American Presbyterian Church has been in liveliest sympathy since its foundation, forty-seven years ago; and its method of adjustment is likely to be followed. Much better than the method of loose subscription or of double statement, it is still much inferior to that of the Engsh Presbyterians, who have formulated and are likely to adopt an entirely new Confession, in much better keeping than the Westminster with the actual opinions and beliefs now held by Presbyterians, though still removed almost immeasurably from a truly rational statement of religious faith and hope.

But let not those who think they have arrived at such a statement for themselves, or, if not to a statement, to a general rational order of belief, count it a little matter that this agitation in the Presbyterian Church is going on. It is the beginning of the end. Though at the next General Assembly the majority should be against revision, the majority will be so large, and its temper is so firm, that it will not relapse into obscurity. It will live and grow. But the chances are that something will be done, and the something is hardly more likely to be meaningless subscription or a double statement than a thorough-going change from the old Confession to one entirely new. It is likeliest to be a revision by omission and modification of the obnoxious articles. But, once entered on this path, the spirit of reform will not become quiescent with the achievement of its first noble victory. It will go on and on to a revision far more radical than that of the English Presbyterians. The extreme conservatives are well aware of this. They know perfectly well that "their strength is to stand still"; that, if they begin to move, there is no telling where they will stop. Meanwhile, how good to see the leaven work!

The most surprising special circumstance in the whole course of the debate has been the inability of the most liberal to vitally appropriate the result and meaning of that scientific criticism of the Bible which has now been going on with steadily increasing volume and momentum since Astruc's great discovery of two documents in Genesis, in 1753. It is true that one impassioned disputant declared that he would tear his Bible into shreds if it taught anything so horrible as the decree of reprobation and the damnation of infants. That was a very foolish thing to say; for, if the Bible teaches those things, it teaches many others that are altogether sweet and good. Moreover, it was written by

different men at different times, along a period of at least
a thousand years; and it would be far less absurd to hold
Chaucer responsible for Walt Whitman or *vice versâ* than to
hold the earliest writers of the Bible responsible for the
latest or the other way, or the whole responsible for any
special part. But the debaters have been generally agreed
that, if it could be shown that the Confession has Biblical
warrant, that would establish it forever. "If it were in
God's word," says Dr. Crosby, "we should accept it, however horrible it might be." But why? Even if there were
a text for every word of the horrible decrees, the grand contention of Matthew Arnold that the Bible is *literature*, and
not *dogma*, should stay the hand that sought to build its
tropes of rhetoric into an iron creed. But, were it as dogmatic as Calvin or Edwards, it is high time for every graduate of the most orthodox theological schools in the United
States to know that there is nothing in the origins of the
Bible, so far as we can make them out, that affords a parti-
cle of justification for making it the final court of appeal.
Yet even a thinker so cultured and intelligent as Dr. Abbott
writes of the theological movement of the time as an appeal
from tradition to the Bible. As if the Bible were not itself
a crystallized tradition! As if there were any reason under
heaven for making a set of writers (nearly all of them anonymous) for eight hundred years before and two hundred after
the time of Jesus a more absolute authority than the writers
of the next thousand years! If this is not clearly seen
to-day, it will be clearly seen to-morrow; and, when it is
clearly seen, the Faith of Reason, like jocund day, will
stand upon the misty mountain tops,— the clouds will break,
the shadows flee away.

But the appeal from the Confession to the Bible is not
altogether vain. Paul's doctrine of election was a doctrine
of breadth and liberality, not a doctrine of narrowness and
exclusion. He said, substantially, God can choose anybody
he pleases, and he has chosen not the Jews only, but the
Gentiles, for the kingdom of his love. But there is better

than Paul in the New Testament, even the man of Nazareth. And the Westminster Confession is the work of men to whom the Synoptic Gospels were sealed with seven seals. Did they ever look into them? Certain it is no air from their cool spaces ever blows across the arid waste of their Confession. A table of logarithms is not more unlike the poetry of Whittier and Longfellow than the articles of the Westminster Confession are unlike the parables and beatitudes of Joseph's peasant son. Yet of all that is ascribed to him there is not one sentence that we can be sure of as certainly his own; and not one that has any authority for us in excess of its intrinsic rationality, or would have, though we knew we had his *ipsissima verba,*—the very words he spoke.

It is the Twilight of the Gods, that *Götterdämmerung* of the Norse mythology, a legend strange, mysterious, appalling, come true again in our own time. Have we not had our Jotunheim of critical investigation, from which has come an air so clear and cold that it has made the gods and heroes of the old mythology shiver upon their thrones? Have not our gods of sword and hammer, our mechanic deities, gone down in battle with the frost-giants who have come from Jotunheim to contend against them? Have we not come upon a dim and formless time, full of all vaguest possibilities? "Let not your hearts be troubled, neither let them be afraid." After the Twilight of the Gods there was a new and fairer order in the world. The All-Father was not dead, nor any god deserving of men's reverence. So is it here and now. The twilight has been shorter than sometimes in that Land of the Midnight Sun, where some of you have been, and seen, before the sun had hardly set, the new day begin to make itself an awful rose of dawn. He comes again who has not gone away, the great All-Father, the Inmost Life of everything that is, He who reveals himself in every aspect of the universe, in every law which science reads aright, in every aspiration of the soul. My heart and my flesh faileth; but God is the strength of my heart, and my portion forever.

THE GREAT COMMANDMENT.*

By the great commandment I mean that which is so called in Matthew, the form of which is somewhat varied in the three Synoptic Gospels, in which only it occurs. In Mark it reads, "Thou shalt love the Lord thy God with all thy heart, and with all thy soul, and with all thy mind, and with all thy strength." Now, what I wish to ask, and, in the frankest manner possible, is whether there is anything in the experience of a reasonable faith that corresponds to this commandment. There are some things that cannot be given up without a pang. But, above all, we must be honest with ourselves and with each other. We must not pretend to emotions which we do not actually feel, to beliefs we do not really entertain. If this is lost, this passionate love of God, it does not follow that all is lost. There is a second commandment, Jesus said, which is like unto the first and greatest. It is that we shall love our neighbor as ourselves. This would still remain to us, although the first were gone; and to obey it would be no holiday affair. If you imagine it is easy, keep it for one whole day, and then see what you think.

But why suggest a doubt that to love God is now any

* When this sermon, which was first preached in Brooklyn, was repeated in Chesterfield, Mass., last summer (1889), it was introduced as follows: "I have assumed, perhaps unwarrantably, that the audience I should address this morning would be mainly friends in general sympathy with my habitual thought, and, therefore, I have chosen my sermon with some reference to their natural desires. But those friends and neighbors who have been drawn here only or mainly by the sweet habitudes of the place will, I trust, appreciate the compliment I pay to their liberality in aiming rather at a clear expression of my habitual thought than at something, easily possible, in which we might all agree."

more difficult than it has ever been? We do not suggest it. It is forced upon us by the changing attitude of religious thought. The thought of God is now so different with many from what it ever has been in the world before. Our great commandment first appeared in Deuteronomy about six hundred years before the time of Jesus. It was addressed exclusively to the Jewish people. For them to love the Lord their God was an easy matter, for the simple reason that he was *their* God, and they were his people. He had brought them up out of the land of Egypt. He had cherished them with a peculiar care. All other nations had been colonial dependencies, or even less than that upon his rule. All these things they believed. But in course of time Christianity translated the Old Testament phraseology of a favored nation into the language of sectarian self-satisfaction. The God of the Calvinists, the Baptists, the Methodists, was *their* God as much as Jehovah was the God of Israel. For his own elect to love him was surely natural, seeing that before the foundation of the world he had chosen them without any reference to their moral qualities. Equally natural and easy was it for those to love him who conceived that he would save those, and only those, who held fast to their doctrines of baptism and conversion, and so on.

Then, too, we must consider that the love of God has in past times been much assisted, and is still, for many by the thoroughly anthropomorphic, human, manlike aspect under which he has been conceived. For hundreds of years art contributed immensely to this conception by its representation of the Deity as a benignant old man. This representation was in exact accordance with the Hebrew term which the King James translators very shrewdly translated Ancient of Days, one of the most imposing synonyms of Deity that we have ever had; and yet it only means Old Man! The identification of Jesus with God has done much to make the mental image of Deity a human image. Good people who expect to see God when they die think they shall recognize him by his resemblance to the conventional representation of Jesus, little knowing what a risk they run of confounding him with Plato, upon a bust of whom the conventional representation of Jesus would seem to have been based. The young lady educated in the strictest manner of her sect, who expected to see God as an individual up in heaven, and always thought of him as looking like Jesus *until she was engaged*, was no doubt sufficiently absurd; and yet she was not distant in her thought from many thousands of religious women all along the past, to whom God was the heavenly lover, if not God the Father, God the Son. Saint Catherine of Siena was not the only woman who imagined herself united in a mystic marriage with the Eternal Son. A like imagination — and I am glad that they could cherish it — was the consolation of thousands of tender women cut off from earthly love and marriage by a monstrous and degrading superstition. There are survivals* of the old imagination in a hundred hymns, like "Jesus, lover of my soul, Let me to thy bosom fly."

The conception of God has been dehumanized, made less manlike, for many, by the enlargement of the world by astronomical science. So long as the Ptolemaic conception of the universe held its own, and the earth was regarded as the only sizable body,— the others intended simply for its ornament and use,— when it was a daring suggestion that the moon might be as large as all of Greece, the God of such a universe as this, made solely for our good, was not so vast, so formidable, as to seem incapable of loving us and of being loved by us with any natural affection. But when we have learned that Jupiter is thirteen hundred times as large as our little earth, and that seventy-five million stars have been already counted, whose planets, though perhaps as large as Jupiter, are all invisible to us; and that the sun is so big that the moon's circuit of the earth could be inside of it, with room to spare; and that the sun is but a baby-sun to Sirius and many another star that kindles in the vault of

---

* "Survivals" are those forms of speech and action which have no longer their original use or meaning.

heaven; and that, while the earth is swinging round the sun, the sun is swinging round some infinitely distant star as much vaster than the sun as the sun is than the earth; and that all this mighty pageant must have been substantially the same for millions of years before there was a man or any living creature on the earth,— when we have learned all this and a hundred times as much that is like unto it, and have come to vitally imagine what it means as to the Being who is the Life and Heart of such a universe, its All in All, our awe, our reverence, our adoration, may be vastly greater than these sentiments in earlier times; but what reality can be connoted by the great commandment, "Thou shalt love the Lord thy God with all thy heart, and with all thy soul, and with all thy mind, and with all thy strength"?

I answer, A reality higher and sweeter every way than that of any former time. I answer that there was no impulse to the love of God for those who thought of him as devoted wholly to their nation or their creed, for those who thought of him as a dear old man or as wearing "the express image" of Jesus, which is not multiplied a thousand-fold by that enlargement of the universe which makes such thoughts of God impossible and monstrous and absurd. For you will observe that the greatening of the universe has been accompanied at every step by an increasing unification of its processes and parts. Unity is the creed of science. The geologists, the biologists, the physicists, are all such Unitarians as Channing never was and could not be. The old lines of difference remain as clearly marked as ever, but they are like a net let down into the sea: the infinite ocean of God's unity streams back and forth through them without any let or hindrance whatsoever. There is no uniformity. One star differeth from another star in glory. So mineral differeth from mineral, and flower from flower. The number of classified varieties of plants has been increased within my recollection from one hundred to three hundred thousand. God does indeed fulfil himself in many ways. But the less the uniformity, the more the unity. Like principles disclose themselves in the most different forms. The apple-blossom is a rose; the whale's fin is a hand; the melons, the oranges, the peaches, are "nothing but leaves," each fruit a modified leaf; and, through the spectroscope as through a telephone, the constituents of our own planet shout from the sun and infinitely more distant stars with irrepressible hilarity, "Here we are again!" There are thousands and ten thousands of these resolutions of apparent difference into Essential Unity. And, in their final summing up, what they amount to is that the universe and God are One. This, or no God at all. Of a world *made* there is not a hint or sign. Of a world organically developed, there are a hundred million signs.

> "All are but parts of one stupendous whole,
> Whose body nature is, and God the soul."

And so it happens that the infinite greatening of the world has not set God apart in incommunicable grandeur. It has brought him nearer to us than he ever was before. The universe is not a great machine which he constructed long ago, and to which he communicated perpetual motion, and then retired forever from the scene. It is the revelation of his constant presence, the manifestation of his constant life. Its ether is his breath. Its ocean currents are his circulation. Its galaxies are the molecules of his teeming brain. And still, although I have implied, I have not named the unity that does most to neutralize the overpowering vastness of the scientific conception of God. His unity with nature has brought him near; but, the nearer, the more crushing to our littleness, until we have learned that, when Jesus said (if indeed he said it), "I and my Father are one," he only said what every one of us can say, *must* say, in virtue of our unity with the whole material universe. We have the word of science for it that, of our physiological functions, a good part is strictly vegetable. Cut us off from other vegetable and animal growths, and straightway we should droop and die. Our relation to the inorganic world is not less close. More than half our bodies is lime, phosphorus, sodium, or some other inorganic substance. With every breath, we take in a new stock of inorganic matter, exchanging it for other. How strange, moreover, that the inorganic matter by which we live is just as inorganic, just as dead, while it is nourishing our life as when it is in the atmosphere, before or after its essential contribution to our physical vitality! In ten thousand delicate and subtile ways, the human organism is implicated in that organism of nature which is none other than the Word becoming flesh and stone and tree. "Take, eat, this is my body," speaking by the mouth of Science, says the Eternal Master of the world, as we sit at joyful feast with him in this upper chamber of the world's latest thought, with his disciples — Copernicus and Galileo, and Newton and Herschel, and Lyell and Darwin — sitting round about, a glorious company; we at their feet for patient listening and reverent thankfulness.

So the great gulf is bridged. So the infinity of God that would crush us if it were apart from us sustains us because we are a part of it. So the love that an infinitely gigantic mechanician would repel is invited by the infinitely unfolding life of which our lives are evermore a part. So is satisfied, at length, that craving of the soul for union with the Eternal Oneness which is the heart of all religion.

But, by the canons of this new interpretation, is not God as much too near as he was before too far away? How can we love that of which we are ourselves a part? How but because, though never separate, we are distinct, as the citizen from the State, as the leaf from the tree. If the leaf were conscious of the great life of which it is a part, might it not love it well and try for good received in vital sap to render back whatever it can pluck from earth and air to help the general life. The individual is little wiser than a fool who does not know how worthless his own life would be cut off from the great social whole. The certainty of his unity with that is the ground of his fidelity, the spur of his devotion, the inspiration of his good endeavor. And so the great commandment does not fail. More than ever, a thousand times more than ever, because thou art inseparable from God, "Thou shalt love the Lord thy God with all thy heart, and with all thy soul, and with all thy mind, and with all thy strength." Thou art a leaf of this tree Igdrasil, whose other name is God. Through thee its vital juices stream. Dance thou in sun and rain; ay, dance for joy that thou art part, though but a million-trillionth of a decillionth part of the great whole,— nay, not so much as that. And, if there is anything that thou canst do for any fellow-leaf, for any fruit that needs thy bit of shade, for any bird that wants thy fibre for his nest, then do it with thy might.

When Jesus gave the great commandment, I do not imagine that the terms he used, "heart, soul, and mind, and strength," were terms of definition. They were terms of emphasis, of intensification. And yet they carry with them — some of them, if not all — suggestions that we may profitably heed. Seeing that by the canons of our new interpretation God is no mere abstraction, no mere individual, no heavenly Jesus, or benignant king celestially enthroned, but both the immanent and transcendent wholeness of the world, we love him when we love anything which manifests his life. According to the old interpretations, he must be loved with an exclusive, according to the new with an inclusive, love. According to the old interpretations, he was a jealous God. We must beware of loving any human friend too much, of loving wife or husband, child or friend or lover, more than God. If we were not careful about this, the first thing we should know, God would take away the beloved person from our sight, from our embracing arms, and leave us desolate. I doubt if this way of thinking ever made men and women love their dear ones any less, but it touched their love with fear and trembling. That it ever made anybody love God any more, it is impossible to conceive. It made men and women oftentimes curse God and die. John Carman of Carmantown, who burned down the village meeting-house because they told him God had taken away the little child he loved so much, because he loved her so much, was a representative person. I wonder that, till very recently, a church in Christendom has been allowed to stand. But now "Thou shalt love the Lord thy God with all thy heart" means, or should mean, that we must love him with all the love we have for anybody or for anything. We are in no danger of robbing him. Seeing that all things are in him, we cannot love anything or anybody with a high and noble love without loving him. Whether we love the beautiful things of nature or the beautiful things of art, the mountains or the sea, the music of Beethoven, the sculptures of Michel Angelo, the paintings of Raphael, whether we love our country or our friends, our parents or our children, our wives and husbands, or those whom not having seen we reverence and admire, unconsciously or consciously we are loving God. And the commandment to love him with all our hearts will then be best obeyed when we devoutly recognize that all our love for anybody or for anything, so that it be high and pure and noble, is verily the love of him. We shall love him with a wiser love when we abandon ourselves completely to this spiritual method than when we try to isolate him from his world and love him in that isolation. But why talk of loving God at all? Why not love the beautiful things of nature and of art, the dear ones of our home, the youth and maid each other with those eye-beams that imparadise the heart, the country for which a million men have gladly died, the cause that we delight to serve,— why not, and leave it there? Because each separate love will be ennobled when we see in it a part of that great love of the Infinite and Eternal God which is exclusive of no generous affection, but inclusive of each and every noble passion that can fire our hearts. I do not mean that every generous affection, every noble passion, is converted into the love of God by being deliberately so regarded. Whatever we may think of them, they will be that. But we shall touch them with a finer grace if we associate

them in our thought with Him who is the source of all perfection, beauty, love, and joy.

After heart, the next word by which Jesus climbed to the
expression of his thought was soul. "Thou shalt love the
Lord thy God with all thy soul." Now, it is evident that
there are meanings of the word "soul" which would not
greatly help us here; *e.g.*, the continuous conscious self, or
again the unity of all our intellectual and moral faculties.
In the former we have something purely psychological, and
in the latter nothing that would not be implied in heart and
mind. But the word "soul" is also used to indicate those
higher ranges of man's spiritual nature which converse with
ideal excellence. Now, as some men have less heart than
others, less emotional energy, some less mind than others,
less intellectual force, and some less strength (of body or of
will), so some have less soul, less spiritual energy. How
much of it your friends and neighbors have might be determined pretty accurately by their admirations. If they find
all they need in Colonel Ingersoll's presentation of religion,
or in Thomas Paine's or in Voltaire's or Benjamin Franklin's, it would be safe to conclude that they were not spirit-
ually-minded persons, that they were not distinctively men
of soul. One can be very much of a man, and have but
little soul in this sense, but little spirituality. But, where
this is lacking, it is a very real lack. There are men to
whose equipment we cannot think of this as being super-
added. And we would not spoil what they are, to have this
added unto them. But, where the nature of a man rises
into this naturally, it crowns his life as beautifully as the
spire of Salisbury or the tower of St. Ouen crowns those
lovely miracles of the builders' joyous art. And, whether a
man has much or little, to him cometh the commandment,
"Thou shalt love the Lord thy God with all thy soul,"—not
merely with so much of it as, cherishing an image of his
infinite righteousness, yearns after ever closer unity with
that, but with so much of it as yearns after any ideal excellence, after any nobleness that we have seen in any living

friend or in the recorded life of any man or woman enamoured of perfection and seeking it with a resistless will. For the Eternal is the source not only of all outward fairness, but of all beautiful ideals. Their attraction is his attraction, whether we think of it or not. If we think of it, so much the better. Then every stream of spiritual aspiration takes its way with conscious joy to swell the flood of our rejoicing in the Infinite Righteousness. But, if it is not so, that "they who are in sin are in the punishment of sin" is not more true than that they who are in the love of ideal excellence are in the love of God.

The next word by which Jesus endeavored to intensify his great commandment was mind. Here, as in the previous cases, I do not wish to attribute that to Jesus which he did not have in mind. But here, even more obviously than there, there is a suggestion in the word that would not have been unworthy of the man who said, "My judgment is just, because I seek not mine own will." *There* was a perception of the ethics of the intellect to which not many of the followers of Jesus have attained. What is it to love God with the mind? It is to love truth; it is to love the paths which lead to the discovery of natural laws and of the constitution of the world. "Thou shalt love the Lord thy God with all thy mind." Not such has been the method of the Christian centuries. With so much of it, the churches have declared, as will lead to a foregone conclusion. To love truth with *all* the mind, to endeavor only to see things as they are, however little the result agrees with the established formulas of Christianity,—this has ever been a miserable and accursed thing in the eyes of preachers, priests, and popes. The Church has said, "Thou shalt love God with all thy theologic mind, endeavoring therewith to confirm thyself in what thou hast received from us; but if, ceasing to be an advocate, thou shalt attempt to be a judge, thou shalt have hell hereafter and as much of a foretaste of it here and now as we can manage to give thee with our racks and wheels, our thumb-screws and our iron virgins, our loathsome prisons

and our torturing flames." The penalties are not the same
to-day that they have been in the past, but they are still
serious enough for sensitive and eager minds. "I verily believe," Prof. Huxley says, "that the great good which has
been effected in the world by Christianity has been largely
counteracted by the pestilent doctrine on which all the
churches have insisted, that honest disbelief in their more
or less astonishing creeds is a moral offence, indeed a sin
of the deepest dye, deserving and involving the same future
retribution as murder and robbery. If we could only see,
in one view, the torrents of hypocrisy and cruelty, the lies,
the slaughter, the violations of every obligation of humanity
which have flowed from this source along the course of the
history of Christian nations, our worst imaginations of hell
would pale beside the vision." *

That does not seem to me too strong a statement of the
case. And how different the history of Christianity would
have been if men had loved the Lord their God with all their
mind ; the Lord their God,— the simple truth of things, the
divine and infinite fact ; with *all* their mind, not with so
much of it as remained after the Church had drained away
all of its better part to keep in motion her machinery of
ritual and doctrine ! Who are the men in our own time who
are loving God with all their mind? They are not those
who are endeavoring to force from science a confession
favorable to the claims of the traditional theology. They
are not those who are trying to force from the Bible and the
creeds a confession favorable to the claims of science.
They are those whose hearts are singing "Nearer, my God,
to thee," and who dare believe that nearer to him is nearer
to the fact. They are those who cannot think that it is reverence to imagine that our preconception may be better than
that which actually is ; for what actually is, is God.

They that love God with all their mind because they love
truth with absolute simplicity may not be conscious of the

* Months after my first use of this quotation in my sermon, I found it quoted with
approval by Professor Momerie, a distinguished preacher of the Established Church of
England, in a sermon on the Athanasian Creed.

divine quality of their affection. They may not connect their passion for the simple truth of geology or biology or anthropology or history or political economy with the name or thought of God. Happy are they, if they do. If they do not, still happy, in that, even as they who are in the love of beauty or ideal excellence are in the love of God, so are they also who are in the love of Truth, though all the churches cast them out.

"With all thy strength," said Jesus, crowning so his thought. "With all thy weakness" has been the more common thought of Christendom. The sickly body, the enfeebled mind, the passions of the natural man thwarted as in the monk and nun, or, what is worse, shamefacedly indulged, passive obedience,— the will subjected to some spiritual director standing in the place of God,— such have been the ideals of the Church, such the offerings with which it has imagined God well pleased. So deep the poison works that even in our liberal churches there are men, and preachers of religion, who would not lie or steal, whom wild horses could not drag to such offences, to whom the laws of health writ in their bodily constitution are of no account. Nor is the spiritual pride of Saint Simeon Stylites on his pillar entirely absent from the bosoms of these modern saints. But still the great commandment stands, and this part of it, "with all thy strength," as much as any other. Not as feeble, passionless, emasculated, weakly obedient to another's arbitrary will, does any true man show himself a servant of the highest. That he that made us also meant us is a saying worthy of all acceptation. So long as the material universe, including our material bodies, was imagined as something opposite and antagonistic to the divine power, or at best a manufactured article, it was natural for men to view the whole material order, including their own physical organization, with frank contempt or qualified admiration. But what foothold have these sentiments in a physical universe which is the ever-present manifestation of the Infinite and Everlasting God? "I touch heaven," said Novalis, "when I lay my hand upon the human body." Alike the beauty and the wonder of it justify the word ; and Browning's, too, which you have heard before : —

> " Then let us no more say,
>   Spite of this flesh to-day,
> I strove, made head, gained ground upon the whole.
>   As the bird wings and sings,
>   Let us cry, ' All good things
> Are ours; nor soul helps flesh more now than flesh helps soul.' "

How, then ? Does it not appear that for us, as for no men before us, the great commandment has a meaning full of inspiration ? Thou shalt love *the manifested God* with all thy heart, and with all thy soul, and with all thy mind, and with all thy strength. And he is manifested in the beauty and the wonder of our material frames, in the beauty and the wonder of the whole material universe, in the love of every faithful heart, in the passion for perfection of all noble souls. Wherefore, we can obey no law of health, we can exercise no godlike passion, we can seek no truth of science, we can love no beauty of nature, no blessed human friend, without loving at the same time, and by divine necessity, the manifested God. Better were it a thousand times to love the manifested God in these high ways, though breathing not his name, though absent from him in our thought, than to spend all the energy of our devotion on some vast abstraction or some gigantic individual being throned beyond the stars. But it were best of all to live in daily consciousness of the Unifying Force from which proceed so many streams of blessing to mankind. Then, as the dying Bunsen saw the Eternal in the face of his beloved wife, we shall see it in the face of every fair and precious thing. What worship of the churches shall then sufficiently express the worship of our hearts ? "Be still," the spirit of the universe shall say to us in the bird's song, and in the sound of falling waters, and in the voice of every dear and noble friend, — "be still, and know that I am God."

THE REJOICING HEART.

WHETHER Paul did or did not write the Epistle to the Philippians is one of the questions of New Testament criticism that are not easy to decide. That great critic, Ferdinand Christian Baur, who allowed to Paul only four of the fourteen epistles that are commonly ascribed to him,— Romans, the two Corinthians, and Galatians,— was certain that Philippians was not his; but even his most loyal followers of the Tübingen school have been much less so. Baur found in the epistle hints of the Gnostic speculations of the second century, and ascribed the epistle to that time. But Paul's mind was always on the move. The nature of Christ was to him a matter of free speculation; and, assuming that Philippians and Colossians are from his hand, they do not exhibit a greater advance upon his Christology in Romans than Romans does upon First Thessalonians, the first epistle that he wrote, or rather that has been preserved. I find it easier to believe that we have in his latest epistles the dawn of Gnostic speculation than that they present to us a reflection of that speculation when it had climbed to its meridian height. I do not find it easy to believe that his personality could be reproduced so vividly by an imitator of his style. In Philippians I find the very man who wrote Galatians, which is unquestionably Paul's,— the same impetuous and fiery soul.

Taking the epistle at its face value, it was Paul's last epistle, written in Rome, in prison, only a little while before his death. It was not a cheerful situation. You have visited, perhaps, the little subterranean church in Rome, just at the corner of the Forum (San Pietro in Carcere), which they give out was the prison in which Paul and Peter were confined. But Peter never was in Rome, and the only reason for supposing that Paul was imprisoned here is that no other prison of his time has been identified. This was a prison of his time and earlier; and here Jugurtha, the Numidian royal captive, was confined (106 A.D.), and later Vercingetorix, of whom Cæsar's Commentaries tell. That Paul's prison was any better we have no reason to believe. It was probably much worse. Dark as it was, it was made darker by the shadow of impending death,— such death, perhaps, as theirs whom Nero swathed in pitch to light the streets of Rome. And then, besides, the "perils of false brethren," their jealousies and machinations, were present with him always, daring him to think one cheerful, happy thought. So circumstanced, what kind of a letter did he write to the Philippian Christians whom he loved? A letter that was a psalm of joy! Like a composer's theme, the joyfulness continually appears. It is in the opening sentences; and, when he thinks that he is near the end, it rings out, "Finally, brethren, rejoice in the Lord!" But he has more to say, much more; and in a little while, as he goes on, he breaks out again, "Rejoice in the Lord always; and again I say unto you, Rejoice!" Could the most protected and secure and pampered citizen of Rome have written a more radiantly cheerful letter in that year of God, eighteen hundred and twenty-seven years ago?

Now, it were an easy thing to account for Paul's rejoicing in the Lord by saying he had supernatural support, that he was an inspired apostle, and that beyond the darkness and the danger of the immediate present he could see, with awe-struck face, the glory of Christ's second coming, and his heart could sing, as our own Lowell's did in a most miserable and monstrous time,—

"Though the cause of evil prosper, yet 'tis Truth alone is strong,
And, albeit she wander outcast now, I see around her throng
Troops of beautiful tall angels, to enshield her from all wrong";

but my own persuasion is that the apostle's happy heart, his radiant cheerfulness at a time when there was so much in the circumstances that environed him to cast him down and break his spirit, was not peculiar to himself nor the result of any special grace that he enjoyed. Not because he was different from other men, but because he was like them, in the midst of sorrow and anxiety and the gravest possible anticipations his heart brimmed over with contagious joy. The lives of men and women continually present this paradox,— that it is not the most favored and most fortunate, those who have everything they want, every comfort, every luxury, who are the most joyous and serene : it is quite as often those who have been wounded grievously by the slings and arrows of outrageous fortune. The impatient and dissatisfied are often those who have the most. The farmer-folk I meet in Chesterfield, and round about, work hard, and have very little money,— not a hundred dollars a year in cash, upon the average, I am credibly assured. But, somehow, their faces and their talk brighten the sunshine for me every summer day. They have no envy of my idleness ; would not exchange for it their strenuous toil. When their crops fail, as frequently they do, they shame me by their cheerful acquiescence. When my mind's acres are unfruitful, yield nothing to my drudgery, I show, I fear, a less untroubled mien. Would the same number of millionaires, taken as they might chance to come, show a more cheerful spirit than my farmer-folk ? I doubt it very much.

But you will say, and rightly, too, that I am looking at this matter in a very narrow way. I have no right to make a purely local situation, and my own casual impression, even of so much, a standard of things wide and general. No, I have not. So I will take the widest aspect that I know, the total aspect of modern civilization, of the intellectual and social world. There never was before a time of so much wealth, of so much comfort, of so much luxury, as this time of ours. The increase of wealth has been greater in the last century than in a dozen centuries before. But with increase

of wealth there may be such unequal distribution that, while
Dives has abundance, Lazarus is starving at his gate.   Yes ;
and this is something that should be carefully considered.
An enormous aggregate of wealth cannot console us for the
ruinous poverty of many, while the few have piled their
fortunes mountains high.   At the same time, the formula,
"The rich are growing richer and the poor are growing
poorer," is a misleading one.   The only general truth in it
is that the poor are growing relatively poorer.   Absolutely,
the poor man of to-day has comforts and advantages that the
kings and queens of Europe could not boast three or four
centuries ago.   And, taking the social order as a whole,
never before at any time was the average of wealth, of comfort, of luxury, so high as it is now.   Never before were the
advantages and opportunities of life so great.   But, if literature is at all to be relied upon as an exponent of our social
life, for all its wealth and comfort, for all its luxury, for all
its advantages and opportunities, it is not happy.   It is very
far from being so.   Pessimism is the characteristic note.
Says Mr. Howells, in his introduction to Signor Verga's wonderfully sad and beautiful story, "The House by the Medlar-
tree," "Life was mainly sad at Trezza because life is mainly
sad everywhere."   That is the opinion of all the greater
novelists,— that life is mainly sad everywhere ; and the
lesser ones, of course, take up their dolorous strain.·   As if
it were not sad enough, they write novels that make it sadder
still,— novels that are infinitely depressing.   The artists,
too, must be forever painting pictures that suggest or baldly
represent the misery of human life,— pictures of brutality
and vice and crime that brutalize the men and women who
hang them on their walls.   Reading such novels and seeing
such pictures, one would think that they were written and
painted by men on whom the bludgeonings of fate have
rained incessantly, or men who have satiated themselves
with every grosser pleasure and are suffering from the reaction which always follows hard on such satiety.   But they
are not such.   They are successful men,— men who have

wealth, honor, comfort; whose houses are full of beautiful objects; who are fed daintily and exquisitely served; who have friends to praise them, love them; and, while it is impossible to believe that such a pessimism as that of Tolstoï is not the scum arising on the stagnant stream of jaded passion and excess, no such explanation covers all the facts. In art and literature, as in the world at large, there are good men to whom life, however choice and sweet their own, seems full of bitterness,—"a restless weariness, a clinging curse." Lame, indeed, would be the logic that from this state of things (so obvious, so rampant, in our time, that no one who is not wholly immersed in his own narrow, selfish interests can help seeing it as it is) should deduce the necessity for the ends of happiness of a barren, meagre life; but it does seem to show that for the community as for the individual the external things of wealth and luxury have no infallible charm, no absolute power, to bring us joy and peace. For there is nothing in our modern life so obvious and striking as the contrast between the splendor of our material successes, our wealth, our luxury, and the world-pain, world-weariness, the languor and depression, that infect the mind of art, the mind of literature, the average thought of the most fortunate and successful men.

I have said we often have the seeming paradox of men in sorest straits lifting up, as Paul did in his prison, a heart of joy; but it is not because they are in sorest straits that they are bright and glad, as it was not because Paul was in a loathsome prison, death impending, and false friends about him, that he sang his psalm of joy. The natural operation of good fortune is to make men cheerful and happy, and the natural operation of ill fortune is to make them miserable and sad. And, therefore, when it happens that men whose good fortune is conspicuous are not happy, you may be sure that in their experience there is some root of bitterness; and, when it happens that men whose ill fortune is conspicuous have still in them a heart of joy, you may be sure that somehow, somewhere, high up or deep down, un-

derlying or overarching their pain and sorrow, there is a
great satisfaction, strength, and peace.   Sometimes we cannot fathom the mystery: we only know, because the joy is
there, there must be something higher than itself from which
it flows.   But here and there in the wide range of human
life the source from which the joy in sorrow flows is evident
as the joy itself.   It was this way with Paul there in his
Roman prison, with death not far away,— not quiet, natural
death, but some sort that Nero would devise to give his jaded
appetite a pleasant thrill.   Doubtless, he thought *his* emperor
would soon be coming back to earth again, and that before
his face Nero and all his crew would be like leaves in autumn weather whirled away by the strong wind.   But, if he
had cherished no such expectation, there would still, I think,
have been in him a heart of joy.   And why?   Because he
had in him a great enthusiasm for a great cause.   There is
nothing likelier than that to make men happy and rejoicing
in the face of monstrous opposition, in despite of poverty
and misery and pain and death.   You know well enough
what Latimer at the stake cried out to Ridley in the flames :
"Be of good cheer, Brother Ridley; for we have lighted a
candle this day in England that can never be put out."   You
know what balm for his great sorrow Richard Cobden recom-
mended to his friend, John Bright.   There never was at any
time a happier set of men and women than the abolitionists
whom Garrison grappled to his soul with hooks of steel.
They were hated and despised.   Not many rich, not many
fortunate, were found among them ; and not even wealth
or bluest Boston blood could save them from indignity and
rude assault.   For them, too, there were often perils of false
brethren ; for, whatever happened to the slave, Christ and
the Church must have the first and last consideration.   But,
while others tired of their persistency, they were sustained
by their idea.   Through all their private correspondence,
through all their personal intercourse, there runs a strain of
sweet and lofty cheer, a strain of joy.   Can old age ever be
so beautiful again, now that it cannot have that life of con-

flict overpast, turning to peace and quietness, to placid beauty, absolute serenity, as it did in the lives of Garrison and Lucretia Mott? I speak that which I know, and testify to that which I have seen. A stranger would have imagined that these people had never known an anxious thought, that they had been always shielded from the rougher winds and harsher tumults of the world.

The same truth came out for me strikingly this summer in the life of Captain Cook. It is very interesting to contrast his journal with that of one of the professional corps attached to the exploring expedition. It seems hardly possible that the two can be detailing the same order of events, Cook's is so bright and cheerful, the other is so melancholy and foreboding. Once, where this reports Cook as very dangerously sick, his own subsequent account is the most casual and indifferent. And, as they sailed further south, and the fogs and icebergs thickened about them, and the possibility of ever getting back seemed slighter every day, Cook's health grew perfect, and his spirits rose and reached their climax as they came upon what seemed a continent of ice, with icy mountains rising from its general elevation, whose shore they skirted, seeking vainly for some inlet many a blinding day.

One of the newest books demanding your attention is the Life of Dorothea Dix, which my friend, Francis Tiffany, has written excellently well. It is a book which those of you especially whose hearts have at any time, by any personal experience, been touched with a feeling for the infirmity of those whose minds have lost their healthy, natural motion should get and read, and thereby quicken your gratitude to one who, "in journeyings often" with marvellous patience and persistency, did more for the right treatment of the insane than any of the many others who have gone upon this arduous crusade. Her biographer finds in her another illustration of the truth contained in the familiar saying that "the world's work is done by its invalids." But what interests me in this connection is the fact that but for her great idea, but for her holy cause, Miss Dix would probably never have been anything but an invalid, lying round helplessly upon sofas, so useless and forlorn as to excite the mild derision of her friend, Dr. Channing,— himself a valetudinarian of the most aggravated type. Grandly inspired, she gathered up what little strength she had, and with that little did as much, apparently, as if she had had the muscles of an athlete and the digestion of a stoker at her service and command. "When I am weak, I am strong," the great apostle cried. And so might she have done if she had had time to think over-much about herself. As it was, in the rushing stream of her enthusiasm for those whom God seemed to have forgotten, she was almost as forgetful of her body as Clarkson was of his soul. "I had forgot that I had any," answered he to Wilberforce's anxious interest in that abstraction.

I know what you would say,— that great causes are not as "plenty as blackberries," which, by the way, were never plentier than they have been this last abundant summer. No: they are not; and some that are accounted great will perhaps grow small by degrees and pitifully less on a more close acquaintance. But, if I am not mistaken, there are still causes in our politics and social life great enough to pique the energy and enthusiasm of a countless multitude. If the great cause that shall enlist our sympathy and co-operation must be something picturesque, something romantic and poetic, then it may be hard to fit us with exactly such a halo as we want. But it is only, for the most part, in the long perspective of succeeding time that any of the great causes are picturesque, are romantic and poetic. Those that appear so at the time are very apt to dwindle in that long perspective "from the smallness of a gnat to air." But there is many a cause which is not intrinsically great which has the power of greatening those whom it attaches to itself with a disinterested passion. These various schemes for the amelioration of labor and the salvation of society,— they cannot all be sound because some of them are contradictory. If the socialist is right, the anarchist is manifestly wrong, or at least one must be an Hegelian in philosophy, and believe that two opposite propositions can be asserted with equal truth to suspect the truth of this. And, then, it cannot be disguised that for many persons caught in the swirl of these ambitious schemes the animating motive is a purely selfish one. It is to get even with somebody, to make one's self felt, to hear one's self talk, to exercise a little brief authority, to get more money with less work or none. But all this is but a part of the whole story; and some, who ought to know much better than I do or can, assure me that it is the smallest part. I hope it is. I know there is another part. I know that there are many drawn to these schemes of social reformation by the pain they have in their brother's side, by their sympathy with the crushed and overborne; and I know that, to which-ever of the various schemes they may attach themselves, their enthusiasm and devotion are an honor to themselves and a shame and accusation to the many young and old who have no thought except for their own profit or pleas-ure. Better attach one's self with enthusiasm and ardor to the most mistaken social scheme than be devoted entirely and forever to one's own advantage! The enthusiasm and the ardor will at least produce some fruit of private charac-ter; and from out the clash of rival theories there will come some light upon the darkness of the sad and troubled time.

But it is not as if the only resource were a high and honor-able devotion to some scheme for realizing the ideal of social justice, of political integrity, of religious sanity, of indus-trial reform. These schemes, real and unreal, await the patience and the courage of all those who have the will to grapple with them in a downright serious way. But, while the realization of the ideal thus beckons from afar, the ideal-ization of the real is a more homely possibility which is ever close at hand,—to make one's home, one's business, one's relations of friendship and affection, one's social life, as gen-uine, as true, as helpful, as kind, as earnest, as sincere, as they can possibly be made. If such idealizing of the real appears to you a little matter, hardly deserving of the full-grown energy of a man or woman in the enjoyment of both physical and mental health, I would suggest that you should give it a fair trial for one year, or one month, or one week, or even for one day.

"Rejoice in the Lord always; and again I say unto you, Rejoice!" Now, "the Lord" of Paul's rejoicing was not the God of heaven and earth. He was Jesus of Nazareth, or at least the ideal personality whom Paul had evolved from his own inner consciousness, and called by that beloved name. It is one of the great misfortunes of Biblical nomenclature that the Old Testament title for Jehovah and the New Testament title for Jesus, *Kurios*, are both translated Lord. It is a pure coincidence. The Old Testament Lord and the New Testament Lord have no common meaning whatsoever. But this coincidence has been immensely fruitful of misconception in the Christian world. It has gone far to make the opinion prevail that the Lord (Master) Jesus was the Lord (Ruler) God. All this is by the way. When Paul cried to the Philippians, "Rejoice in the Lord!" he was, as I have said, thinking of Jesus, not of the Almighty. But generally, when we quote his words, we think of the Almighty. Take it whichever way you will, the injunction is for you not less than for those to whom Paul wrote his letter eighteen hundred and twenty-seven years ago. To rejoice in Jesus of Nazareth is still possible, even for those who have recurred to the humanitarian conception of his life which was antecedent to the vast theological idealization and distortion which, for nearly the whole course of Christian history, has concealed from men the aspect of their brother man. How should we not rejoice in one whose moral greatness, whose immense compassion, whose filial trust, and whose fraternal love give such expansion to our sense of spiritual things as comes to us from no other personality in all the range of human excellence! But Paul's sense of the personality of Jesus was extremely weak. He had never seen his face.

He had never listened with the twelve or with the multitude
to those lovely parables which proclaim Jesus first among
the poets of Judea, as he was first among her prophets and
her saints. It was the spirit of Jesus in which he rejoiced,
the spirit of compassion, trust, and love. And it is not as
if Jesus had exhausted this spirit, as if he could.

> " Whene'er a noble deed is wrought,
> Whene'er is spoken a noble thought,
> Our hearts in glad surprise
> To higher levels rise."

And there is something here that will enable us, when things
go hard with us, to rise above our disappointments and our
sufferings and rebuffs into an atmosphere of peace and joy.
The literature of pessimism, of contempt for human nature,
of the worthlessness of life, was never so abundant as at the
present time ; and there are many who rejoice in it for what
it is. But there is other literature ; and, if we are wise, we
shall rejoice in that, and, doing so, we shall rejoice in the
Lord,— in the Master, as his disciples called him ; as *you*
called *your* teacher in the village school,—alas, how long
ago !— we shall rejoice in him with as distinct reality as if
we rejoiced in some word or deed recorded of him in the
New Testament. For we cannot read of any nobleness of
speech or act, however imaginative the form, and not know
that equal nobleness is possible for breathing men, and has
been actual a thousand times. But it is not as if we were
confined to the literature of imagination. I count myself
happy in no mean or paltry fashion that I have always loved
to read the biographies of great and influential men, and
even of those not great or influential. There is but one
better way to fortify the heart against the scepticism of the
many who are crying, "Who will show us any good ?" Say
to them, "Here, here, and here." Here in this life of Channing, here in this life of Parker, here in this life of Darwin,
in this life of Garrison, in this life of Gannett, in this life of
Lucretia Mott, in this life of Dorothea Dix, in this life of

Mrs. Somerville, or George Eliot, or Lydia Maria Child!
Oh, but there are hundreds of these books! Only one better way, I said, of fortifying ourselves against the pessimism
that is coming in upon us like a flood ; and that is, to remind
ourselves what good and truth, what tenderness, what compassion, what fidelity, we ourselves have known, and then
that everywhere there are men and women who can rejoice,
as we do in our own, in men and women to whom all things
are possible, all things that make for righteousness and truth
and love. Love is the Lord of Life. It is the same love
that was in Judea, is now, and ever shall be. Rejoice in
that always ; and again I say unto you, Rejoice !

FREDERIC HENRY HEDGE.*

ONE of the happiest fortunes of my life has been to enjoy
the friendship of several of the most venerable of our Unitarian ministers,—the most venerated, too,—Dewey and
Furness and Bellows and Bartol and Hedge. I must be
careful how I speak, or I shall be allowing myself old; for,
when I came to Brooklyn, Dr. Bellows was exactly of my
present age, Dr. Furness was sixty-two, Dr. Bartol fifty-one,
Dr. Hedge fifty-nine. Dr. Dewey was born in the same year
with his friend William Cullen Bryant (1794); and he was
already seventy when I met him for the first time, right here,
as full of tremulous anxiety at the prospect of his morning
service as if it were to be his first attempt,—no sign of age,
for he told Dr. Bellows that his knees always smote each
other when he entered the pulpit. There is among you one
who was an habitual hearer of his preaching seventy years
ago, in Gloucester, when he was wavering in his Orthodoxy,
which shortly after he abjured. In his society, I seem to
be in touch with the beginnings of Unitarianism in America;
for it was only six or seven years after the outbreak of the
Unitarian controversy that he was (informally) invited to be
Channing's colleague, but declined, perhaps because with
Dr. Channing in the pulpit it was impossible to realize the

* At the request of friends, I allow this discourse to be printed in my sermon series,
not without hesitation, lest its undrest, familiar style, especially in the former part, should
seem below the dignity of my theme. It must be understood that it was prepared as a
confidential talk with my own people. To eliminate the matter personal to them and
myself would require such recasting of the whole as I have neither time nor courage to
attempt. I cannot " mar my work, though vain." This discourse was preached October
5, and I have since been confirmed in some of its judgments by those of Mr. Allen in his
admirable article on Dr. Hedge in the October *Unitarian Review*. No one had better
opportunity than Mr. Allen to know Dr. Hedge's mind and life, and after him I speak
with bated breath.

ideal of the apostle,—"forgetting the things that are be-hind."

If I had enjoyed no personal relationship with Dr. Hedge, I should have felt it right to speak to you, some time, of his life and work ; for he was one of our leaders, one of our greatest men, one of the principal actors in a great drama of progressive thought. But, had he been the least of the apostles, I must still have thrown my pebble on his cairn, because he sent me here in 1864, with the assurance to your committee that I was the man you wanted for your minister, your noble Staples being dead. I have often told you he had never heard me preach, and hence, perhaps, his hearty commendation. But, as my Professor of Ecclesiastical His-tory in the Divinity School, I had read to him essays on Justin Martyr, Tertullian, Saint Bernard, and Calvin ; and it was my passionate interest in biographical studies that first won for me his warm regard, as it was his magnificent por-trayal of the great men of Christian History that first won my boundless admiration. I am very certain that the proud-est day of my whole life — I do not say the happiest — was that in my second year, when he asked me for my essay on Tertullian for the *Christian Examiner*, of which he was then editor. I sat in my pleasant room, where Theodore Parker had "toiled terribly" for two years in his young manhood, and received the homage of my fellow-students, and recalled the saying of the dying emperor, "I feel myself becoming a god." Not long ago I tried to read that essay ; but my powers of comprehension were not equal to the task.

At the time of my graduation, he preached a sermon to my class, and it proved to be the most provoking of discus-sion and dissent of any sermon he had ever preached. Since Theodore Parker's "Transient and Permanent," in 1841, only Dr. Bellows's "Suspense of Faith," five or six years before Dr. Hedge's, had made such a sensation. There was a war of articles and pamphlets over it ; and Mr. Longfel-low, at my ordination six months later, made it the object of distinct animadversion. To my dismay, it was a vigorous

condemnation of "Anti-supernaturalism in the Pulpit," —
this the title that it bore; and, as I was self-consciously
the anti-supernaturalist of my class, I seemed to suffer
public punishment. I afterward discovered that a man in
the next class was the animating cause of the attack. I
trust that it was sanctified to him. For myself, as his
preaching the sermon was conceded by my classmates to
my wish, I felt much as my little sister did when she pre-
sented her teacher with a "clapper" and was the first to
feel its sting. When, a few years ago, I sent Dr. Hedge
a sermon on Supernaturalism, premising that he would not
like its tone, he wrote expressing his entire accord. "Perhaps," he said, "you were thinking of my misunderstood
and ill-fortuned address, 'Anti-supernaturalism in the Pulpit,' which caused such a flutter among some of my old
friends. By anti-supernatural in that address I meant to
designate the position which holds that every-day experience is the measure of possibility. I never meant to imply
that Nature is not up to the most uncommon — in loose
phrase, 'the supernatural' — as well as the most common.
Your sermon has in all its positions my hearty assent."
Nevertheless, I fear that those who cried over the doctor's
sermon, "He has become as one of us," would find it very
hard to reconcile it with my sermon and the statements in
his letter.

The monthly publication of my sermons was the occasion
of a more intimate relation with my teacher, who had never
permitted me to imagine that his interest in my welfare had
grown dull and cold. In sending them to him, I begged
him to criticise their faults as freely as if I were still his
pupil in the musty lecture-room at Divinity Hall, however
sparing he might be of praise. And to this compact he was
always true. Some seventy of his letters I have valued as
the most instructive criticism of the form and substance of
my work that it has ever had. Greedy for praise I must
have been, if I had asked for more than frequently he gave;
and many a time it lifted up my heart when it was very low.

But he did not spare what seemed to him my faults of thought and style, my distrust of metaphysics, my liking for Spencer, a certain polemical habit (which I am not conscious of possessing), my subjection of Christian history to ideal standards, my political independency, and so on. My disuse of the word "Christ" as a synonym for Jesus was always an offence to him, and he returned to it again and again. Because Mr. Longfellow enjoined me to such disuse in his ordination charge, he held him responsible for my folly. He had his laugh about it, too; writing me once, "It must have cost you a pang in the poem, 'Gifts in Sleep,' to have used the word 'Christ.' But Mr. Sam. Longfellow, if he sees it, I think will forgive you in consideration of the metrical exigency." That shows a great misunderstanding of Mr. Samuel Longfellow, who would sacrifice the most perfect metrical arrangement ever framed to his theological sincerity. Here is a drive at my polemics: "There is still [in one of the sermons] but half suppressed the old growl at Christian tradition, your eternal *bête noire*, which I wish you would get to understand at last: then it would no longer be a *bête noire* to you, but a necessary moment of the great evolution, and you would be reconciled to it, viewing it historically, not pragmatically. But with your impatient Donnybrook-Fair temper you cannot help hitting it whenever it comes in view." I could not acknowledge the unqualified justice of this criticism, being too good an evolutionist not to appreciate the value of things as a "Becoming" which as finalities I might deplore. Positivism and evolutionism help us pre-eminently to appreciate the past. It was the positivist, George Eliot, who wrote,

> "The soul of man is widening towards the Past;
> He spells the record of his long descent,
> More largely conscious of the life that was."

Again, still harping on my warlike disposition: "I dreamed of you the other night. You seemed very meek and tolerant and Christian-like. I felt uneasy all the next day for fear you were not going to live long. They say such changes are ominous. Have you experienced any ugly symptoms lately?" Sometimes my dulness or my opposition irritated him a little; but that insured the perfect sweetness of the next following letter. Once he charged the irritation to his difficulty in deciphering my letter; and I wrote the next one legibly enough, you may be sure, and got my meed of praise. His own handwriting was extremely angular and stiff, its carefulness a symbol of the slow and patient process of his thought.

Do not imagine that his letters dealt exclusively with my own small affairs. They took a wide range. If I should print them, they would prove very interesting,— only, alas! some of the best things, the personal judgments, would have to be left out. They contain many touches upon Emerson, Alcott, Margaret Fuller, Bellows, the poets and philosophers, alive and dead. They preserve the spoken phrase concerning Alcott, "and Trismegistus spins his endless yarns," omitted from the printed tribute to Emerson and Bellows, than which the carbon of a diamond is not more compact. He knew whom and what he liked, whom and what he did not like equally well. He had his prejudices: could never say a good word for Spencer or Tyndall; did scantest justice to some of our own men; for Parker had little appreciation on his intellectual side; of Wendell Phillips less; for Joseph Cook, as well he might, an absolute contempt. When there was talk of our greatest poets a few years ago, and of the order of their genius, and Mr. Gosse proposed to head the list with Poe, he wrote, "I consider 'Thanatopsis' our greatest *poem;* Emerson our greatest *poet;* Poe *nowhere.*" There is humor as well as pathos in his frequent allusions to the fulness of his years and the increase of his infirmities. Thus, three years ago: "Abraham Cowley writes,

'The soul's dark mansion, battered and decayed,
Lets in new light, through openings Time has made.'

I would trouble Abraham for some of that *new light.*" With the firmest courage there was something of noble shame at the abridgment of his physical and mental powers, in the latter case extremely slight.   In 1878 he wrote: "As for me, my writing days are well-nigh past, and the nearer roll of 'the mighty waters' is in my ears.   George Bancroft, in a letter I had from him yesterday, reminds me that 'it is the sixtieth year since you and I went together on board ship, to travel towards the sources of wisdom.'   He a recent graduate, not quite eighteen, and I, intrusted to his care, a child of twelve.   Dear me !   How can people talk of the shortness of life ? measured by my experience, it is so immense !   I cannot sympathize in the wish of Elia, in the New Year Essay.   I have no desire to 'lay my ineffectual finger on the spoke of the great wheel.'   Let it drive !   *Cras ingens iterabimus æquor.*"   No, not "to-morrow" would he cross the great sea.   Not for twelve years.   And they were years in which he did some notable things : five years later his great Luther oration, delivered *memoriter* without hitch or halt ; seven years later the *De Senectute* at the banquet tendered him on his eightieth birthday ; and, in default of novel germs, there was much ripening of the unfallen fruit.   But there were also novel germs.   A stereotyped opinion was for him impossible.   Better go wrong than not go on.

The circumstances of my life forbade my having frequent speech with Dr. Hedge.   This I regret the more, because the opportunities I had were painfully convincing of my habitual loss.   Once I had him under my own roof for a few days ; and at another time, when I was to preach in Cambridge,— this shows the goodness of his heart,— he came up from Newport in the summer heat, in order to receive me in his house.   He was no monologist ; but my own part of the conversation that went on through all the afternoon and evening hours was mainly interrogative.   That night I jotted down some of the thousand wise and witty things that he had said ; but how meagre was my salvage in comparison with all the themes that he had set afloat, laden with his wisdom, gay with all the flags and streamers of his wit !   Those who knew him only as a writer and preacher could have little apprehension of the brightness of his spirit. For all his culture, he was "human at the red-ripe of the heart," with something, too, of the immortal boy in him. He liked Munby's realistic "Dorothy" much better than Tennyson's "Idyls of the King." When he came to New York, and Dr. Bellows asked him what he cared to see, "The circus," was his uniform reply. Mr. George William Curtis, who travelled with him a good deal in Italy in 1848, remembers "Henry Hedge" — so his earlier contemporaries always called him — as overflowing steadily with wit and humor ; as having a wonderful stock of mirth-provoking reminiscences and stories, and delivering them with infinite zest. Once, at my own table, I attributed to another that group of happy sayings supposed to express the sentiments of different Unitarian clergymen on their arrival in another world, when, with an ingenuous blush, he said, "But those are mine." Dr. Pierce, proud of his walking always, was to say, "Just 15 minutes from earth; walked all the way!" Andrews Norton : "Spinoza here!" or "A very promiscuous assemblage." Dewey was to rejoice over the absence of any distinction between clergy and laity ; another, if there was any likelihood of a vacancy in the Trinity, was to aspire to fill the same. (This Dr. Hedge protested was an addition by a later hand.) What he would say himself he left another to invent. The fire in the parlor grate had a habit of going out, which annoyed him a good deal ; and it was suggested by a friend, whom perfect love made bold, that his first exclamation in another world would be, "Well, I'm glad to be somewhere at last where the fire doesn't go out."

He was so strong and masterful that there was something infinitely pathetic in his increasing feebleness. The man whom we had known was almost concealed from us at last by the full, snowy beard and cap that covered his great dome of brow. The voice which had lost its strength still kept its characteristic modulations. At our last meeting, three months before his death, I spoke to him of Martineau's new book, "The Seat of Authority in Religion." "It is nowhere outside ourselves," he said. "It is in the individual soul." Then, as we parted, he spoke to me words of such sweet affection that I almost forgot my natural foreboding in my pride and joy.

———————————

I trust that by the personal tone of my discourse so far I have not obscured the man whom I would fain reveal to you "in habit as he was." But, for the rest, I will endeavor to briefly indicate the course of his experience and his relation to the great movement of New England thought, all of which he saw and of which he was a great and honored part. He was born in Cambridge, Mass., Dec. 12, 1805. The roots of his life struck deep in scholarly and theological soil. His great-grandfather on his mother's side was Edward Holyoke, the first minister of my own home church in Marblehead, who became President of Harvard College in 1737. His paternal grandfather, Lemuel Hedge, was minister of the church in Warwick, Mass., from 1760 to 1777, where he died, October 17, the day of Burgoyne's surrender, which might have convinced him of the ability of the colonists to maintain their liberties by force of arms. His doubt of this was expressed in a letter to Joseph Warren, his classmate and friend,— a letter found upon Warren's person after his death at Bunker Hill. This doubt constituted him a Tory in the eyes of his patriot townsmen, and they voted to disarm and confine him, also to dismiss him; and a mob of the more thoughtless hustled him to Northampton, hastening, if not causing, his early death by their indignity. The real Tory ancestor was the Grandfather Kneeland, who married Holyoke's daughter, though it may be doubted whether he could be called an *active* Tory, seeing that he slept right through the march of the British past his door, on their way to Lexington and Concord, on the night preceding the eventful April day. Dr. Hedge's father was Levi Hedge, for many years (1810–32) professor of logic, ethics, and metaphysics in Harvard College. His text-book, "Elements of Logic," was long a famous book; and when

Dr. Hedge was introduced to Mr. Blaine by Mr. Curtis in 1875, at the Concord celebration, Mr. Blaine said, with the happy assurance of the man who knows exactly the right thing to say: "I am very glad to meet Dr. Hedge. He is no stranger to us. We all know his *Logic*." And Dr. Hedge replied, "I am an old man, Mr. Blaine, but not old enough to be my own father." This incident did not prevent his thinking highly of Mr. Blaine, who had in 1884 no sturdier protagonist.

From certain "Reminiscences" furnished me by Dr. Hedge, I gather these particulars of his youth and early education. He was a timid and somewhat puny child, fond of reading, poetry and stories having for him an equal charm; reading at the age of nine Pope's "Essay on Man" with great delight, at the age of eleven "Don Quixote" over and over again. He was fitted to enter college in Latin and Greek the following year. One is reminded of the elder Mill's demands upon young John Stuart by Professor Hedge's on his son's intellectual and moral powers. Sent to Germany in his thirteenth year, in the care of George Bancroft, he was too young to appreciate the advantages that he enjoyed. "As a foreigner," he says, "I was indulged and left too much to my own devices at an age when I should have been subject to discipline. . . . The only substantial benefit I derived from my German years was a thorough knowledge of the language, some acquaintance with its literature, and an early initiation in the realm of German idealism, then to our people an unknown world." But seeing that through him, as through no other, that world was afterward made known, as it could not have been without the experience in Germany, it would appear that his exacting recollections did less than justice to its contribution to his mind and life.

Returning to America, after five years abroad,* he entered Harvard two years in advance, and graduated in 1825, in his twentieth year. His college standing did not satisfy his

---

* See a delightful account of this period from his own hand in the *Unitarian Review* for October, 1890.

father, owing to his "strong distaste and natural incapacity for mathematics," but in the retrospect the Harvard years left no such painful impression as the preceding period. His college ambition was to be a poet, and nothing short of an epic would satisfy his generous hope. Class poet he was, and poet of the Phi Beta Kappa Society in 1828; but, in the ultimate event, not epic largeness, but the compactness of the hymn and lyric, answered best to his ability and taste. Two years ago he sent me with great glee a Philadelphia reviewer's comment on the relative value of his prose and verse: "There are thousands who know him as a poet to one who knows anything about him as a prose-writer." The fact was the reverse of this. The poetical production of his maturity was limited to a few noble hymns, still fewer "short swallow flights" of lyric song, and a larger number, but still small, of exquisite or superb translations from the German lyrists whom he loved. His translation of Luther's Hymn, "Ein' feste Burg ist unser Gott," impresses me as even better than Carlyle's. His hymns are hymns of eloquence, marked like his prose by a splendid and resounding rhetoric. His hymn for Good Friday is a great example : —

> "Not in vain for us uplifted,
> Man of sorrows, wonder-gifted,
>   May that sacred symbol be !
> Eminent amid the ages,
> Guide of heroes and of sages,
>   May it guide us still to thee ! "

In the region of pure poetry, his "Morning Star" shines with the clearest light. Here was not an instance of "emotion recollected in tranquillity." The poem was composed in bed, with the morning star in full view, and afterward written out. His power of immediate memory was certainly remarkable. His Phi Beta poem, which attained to almost epic length, but missed the grandeur, was composed entirely in his head before a word was written. The decade of orations which were the most brilliant fruits of his career, culminating in the Luther oration of 1883, were all given *memoriter*. He had the longer memory, too, both copious and exact; and Mr. Allen has told us how jealously he measured its declining strength with German lyrics that he had learned fifty and sixty years ago.

He wished to study medicine; but his father urged theology, and to his grateful heart his father's will was law. Entering the Divinity School in 1825, he came under the influence of Professor Andrews Norton, "whom," he says, "I learned greatly to respect, though conscious of his limitations and sometimes galled by his intolerance." During the last year of his course he made the acquaintance of Emerson, and gradually became intimate with him. Their relation was one of mutual benefit. Dr. Hedge's admiration, reverence, and love for Emerson were among the most secure possessions of his mind and heart. It was his admiration for Emerson's poems that encouraged him to publish them and to cultivate the gift. In 1834 we find Emerson recommending to Carlyle Hedge's essays on Swedenborg and Phrenology. These were the second and third of Dr. Hedge's publications on a list that stretched to hundreds ere he died, though he was ever slow to print. In the case of "Reason and Religion," it was Mr. Alger's urgency that conquered his inertia and distrust. Somebody's was often necessary. Preceding the essays named was one on Coleridge, through whom the philosophy of Schelling was acclimated upon "the wild New England shore." As this positively, so the essay on Phrenology negatively prefigured the Transcendental Movement, "which was in some sort a reaction against the prevailing philosophy, based on, or basing, phrenology."* Meantime, he was a diligent student of Kant, Fichte, and Schelling, and derived from them "impulses that greatly quickened the speculative impulses of his nature"; but in his own opinion he was "never a votary of any system," and he learned to distrust all systems, as such, at an early day. No one acquainted with his thought can fail to recognize the fairness of these judgments of him-

* Manuscript Reminiscences.

self. For good and ill, German idealism colored all his thought; but it was not the idealism of any single master in that kind. It was, perhaps, more frequently Schelling's than any other's; but there are wandering gleams from all their shifting lights. He was no retailer of their strange and costly stuffs. He made everything his own by the reaction of his mind on others' contributions and by the necessity that was laid upon him to express his thought in beautiful and noble forms. What of obscurity there is in him is central to the problems he attacks or to his philosophic method, confusing what it seeks to clear. He sometimes wished that he had been born under the star of science rather than under the star of metaphysics. Amen to that! He would have found that science lends itself as readily as metaphysics to a poetical interpretation; and it was his poetical interpretation, not his metaphysics in the rough, that was the solace of his mind.

His first settlement was in West Cambridge (now Arlington) in 1829, his second in Bangor, Me., from 1835 to 1850. Our best description of him while at Bangor is from Emerson's letter commending him to Carlyle in 1847; yet I know that there is one of you it•does not satisfy, a girl in his society in those far-off years, in whose mind and heart the echoes of his sermons still go sounding on, for whom in his study and in her home he poured out the treasures of his culture and his thought. It was while in Bangor that he elaborated his monumental work, "Prose Writers of Germany," which is both biographical and critical, with translations from each author, of which many were his own. Hedge did for America very much what Carlyle did for Great Britain as an introducer of German literature and philosophy. As time went on, he had many great allies; but he was the worthiest pioneer, the most completely qualified among the leaders of the German party in the Transcendental Movement. His enthusiasm was contagious, and passed from him to Margaret Fuller, Ripley, Clarke, and others. As early as 1835 he was urgent for a periodical that should represent the idealistic thought of Coleridge and Schelling and their spiritual kin. His removal to Bangor caused delay, but in due time the *Dial* began to register the brighter hours. The "Transcendental Club" was formed in 1836, Ripley, Emerson, and Hedge taking the initial steps. Its members never called it by the popular name, but simply "The Club"; often "The Hedge Club," young Hedge's part in it was so important. One of its irregular meetings was always held when he came up to Boston from Bangor, whither he went on Emerson's recommendation to the parish. "It was," he writes, "a kind of exile, but, on the whole, was an advantage to me, favoring mental independence and allowing a freer intellectual development than I could, perhaps, have attained in a parish nearer home, under the pressure of ecclesiastical influences." But, though remote from Boston, the society was uncommon for its intellectual force. It had lawyers by the dozen and politicians by the score,— once at the same time four candidates for governor of the State. Preaching political sermons must have been a very ticklish business in that year of grace. In 1850 he left Bangor and went to Providence. One of your number enjoyed the privilege of listening to his preaching there; and I can never speak of him that her face does not shine with gladness at the memory of his grandly beautiful and inspiring utterance, which she can never forget. His next and last settlement was in Brookline, Mass., from 1856 till 1872, when he became Professor of German in Harvard University. He had held the chair of Ecclesiastical History in the Divinity School for several years, in connection with his Brookline pastorate. It was only as a lecturer upon German Literature that his professorship of German had any answer to his aptitude and taste. And his work in the Divinity School was no adequate expression of the wealth of his historical knowledge and the brilliancy and acuteness of his thought. For the most part, his lectures were a level tract of arid exposition. Only now and then, when some splendid personality appeared upon the scene, the level tract became a mountain's stairs, inviting us to summits from which the horizon of our thought and feeling widened with infinite expansion on our view. How we longed and waited for those mountain elevations, as we sometimes wearied of the plain! How glad and satisfied we were when he caught us up with him into those mounts of vision!

We must be on our guard lest, in thinking of him as a scholar, a writer, a philosopher, we lose sight of the main region of his intellectual activity and spiritual joy, which was that of a preacher of the Unitarian faith. He held this faith in an entirely independent, individual way, as he could easily do without fear of violating its fundamental principles. In some particulars, his sympathies and beliefs were more Orthodox than Unitarian, as in some they were more Catholic than Protestant; but never for a moment did he cast a longing eye on any other communion as likely to furnish him with more suitable surroundings or a livelier appreciation. He contented himself with the frankest possible statement of our limitations, never happier than when withstanding us to the face. Especially did he feel it incumbent on himself to set us right as to the relative merits of Arius and Athanasius. He was no Arian; why, it is easy to perceive. The Arian Christology was to him "a stubborn anomaly, which the mind can neither historically adjust nor philosophically assimilate." In Athanasius he could find a symbol of his speculative thought. But was it the thought of the great Athanasius? I doubt it very much. "It merely affirms," he says, "what every one believes, who believes in Christianity at all, that God and man wrought together in Christ for the regeneration of human kind." Now, Athanasius and those who fought for him like beasts at Nicæa would have laughed this statement to scorn,— a fact which did not trouble Dr. Hedge. Not what they thought they meant, but what they really meant, was in his eyes the " precious thing discovered late." But that the Athanasian theology preserved the humanity of Jesus as the Arian did not was for him its supreme attraction. He would have preferred the name

Humanitarian to Unitarian as a designation of our sect. Another of his grand contentions was that we are not to look for the completeness of Christianity in the teachings of Jesus, the New Testament, or the apostolic age. The historic Church is more than any one or all of these.

His denominational standing was peculiar and unique. No party, right or left, could claim him as its own. In criticism absolutely free, in speculation bold, daring, even rash, in his practical ecclesiasticism he was as conservative as any, and on critical occasions it was often his practical ecclesiasticism that assigned his place.* This meant no failure to apprehend, in general, the dangers of the ecclesiastical spirit. Writing of Eusebius, he said, "There is not a more hateful creature in human guise than your typical ecclesiastic." There was certainly a frequent incongruity between the narrowness of his ecclesiastical constructions and the breadth and freedom of his thought. He was simply intolerant of the Free Religious Association, which had much in common with his own most characteristic doctrine of divine revelation; and the same is true of his feeling for the Western Unitarian Conference. It was comical and yet pitiful to find him frowning on the audacities of Western men at the very time that he was complacently doubting the personal immortality and relegating the realm of Nature to the devil. It should be said that in neither of those cases had he informed himself of what was going on. Whether this palliates, or more condemns, it was characteristic of his denominational attitude, and also of his larger mental operations. Here, too, he had his intuitions. What he did not like, or thought he should not like, he was at little pains to understand. This was true of his relation to the whole trend of evolutionary science and philosophy.

The radical thinker who is repelled by his formal conserv-

* A notable exception was at the time when Messrs. Hepworth and Putnam were anxious that a creed of their construction should be accepted by the Association, and were confident of success. The slow, deliberate opposition of Dr. Hedge was like the march of a remorseless fate. Quite unexpectedly, Dr. Bellows took the same line in a speech of rushing eloquence. But there was little need. By the solid impact of Dr. Hedge's speech the poor thing was already " dead and damned."

atism, and impatiently lays down his book, makes a great mistake. Let him go on, and he will find that the formal conservatism is the mask of a radicalism quite as intelligent and thorough as his own. "My conservatism," he wrote to me in 1881, "relates to method and position rather than opinion. On the primary questions of theology, I suppose I am as radical in my speculations as any one whose position is not that of a *rangé* denier. As a preacher, my principle has been, in the first place, to say nothing that I don't believe ; and, secondly, in relation to beliefs that I do not share, to proceed not iconoclastically, but to instil into my hearers those broad, philosophic, and fundamental views which will enable them to outgrow those beliefs and thus to emancipate themselves. For I hold that self-emancipation is much more effective than emancipation by another's denial, inasmuch as it applies not merely to this or that particular superstition, but to all doctrines inconsistent with reason." We have here, I think, the clue to that quality of Dr. Hedge's mind which often laid him open to the charge or the suspicion of holding esoteric opinions which his exoteric utterance concealed. He was an intellectual aristocrat, and distrusted the ability of the average man to appropriate the best results of criticism and philosophy. Hence he was violently opposed to opening the doors of the Ministers' Institute to the general public. And hence, when I lamented that Renan's Life of Jesus was so miserably translated, he said : "It should not have been translated at all. It should have been written in Latin, and then only those could have read it for whom it was intended." This, not that the truth was too good for the people, but because a truth seized upon out of its relations is no better than an error to the individual mind.

Again, I must remind myself that he was pre-eminently a Unitarian minister. As such, he did, perhaps, his best and most enduring work,— not that his sermons will be read when his essays and lectures are forgotten, but that they will live in minds made better by their influence. They were not mainly theological or critical: they were mainly ethical, and searched the consciences of those who heard them to the very quick. They were prepared with the same laborious conscientiousness that went to all his other work. Every sentence was measured, every word assayed. Not his the slovenly helter-skelter of the Saturday night or Sunday morning improvisator. We have, in his published volumes, ample means for learning what he was and did, as a critic, as a philosopher, as an orator, as a theologian. What we greatly need is a volume that shall enable us to share with his parishioners their "uplifts of heart and will" in their enjoyment of that gospel preached by him in the various "cures," as he would say, that had the honor of his charge.

It was frequently the poet's love of symbols that held the mind of Dr. Hedge captive to certain ancient formulas. Analyze the symbol, and its contents are generally as rational as could be desired. His love of paradox was another blind for the incautious and unwary follower. He thought contemptuously of Hegel; but he had the true Hegelian passion for reconciling opposites and resolving them into each other. See, for example, his "Way of Historical Atonement" in his volume "Ways of the Spirit." But his philosophical trumpet gave no uncertain sound. He could not be named a Kantian, certainly not an Hegelian, for he thought Hegel a good deal of a charlatan; but he was always clearly with the idealists and the intuitionalists as against the realists and the experientialists. The influence of Leibnitz was, perhaps, greater than any other on his mind; and his indifference to the later speculation could have had no sign more positive than his failure, so far as I am aware, to appreciate Lotze's rehabilitation of Leibnitz's monadology, in which he should have taken much delight. Schopenhauer was an exception to this indifference; and to him he was attracted, certainly not by his pessimism, and probably by his style, always with him a prime consideration. If Herbert Spencer could have had Schopenhauer's style, Dr. Hedge's dislike of him would not have been so great;

and I wonder that John Fiske's exposition of the Spencerian Philosophy never made him a convert by its wonderful lucidity. It was what seemed to him the necessarily utilitarian ethics of the experiential school that most offended him. He found no ground of obligation but the inborn sense of right. But his criticism seems to lack acquaintance with the later aspects of Utilitarian thought, which he vigorously flouts, while adopting much to which its modern statement has attained. A criticism of Bentham, or even of Mill, is not a valid criticism of Sidgwick's "Methods of Ethics," Leslie Stephen's "Science of Ethics," or Alexander's "Moral Order and Progress," in which Hegel and Spencer meet, like righteousness and peace, and kiss each other. As with the moral law, so with belief in God: it was given in consciousness, by intuition. Speculation can only reach a negative or incomplete result. It cannot prove God. It can only analyze the ineradicable belief.

Dr. Hedge loved the force of contrast. He would paint in a dark background, to bring out his darling thought against it the more clearly. He liked to give his hearers a veritable shock, as when he told the Cambridge theological alumni that Dr. Channing was "a good deal of a Philistine" (his humor and his frolic-temper had a part in this); but he liked still better to "pluck up drowning honor by the locks," — to prepare for his hearers a happiness of glad resuscitation, when he had buried them under a torrent of superb negation. The best example of this that I recall is where he says of Dr. Channing, "And curious it was how this man — without learning, without research, not a scholar, not a critic, without imagination or fancy, not a poet, not a word-painter, without humor or wit, without profundity of thought, without grace of elocution — could, from the spiritual height on which he stood, by mere dint of gravity (coming from such a height), send his word into the soul with more searching force than all the orators of his time." Make positive the negatives of this daring characterization, and, with the least necessity for change, you have the qualities of Dr. Hedge's mind. But to make negative the positive we have no call. He had not the ethical supremacy of Channing. His dominant quality was intellectual. But his ethical volume and momentum were not slight and small. We speak of him habitually as a scholar; but he was not pre-eminently that. Not merely that he was no Dryasdust, but also that in his wide reading there was much of touch and go and little of the patient digging in minutiæ which constitutes a talent like that of Ezra Abbot, for example, or Freeman, or Kuenen, or Toy. He was more of a thinker than of a scholar. To develop his own ideas was to him a business more proper to himself than the massing of facts, the tracing of causes. Others must write *mémoires pour servir:* he would make the memoirs serve his thought and art.

That last word, like a herald's trumpet, ushers in the long expected king, the governing idea of Dr. Hedge's intellectual life. As with the great Goethe of his boundless admiration, art was his joy and crown. He aimed to be, and nobly, grandly was, the literary artist, taking his rank not with Emerson as a seer, but with Burke and Gibbon and Arnold and Newman and Ruskin as a sayer; a seer in no mean degree, but pre-eminently a sayer, an artist in words, in thought, a master of style, of classic style, "the grand style," swelling, resonant, Miltonic,— first, last, and always this. He is full of thought, full of suggestion; but sometimes, I think, if he were not, or if he always irritated, never satisfied my mind, I should go on reading him for those majestic swells and falls, those words so full of color, warmth, and fire. But there is no separation of the thought and word, the sense and sound. I remember his quotation in Divinity School days: "Luther was the absolute man. In him soul and body were not divided." That was true of his own style.

> "For of the soul the body form doth take,
> For soul is form, and doth the body make."

It was not merely his love for beauteous form that made him strenuous for the balance and perfection of his style: it was his passion for ideas that obliged him to demand for them the fairest temple he could build for them with words chosen and fitted with the great builder's mastery and patient care.

What he has added to our intellectual life is not any definite system of ideas, no philosophic scheme, no theological finalities, but something much better than any one of these things or than all of them together. He might have said with the apostle, "Not that we would have dominion over your faith, but that we would be helpers of your joy." A helper of our joy he certainly has been in many a session of sweet, silent thought, when the splendor of his diction has so married with the freshness of his idea that there has been born for us a pleasure bright and beautiful as that Euphorion of Goethe's mystic song. But he has been much more than this. We have been baffled by the seeming contradictions of his thought. We have been irritated and provoked by his cherubic scorn of doctrines and ideas that were precious in our eyes. *But he has made us think.* Impossible to follow, he has driven us back with his Ithuriel spear upon our individual strength, compelling us to think out our own intellectual salvation, albeit with trembling and with fear. This is the highest service that one man can render to another in the intellectual life.

> " He is gone who seemed so great,—
> Gone, but nothing can bereave him
> Of the force he made his own,
> Being here ; and we believe him
> Something far advanced in state,
> And that he wears a truer crown
> Than any wreath that man can weave him."

PUBLIC WORSHIP.*

IN our liberal churches, the range of thought concerning public worship is extremely wide. On the one hand, we have those to whom "the enrichment of our public worship," as they phrase it, is a prominent ideal. On the other hand, we have those who would like to come in after what they call "the introductory services," which, to their thinking, merely lead up to the sermon, with which they have no worshipful associations, often naturally enough. The latter class again divides itself into two parts, widely distinguished from each other, one part finding no reality or appropriateness in any prayer or worship, the other holding that true prayer is an aspiration from the alone to the Alone,— a soliloquy which cannot be overheard without impiety.

It follows that the first consideration to which we are called in the discussion of public worship is the legitimacy of private worship, of private prayer. For, if there be no legitimacy here, it would hardly be conceived by any one that a place for public worship can be found. But, if there be legitimacy here, then, whether there is any for public worship is the next step, from which we may go on to ask what manner of public worship is best suited to men's spiritual wants and aspirations.

* A paper read at the meeting of the New York State Conference in New York City, Nov. 20, 1889, and reprinted from the *Unitarian Review* of February, 1890, as a contribution to the debate now going on in Unitarian circles as to the advisability of a liturgical service and the publication of such a service by the American Unitarian Association. Having examined with some care the five sample services that have been sent out, I should greatly regret their publication by the A. U. A.,— they have in them so much of mere survival with much admirable matter,— but hardly less the publication by the A. U. A. of any such service. It would seem a sanction of it that it has no right to give. I wish that those who are of this opinion would make it known to Secretary Reynolds or the Liturgical Committee.

I cannot think of anything more simple, natural, inevitable, than private prayer. It is as simple, natural, inevitable, as awe and wonder, reverence and adoration, as thankfulness for benefits received, as aspiration for the good and true, as yearning for communion with our own who have been received up out of our sight, and all those who have been "friends and aiders of such as would live in the spirit." The prayer of awe and wonder, reverence and adoration, is as much the normal attitude of the healthy soul as an erect posture is of the healthy body. The world might be just as wonderful, just as beautiful as it is; and, if man's mind were different, it might stir in him no sense of mystery, it might awaken in him no delight, no transport of enthusiasm, no rapture of thanksgiving. But, so long as the world and man remain as they are,— made for each other, the mind of man the complement of the material universe,— so long there will be that response of the human spirit to the divine which *is* worship, which *is* prayer, whatever it is called, or however strenuously it refuses to be named.

And just as natural as the private prayer of adoration, quickened by all the infinite wonder of the world, its infinite beauty and magnificence, is the private prayer of thankfulness. I cannot think that this — to live and thrive — demands a sense of the peculiar and exclusive care of the omnipotent power. What we are thankful for is that we are sharers of the universal joy and sorrow of the world. What we are thankful for is that, for all our sorrow and our burden, others may be glad and free. What we are thankful for is that, however stricken and bereft we may be now, we *have* been blessed in ways we never can forget, and that the recollection helps to make us patient, sweet, and brave. What we are thankful for is the great inheritance which has come down to us from the toilers and thinkers of the past and the high privilege of living in such good man-fashion that it shall not be impaired by any fault of ours.

But adoration and thanksgiving do not exhaust the possibilities of private prayer. There is much more than these.

There is aspiration. There is the worship of ideal excellence, which declares itself in every effort to obey the body's law of health and the mind's law of growth, and that law of conscience which we call the Golden Rule. I would not underrate the value of the faintest impulse in the direction of a purer and a better life. But the aspiration which marks the highest possibility of private worship must not be confounded with any such impulse, with any momentary *wish* that we might live more nearly level with the best that shames us from afar. Welcome the mountain height or forest depth, the face of man or woman, the mystery of science or the poet's thought, that for a moment gives to our horizon infinite expansion. But there is private prayer which is more than any thrill of gladness, any rapture of thanksgiving, any momentary impulse of the heart towards what is purest, truest, best. And, what is more, unless the worship that is all of these goes forth to seek embodiment in voluntary act, in habitual life, it cannot be expected to return and animate our dust. Only when aspiration is a constant and unwearied habit of the soul, only when year in and year out we seek not only harmonious perfection for ourselves, but to widen upon every side the skirts of light and love, only then does the Eternal give to his beloved even while they sleep. In town and field, he waits for us in every atom and event, and responds to our fidelity with the best he has to give.

Men's earliest prayers were to their vanished friends. "Come to your home," they cried. "It is swept for you and clean, and we are there who loved you ever. And there is rice put for you, and water. Come home, come home, come to us again!" Men's latest prayers take up that sad refrain. In the quiet places of their hearts, they summon back the friends whom they have loved and lost. They enter into spiritual communion with their love and truth. They shame themselves with their remembered good; and with these there comes a cloud of witnesses, the truest and the best of every nation under heaven. The problem is not how to secure, but how to escape such visita-

tions. They throng our silences, whatever be our wish
or will.

> "Ever their phantoms arise before us,
> Our loftier brothers, but one in blood;
> At bed and table, they lord it o'er us
> With looks of beauty and words of good."

Because such things as these, such adoration, thankfulness,
aspiration, striving, spiritual communion, are as simple, natural, inevitable, as anything can be, I say that private prayer
is simple, natural, inevitable. Does any say, But why call
such things prayer and worship? Because they *are* prayer
and worship, whatever they are called. They are of the
stock and lineage of all the world's best worship and the
world's best prayers. By an unbroken thread they go back
through the labyrinth of centuries to the first motions of the
human spirit on its way to God.

There are those who limit the signification of private
prayer to so much as is spoken audibly. · Some do it to the
prejudice of the silent, conceiving words spoken, or, at least,
deliberately thought, to be essential. Others do it to the
prejudice of prayer, conceiving that a spoken prayer implies
a physically hearing God. The literalism of the latter and
the materialism of the former are equally deplorable. Does
the poet think that Nature physically hears when he lifts to
her his high and holy hymn? True prayer cannot be un-
made by speaking it, nor by keeping silence. I cannot but
think that those are wise who keep some little space apart
for prayerful thoughts and words ; but, even for those who
do, it will very often happen that the prayer-moments which
are of the finest essence are not those which they set apart,
but those of a divine surprise, when something in the face
of nature or in a book or in the deep heart of a friend appeals to them, as if God did beseech them, to put away all
weak and wandering thoughts. Our best private prayers, I
am quite sure, are not on fixed occasions and at home, but
on the street and in the public conveyance, when we are
suddenly confronted with some bestial or angelic face, or

with some gracious memory or perfect trust that shames the
things that we have done. Even our best at home are seldom audible. They are of the kind which thus the poet
sings : —

> " Ere on my bed my limbs I lay,
> It hath not been my use to pray
> With folded hands or bended knees ;
> But silently, by slow degrees,
> My spirit I to love compose;
> In humble trust, mine eyelids close
> With reverential resignation :
> No wish conceived, no thought expressed,
> Only a *sense* of supplication,
> A sense o'er all my soul imprest,
> That I am weak, yet not unblest,
> Since in me, round me, everywhere,
> Eternal Strength and Wisdom are." *

Private prayer and worship being thus natural and inevitable, what shall we say of public worship and of public
prayer? They seem to me as natural, if not as inevitable,
as the other. It is easy to conceive of public worship in a
way that shall commend it neither to the head nor to the heart.
Let a little story serve for illustration. In England, on a
day of days, I met a lady whose husband was the rector of
a church in Australia or New Zealand. She said that he
had services every morning in his church, that often not
more than one or two were present, but that he would have
them just the same if no one came, as they were for the
worship of God. There was nothing singular in this. Nothing has been more common than the idea that public worship
is for God's sake, because he is pleased with adulation, as he
was formerly, or was supposed to be, with the savory smell
of burning sheep and cattle.

In the rector's indifference to attendance on his function
there was also the sacramental idea that the priest worships
in the people's place. If public worship were so bound up
with these primitive ideas that it must stand or fall with

* S. T. Coleridge, " The Pains of Sleep."

them, the sooner it fell, the better. But it is not: it is not
God's need and satisfaction, but our own, that makes public
worship fit and excellent. It is what we have together much
more than what we have in difference and separation that is
the ground of our thanksgiving, adoration, trust, and love;
and so it is the most natural of all things that we should express together these sentiments and emotions of our hearts.
A frequent objection to public prayer is that it is praying *for
others*. If it is, so much the better. The most private prayer
is that, when it is at its best; in the spirit of the Buddhist
declaration, "Never will I accept private individual salvation, never will I enter into peace alone." To pray *with*
others is the highest possible ideal. "O God," said Father
Taylor, "we are a widow with six children." That was to
touch the goal, to identify himself and congregation with the
sorrow close at hand. So, always, when the preacher truly
prays, he is his congregation, the mouth-piece of their gladness and their sorrow, of their peace and pain. As much
sympathy, so much true public prayer, no more. Given the
sympathy, and the minister who prays is the father fretted
with his business anxieties, the mother with her household
cares, the young man or woman struggling with temptation
or with aimless ease, the wife or husband sitting in lonely
darkness, the children who miss everywhere the father's or
the mother's voice and step. Given the sympathy, and all
the people's joy and gladness, as well as all their sorrow,
shame, and sin, will find a door of utterance at the preacher's lips, or in the silence upon which his laboring heart pre-
cipitates itself like a tired child upon its mother's breast.

For all its sacredness, the prayer of public worship does
not disdain some practical considerations. It is not a soliloquy; and, though the temptation is often very strong to
make it this, in any rational conception it is only spoken to
be heard, not overheard, by the congregation; and, when
not so heard, the congregation is defrauded of its right.
We have all heard of certain eloquent prayers "addressed
to a Boston congregation," and have appreciated the sting-

ing satire of the phrase. But, in all sincerity, are not the least eloquent addressed to the people much more obviously than to God, and without requiring an apology for this? "As if God did beseech you"! It is God who prays to us as much as we to him in every truest prayer; and the minister never rises so high as when he knows not whither he is going in his voicing of that prayer of God.

Further than this, let us say frankly that public prayer is the endeavor of the minister to engage his people in a devout and reverent frame of mind, to draw their wandering thoughts together in a common act of adoration and thanksgiving, to bring home to them the appealing loveliness of outward things, and their birthright as inheritors of countless centuries, and the possibilities of holy living which they have failed to seize, and the miseries they might do something to allay, and the wickedness into whose blackness they have sunk, and the goodness to which death has given added power to shame and heal.

But much of this, or all of it, you may suggest, is more the function of the sermon than of the prayer. Not more; yet hardly less. I mean the mystic line is very hard to draw between the function of the sermon and the prayer. I mean that the sermon not less than the prayer is a part of public worship. Some who are ritually inclined, or worshipfully only, take serious exception to the designation of the hymns, the Scripture reading, and the prayer before the sermon as "introductory services," as if the sermon were the king, these but the heralds sounding his approach. The exception is well taken, I am sure. What goes before the sermon, equally with the sermon, stands in its own right, and is often more than that to many who are too tired to think, but not too tired to feel the weary weight of this (for them) unprofitable world. But, if the parts of the service that go before the sermon cannot properly be spoken of as "introductory services," as little can the sermon properly be shunted off upon a siding as a mere train of intellectual lumber, in order that the *express* object of religious meeting

— worship — may have free course and be glorified. My dear young friend raises the voice of lamentation because of "the position of the pulpit in the centre of the head of the church where the altar was before."* The wicked secularism of the time hath done it, we are told. Nay, but it is the secularism of Jesus, an appeal to whom against the centrality of the preacher's function in the church is so unfortunate as to be almost ridiculous. The Christian Church is not of priestly, but of prophetic origin. It derives its characteristic note not from the temple, but from the synagogue. Of the priestly functions of Jesus there is no gospel word. But of his preaching there is much reported; and there is reason to believe that it was very good, and quite as useful as the temple ritual of the time. Not the altar, but the pulpit, has been the central force of Christian history; the preacher, in the line with Jesus and the prophets, quickening a thousand souls to better life where the altar has not quickened one. If the displacement of the latter by the former is, as we are told, "a sign of the desire that the personal qualities of the minister shall prevail over his priestly qualities," it is a good sign. The notion that the functions of the priest are unaffected by his personal character was once very prominent, and what came of it does not admit of public characterization.

But, even if public worship were the be-all and the end-all of religious congregation, the sermon could not properly be set aside of such small account as it appears to many of our priestly ministers who preach very well themselves. They condemn it for excess of intellectuality, but some of us have oftener found too little than too much. I really do not think that this is greatly to be feared. It has an intellectual work to do, a work of sound instruction in revealing the true character of the Bible, the relation of Jesus of Nazareth to his age and to the ages, the course of Christian history, and the development of our own branch of the

* *Unitarian Review*, October, 1887, p. 311.

true vine in which all religions live, the relation of the exigencies of religion to the successive problems of the time. It has a moral work to do which ought to save it the esteem of those to whom its intellectuality is an offence. Is it nothing that it shames men's weakness and frivolity, that it drags their hidden baseness to the light, that it holds a mirror up against their secret sins? Is it nothing that it shows " how awful goodness is, and virtue in her shape how lovely," till men see and feel their loss? Is it nothing in such times as these, when, here and there and everywhere, the social theorist hawks his nostrum for the sickness of mankind, that the sermon steadily insists that there is no other name given under heaven by which men can be saved but private character? Let them lay this " single tax " upon themselves and pay it honestly, and very soon their " looking backward " would reveal a vision full of peace and joy.

And then, besides its intellectual and moral work, the sermon has a work of comfort and of consolation. It is at this point, perhaps, that it passes most naturally and easily into the province of the prayer ; but there is hardly any point at which the two are not as open to each other as the temperate and tropic seas. If, as its critics frequently imply, the sermon had in it no element of worship, it would still hold the first and central place in the public ministration of religion. But, if it had no intellectual force, no moral inspiration, no voice of comfort and of peace, it would still hold the first and central place in public worship. In the judgment which sets apart the sermon from the worship of the congregation there is no justice whatsoever. If it approximates to what it ought to be, and often is, it is more worshipful than any other part of the religious service, however slightly or elaborately ritualistic that may be. At one time or another have we not all listened to sermons which brought home to us the wonder and the bounty of the world, and summoned us to adoration and thanksgiving, more irresistibly than any form of prayer, than any hymn or Bible reading or antiphony, than any eloquence of architectural beauty, or windows blazing with the forms of angel companies? But, more than any adoration or thanksgiving, it is the use of prayer to lift our hearts to ideal excellence, to touch them with divine compassion, to fill them with a tender confidence and glorious hope. Yes, certainly; but does not the sermon do these things quite as effectively as any ritual, hymn, or prayer? One, pleading for a better "door of utterance" than the sermon, has recently inquired among us,* "Can the words of any man's earthly wisdom have such direct force and instantaneous appeal as an illuminated sketch of the transfiguration?" I should say, "Yes, and more; a thousand times as much." I would not give one good sermon for all the stained glass in Europe, and all the religious pictures into the bargain, as a means of instantaneous appeal to men. "Can any argument," proceeds my friend, "however firm and subtile and high-strung, make the heart so quiver with the hope of immortal life as a glowing picture of the resurrection?" "Yes," I should say again, "and more a thousand times; even for those who accept the resurrection of Jesus as a fact." As very few among us do so accept it, to put a picture of it on the walls or in the windows of our churches would be a glazed or painted lie. And George MacDonald has well said, "The hell which a lie will keep a man from is doubtless the best place for him to go to."

As to the constitution of an ideal public worship, I trust that I am not so set and fixed in my own way that I cannot see what good there is in other ways for other people.

> " I may not hope from outward forms to win
> The spirit and the life whose fountains are within."

If others may, I would not hold them back. As an instrument of public worship, the highest place, I should say, belongs to the sermon. If it does not take it and fill it, then it is not what a sermon ought to be. Next I should place the unpremeditated prayer; unpremeditated because only

* *Unitarian Review*, October, 1889.

so,—though not unfrequently it will return to many a familiar phrase, and be the better for so doing,—only so can
it economize the impulse of the hour, that surging of the
people's joys and sorrows through the preacher's heart,
which Theodore Parker said he always felt, no matter how
dull and lifeless he had been before. All are not so fortunate. I know all that can be said against

> "That drony vacuum of compulsory prayer,
> Still pumping phrases for the ineffable,
> Though all the valves of memory gasp and wheeze."

This is, perhaps, the average way. But sometimes the
channel, so often muddy when it is not wholly dry, receives
such glorious access from all the heights of a man's nature,
from all the hidden springs of his experience, that its banks
are broken down, and growths of characters and endurance
that were perishing of drought in other men feel a refreshing
coolness at their roots, and throughout every part the promise and the potency of a divine renewal. To throw away
the possibility of such moments of the "real presence" as
are these would be a dreadful waste. Whatever system of
printed prayers our churches may adopt, I should hope this
postern might be left open for the army of God encamping
round about us to come freely in. I should also hope that
the printed prayers might be left optional by churches using
them for ministers exchanging with their own. Otherwise,
they would make such a line of cleavage in the denomination as we have not had since Clarke and Sargent went outside the wall with Parker, bearing his reproach. And it
will not help the matter for the contracting vestrymen or
deacons to assure the exchanging minister or candidate, who
cannot stomach the damaged phraseology of the liturgy,
that he believes it quite as much as any of the congregation ;
that none of them, in fact, believe it.

"The enrichment of our public worship" is a phrase that
means one thing here and quite another there,—concession
to a vulgar and aggressive secularity, or a deepening of the

spiritual import of the service in its various parts. It is
against the former that we have to guard ourselves with
every barrier we can oppose. Whatever is intrinsically
good, that let us boldly take, scared by no Puritanic warn-
ings of the Episcopalian or Romish dangers of the way.
But let us be very certain that we take it because it is intrinsically good, and not because it is a bid against some
rival church, an "unparalleled attraction," "the peacock's
tail," — it was an advocate, and not an enemy, who named
it so, — "which the people want; and, if we don't give it to
them, they will go somewhere else." Let them go. Better
"churches of two, churches of one," than churches filled by
seekers for mere entertainment for the eye and ear. To un-
spiritualize religion there is no surer way than this. The
temptation comes along with the singing and the music
oftener than in any other way. There is a musical enrichment of the service which is its degradation, — the singing of
pieces in which the triviality of the music is only less abominable than the quality of the words. That these can seldom
be distinguished is a happy consummation ; but, in an order
of worship appealing to the sympathy of honest men, they
ought to be such as might be distinguished without grief or
shame. I know the difficulty of finding words expressive
of a rational faith in connection with good music. Then
have the good music without any words. Then fall back on
congregational singing. There are plenty of good words
for that. And that is not vicarious. I have Theodore
Thomas with me in my conviction that this represents our
best attainment in church music at the present time. But
it is capable of infinite advance. There is not a quartet
in Christendom that could so lift the heart to high and holy
things as a congregation trained to the singing of such
hymns as already make our liberal anthology the richest
that the world has ever known.

The reading of the Scriptures is generally regarded as a
part of public worship. If one portion is read for instruction, another portion is generally read for praise. And,

surely, for the latter there is nothing in the scope of universal literature so good as the psalms and prophets of the Old Testament. So good, and — may I not say with equal truth? — so bad. So good, where there is wise and loving choice of what is sweet and true; so bad, when the reading is hap-hazard, when no anachronism and no imprecation daunts the headlong speed. Here, then, is obviously an opportunity for the enrichment of our public worship in a very real and noble fashion,— by the selection of what is most excellent, most universal, for the help of ministers, who, in the rush of many cares, often let this be crowded out. The enrichment would be greater and more admirable if the selection did not stop short with the Hebrew and the Christian scriptures, though here the personal equation counts for much. It is what *we* love that goes to other hearts. I am persuaded that no Scripture reading I have ever done has been so quickening or quieting as certain bits of modern poetry and psalm with which I have begun the worship of the day.

Closely allied to the matter of Scripture reading is the matter of a responsive service. Indeed, when the enrichment of our public worship is spoken of, this is what is generally intended,— this and a multiplicity of printed prayers. In the discussion of this matter, it has seemed to me that there has not been sufficient allowance for the difference in men and minds. That what is good for one is good for all has too often been the implication upon either side of the debate. Surely, it is not so. As for myself, I doubt if such a service, however genuine, however admirably conceived, would be to me a helpful thing, or, indeed, anything but a weariness. I have found it so with the most beautiful services of England's Church in her cathedral choirs. I have found it so with the beautiful ritual service of James Martineau, which, intellectually and spiritually, left nothing to desire; and human nature has never seemed to me more absurd and despicable than at a service which I saw at Notre Dame in Paris. It was a magnificent service. The feast of color was superb. The singing would have made the angels glad. But what a business for men to be engaged in!

But, because this kind of thing has for me so little attraction, I am not disposed to make my taste a rule for others. Only, if we are to have a ritual service in our churches, let it be real, let it be genuine,— the truth, and not a lie. Let us have honesty in our devotions. That a number of persons reciting in unison what none of them believe produce an effect that is extremely edifying to themselves, and by which God is well pleased, I find no reason to believe. Yet something very like to this is the contention of so many voices near and far that it would seem to indicate some general movement of contemporary thoughts and feeling. We are told that "a tender conscience is a conscience unequal to the struggles of life," * that "we should be suspicious of any conscientious scruples that other good men do not share," * that "we cannot afford to individualize ourselves with respect to outward symbols," † that no "intellectual vexation" with them ought to prevent our use of them, † that "what is gained in accuracy is lost in effectiveness," ‡ that "to decline to read the psalms together" because some passages seem meaningless or false to us is "more likely to develop purism and Pharisaism than sincerity." § All this is pleading for dishonesty in worship. Every one knows that a responsive service which shall express the exact beliefs of an entire congregation is an impossible thing. But is this any reason for flouting scruples, for offering premiums upon carelessness of word and phrase, for pretending that, so long as men say something together, it is no matter what they say? This is to invite the unreality of which we have already had too much,— in Unitarian services, sentences as little applicable to our present needs as "Moab is my wash-pot ; over Edom will I cast out my

---

* Professor Jowett.   † Thomas Hill Green.

‡ *Unitarian Review*, November, 1889, p. 418.

§ *Ibid.*, October, 1889, p. 341.

shoe." No : if we are to have a responsive service, let it be as real, as genuine, as it can be made. For, if we are contemptuous of truth in our devotions, we shall very shortly be contemptuous of it in all the various business of our lives. What a gospel for the political managers and makers of political platforms,— that phrases recited in concert need not mean anything in particular!

For the further enrichment of our public worship, it is suggested that "the whole church, outside and inside, should be made to speak to the eye." It should be cruciform in shape, and its walls and windows should repeat the stories of Old Testament and New. In all of which, as opposed to the preacher's living word of comfort and rebuke, I find a plea for unspiritual religion, for soft and sensuous things in place of the realities of truth and love. I would not be ungrateful that my own little chapel has the regulation shape ; but I am compelled to recognize that its acoustic properties are the worse for it, and I would have it modelled on a brick to-morrow, if with the transformation there might come some space and some convenience for our parish work. If memorial windows are put in by anybody who can pay for them, whatever they depict they are hardly likely to improve the morals of the congregation. The man who is too drowsy to hear or listen to the preacher's voice might profit more from "forty winks of sleep" than by a glow of color that would have for him no other than a sensuous or æsthetic charm.

I would be understood. I have yet to see the church that is too beautiful for the housing of a congregation bent on doing justice and loving mercy and walking humbly with their God. But the beautiful church must ever be the least of all the helps to the religious life ; and the religious life which cannot dispense with it unreservedly is still a child, still in the go-cart stage of its development. Whether the congregation meets in a barn-like meeting-house or in a temple where form and color equally entrance the eye, its worship will be of the best if sermon, hymn, and ritual, and prayer conspire to make men feel the wonder and the glory of the world, the greatness of their opportunity, the shame of their self-seeking ways, the need they have of one another, and the sufficiency of righteousness and truth and love for every possible event.

THE POWER OF AN ENDLESS LIFE.*

"THE Power of an Endless Life" is one of the great phrases of the New Testament. We know not whose it is, for it occurs in the Epistle to the Hebrews; but it is just as admirable as if Paul had written it, as the Christian world imagined he had done until quite recently. It is of the power of an endless life, not as a fact, but as an idea, that I propose to speak to you to-day. As a fact, it might well engage the imagination of the preacher or the poet, the serious attention of any moral or religious soul. It touched the verse of Tennyson with its suggestion, and he sang,—

> " Rapt from the fickle and the frail
> With gathered power, yet the same,
> Pierces the keen seraphic flame
> From orb to orb, from veil to veil."

Truly, there are lives that are so mean and petty here and now that their indefinite continuance would not contribute any appreciable amount to the world's good. But let alone the great and famous ones of history, and consider some of the lives that you yourselves have known, lives of men and women of the kind that every village has a dozen or twenty of, every town a hundred, every city a thousand,— ten thousand as it mounts from the little city to the big,— and try to imagine the good that such might do with an immortal opportunity. What waste places of the universe they might redeem! If there were really any hell, they might, as Father Taylor said of Emerson, change the temperature of the place, and the emigration might set that way. I know that the traditional conception of the immortal life has been that of a life without effort, without pain, without sorrow, without

* This sermon was preached July 27, 1890, at Lake Pleasant, Mass., to the New England Camp-meeting Spiritualists' Association.

any tragical implication whatsoever. It must have been of
such a heaven as this that good old Origen was thinking
when he imagined the angelic company tiring of its immense
satiety, and from the necessity for change and variation falling from unendurable grace. It was such a heaven as this
that Emerson repudiated, when he said, "I do not wish to
live to wear out my old boots." And it was such a heaven
as this that John Weiss, that incomparable genius, visited
with all the lightnings of his intolerable scorn. "What a
heaven it would be," he says, "if the elements which stim-
ulated a Shakspere to make his great appeal to souls, a
Beethoven to travail with harmony, and reduce to expression
the crude music of the spheres, were all left behind, if man
had forgotten to carry with him his sublimest emotions, or if
deity had neglected to provide the circumstances which force
them from us as at the point of a celestial sword ! A heaven
not worth dying for, and only not a place of torture because
the nerves which can be wrung and the sinews that can be
stretched have been drawn out of the frame of the soul.
Let us hail a better, a more heavenly hope,—that the elements will continue to challenge our maturest powers, preserve them in the pains and exercises of a lusty manhood,
furnish imposing situations, tragic moments of collision,
romances of love,—thus triumphing forever over death and
the grave."

I am tempted to still further violate my chosen limitation,
and endeavor to imagine what a power of help and healing
there might be in an endless life for men and women who in
this life have felt the blows of adverse fortune in a steady
rain on their defenceless heads. And here I do not mean
the power which many seem to think will be acquired by
disembodiment, by getting rid of what Paul called "the
body of this death." His notion that "in his flesh dwelt no
good thing " never appealed so persuasively to me as Browning's doctrine, "nor soul helps flesh more now than flesh
helps soul." "Not that we would be unclothed, but clothed
upon," said the apostle in some better hour. That is the

ideal. In the new life that awaits us we must, I take it, have a body of some sort ; and such a one as we have here would be entirely satisfactory to me if it answered the conditions of the time and place. Whether we view it from the anatomist's or from the physiologist's or from the artist's point of view, it is curiously and wonderfully made ; and I think that Michel Angelo was right, when he sang out in one of his great sonnets,—

> " Nor hath God deigned to show himself elsewhere
> More clearly than in human forms sublime."

Not in the power of disembodiment, but in the power of changing scene and circumstances do I have confidence for the betterment which immortality may bring to bruised and broken lives. It *does* seem that in this life there are many, a great many, thousands, ay, and millions, who haven't a fair chance. And if all the analogies of nature, and all the arguments of science, were against the personal immortality, and all the Spiritualist's assurance should be resolved into the play of psychological forces that have their limit on the hither side of death, I should still go on hoping unconquerably that somewhere " beyond this place of wrath and tears " there looms the possibility of an immortal life freighted with all the glorious opportunities of a divine renewal. And not only so ; but, while I recognize that the fruit of every action is immediate, I crave for many faithful souls some outward comfort in addition to their peace of heart. I want to see good men who have been cruelly maligned, and have gone down to death unable to relieve themselves of the unjust opprobrium, enabled, in a world of clearer light and more serene intelligence and more patient listening, to make their vindication absolute, their righteousness shine forth without a fleck or stain ; and, so long as I live, I shall go on hoping that such things may be some day.

Coming now to my true subject, the power of the idea of an endless life, the first thing that is evident is that this idea has not been anything like so universal as has been commonly believed of late. The argument for its validity from its universality is a very doubtful one, so many deductions must be made from the completeness of the universal faith or hope. Not to consider this too curiously, what an enormous deduction is that which must be made on account of the Hebrew frame of mind! The first gleam of the resurrection doctrine, which was the first Jewish form of the doctrine of personal immortality, is in the Book of Daniel, which now, we know, appeared about 165 B.C.,—the doctrine a Persian importation, which, once it had appeared, spread very rapidly. And, while remembering that the most religious people of antiquity did not share this hope, we must not forget that in our own time there are many individuals who at least imagine that, if their preferences were consulted, they would have their be-all and their end-all here. I often please myself with imagining the surprise of some of my habitual hearers, who are manifestly bored by my recurrence to this theme, when they discover that they are immortal, after all, and how confidently they will expect to have me say, " I told you so "; but I trust that I shall meet them with a better grace.

A much more important fallacy than the attribution of universality to the idea of immortality is the assumption that the power of this idea has always been a power of comfort and of consolation to mankind. On the contrary, it may well be doubted if the human mind has ever entertained any other idea that has been to it the occasion of so much anxiety, so much agonizing doubt and fear. The idea of immortality attests its vigor in no respect more grandly than by its persistence for so many centuries, in spite of all the terrors that it has carried in its train. It needs no ghost revisiting the glimpses of the moon to say to us,—

> "I could a tale unfold whose lightest word
> Would harrow up thy soul, freeze thy young blood,
> Make thy two eyes, like stars, start from their spheres,
> Thy knotted and combined locks to part
> And each particular hair to stand on end,
> Like quills upon the fretful porcupine."

No ghost returning could relate things more horrible than those which have been imagined by the preachers and the poets of the Christian world. There is, perhaps, no better way of judging of the relative amounts of pain and pleasure associated with the doctrine of a future life along the Christian centuries than a comparison in Dante and Milton of the vividness of the terrors that are multiplied with the splendors of the beatific vision. The imagination of the poet would seem to have exhausted itself upon the former, and to have approached the latter "fat and scant of breath." Such images as those of Dante's spiral hell and purgatorial stairs must have made life a burden and a curse to thousands, where his description of the mystic rose of heaven had no fragrance of suggestion for the mind and heart. Indeed, the endless disquisitions of his saints in light have sometimes seemed to me an evil to be feared more than the torments of his infernal tunnel or his purgatorial hill. With the prosaists as well as with the poets there has been no genius in the picturing of heaven approximating to that with which they have pictured hell. Let Boston's "Fourfold State" or Jonathan Edwards's sermons witness to my words. Swedenborg's hell is made horrible enough, but his heaven is about as bad. If we paid our money, it would be hard to take our choice. And then, too, we must consider that heaven has been for the few, hell for the many all the way. Chrysostom doubted if one hundred of one hundred thousand citizens of Antioch would be saved; and what his golden mouth delivered, many throats of iron and brass have clamored forth. Massillon was never more eloquent than when preaching on "The Small Number of the Saved," and two centuries ago an English preacher urged that one person saved out of every million would be a liberal calculation. Surely, an idea which has had these implications must have been more powerful for the creation of human misery than for anything else. To think otherwise would be to think a man the most insensible of brutes.

"Every religion which is worthy of the name," says Lecky

"must provide some method of consoling men in the first agonies of bereavement, some support in the extremes of pain and sickness, above all, some stay in the hour of death." And he assumes that the absolution of the Roman priest and the Protestant doctrine of justification by faith have been efficacious to these ends. If they have been, it has been only by dispelling terrors which the Christian theologian has invoked. In so far as the idea of immortality *as such* has been a source of comfort and of consolation to mankind, it has been so, thanks to no Bible revelation, nor to any traditional Christianity, but thanks to the softening influences of Universalism and Spiritualism and Unitarianism, and Rationalism in general, on the ancient creed. The consolations of the churches are the gifts of those whom they despise and fear. It was only yesterday that Gardiner Spring did not exceed the average temper of his sect in saying, "When the omnipotent and angry God, who has access to all the avenues of distress in the corporeal frame and all the inlets to agony in the intellectual constitution, undertakes to punish, he will convince the universe that he does not gird himself for the work of retribution in vain"; and "it will be a glorious deed when he shall cast those who have trodden his blood under their feet into the furnace of fire." Nothing is more common than for men to talk as if the idea of immortality had always been a source of comfort to mankind. But, so far as comfort is concerned, humanity would have been much better off without it. It is only recently that immortality, as such, has been a comfortable object of regard. And it has been made so by the intellectual forces and the heretical developments which the traditional Church has visited with her dreadful ban, which is not dreadful any more.

Has the moral bearing of the doctrine, heretofore, been such as to atone for all the terrors it has had for the imagination and the heart? Doubtless the penal cruelties which men imagined in another world were reflections of the cruelties they practised steadily in this. Men who could devise the horrors of the inquisition and of the penal civil codes of whose cruelties it availed itself (and often bettered their instructions) could easily devise the horrors of an eternal doom. It has always seemed to me an admirable touch in Alger's monumental " History of the Doctrine of a Future Life," where, speaking of Calvin's monstrous view of the hereafter, he says, " His character enabled him to believe it." And what was true of him was true of many : actual begot ideal cruelty ; they made God in their own image,— in the image of their cruelty and hate. Having done this, however, the reactionary force of their imaginations was immense. From their imaginary hell there came a foul, contaminating breath, poisoning not only those who hollowed out the pit, but many innocent of their offence. Thus the ideal power of an endless life was for many centuries a power of moral hardening. The cruelty of its imaginations was actualized in men's daily lives. From the preacher's sermon they went out, from the sulphurous book or parchment they rose up, to smite and slay. Then, too, it must not be forgotten that the strength of persecution was this same ideal power. The foundations of that monstrous system were laid deep in the conception of a never-ending life. The bed-rock was the idea of the moral heinousness of an unorthodox belief. But, if that heinousness could have worked itself out within the limits of the present life, the enginery of persecution would never have attained to its historic violence. It was the idea that men's orthodox or unorthodox opinions determined their eternal state for good or ill that did for the capacity of persecution what the application of steam to industry has done for that,— multiplied it a hundred and two hundred fold. This inspired the infernal ingenuities which some of you have seen in the torture-chambers of Nuremberg and Ratisbon,— things so ingenious in their cruelty that it would seem that only a devil could have invented them ; and this it was that nerved the arm to turn the torturing wheel, screw on the iron clamp, or shut the victim in the Iron Virgin's fell embrace. What suffering too great, too horrible, if haply it might save the victim from the torments of an endless hell ;

or, failing to do that, would shut up his heretical mouth forever and be a fearful warning to his fellow-men!

To discourage thought, to encourage general immorality, was the natural operation of the idea of a future life, as cherished throughout Christendom, down to the very threshold of the present time. The doctrine of purgatory was originally a demurrer put in on behalf of the varieties of human character, the different degrees of sin, and the remedial character of punishment. But in its historical development it proved to be the infallible device of hierarchic selfishness. This was the instrument that fleeced the lambs, in order that the shepherds might be sumptuously clothed and in order that such sheep-folds as Saint Peter's might be glorious in men's eyes. Glorious in men's eyes they are; but it takes something from their glory to think they were so often built with money that was the price of tolerated sin, or went to buy release of friends in purgatory from their pains. But not all the other influences of the Church combined did so much to keep men out of hell as this mercantile basis of salvation. For souls in hell had no pecuniary value for the Church. Once *there*, it was forever. It was then, you see, wholly for the interest of the Church to have as few in hell as possible and as many in purgatory. And so it happened that the Roman Catholic hell was mainly peopled by Protestants and heathen beyond the jurisdiction of the Church, and by those who had no "property qualification" for election to the upper house.

The ideal power of immortality in the Middle Ages was "the power of the keys": "that which is bound on earth shall be bound in heaven." This armed with the right of investiture — no king a king but by the pope's allowance — made every king as servile as a slave, and blocked the path of human liberty and political development with a bulk which many centuries of labor and convulsion have not availed to wholly clear away.

If I seem to keep your gaze too closely fixed upon the mother Church and mediæval time, it is not because I cannot give it ampler range. There is at least one aspect of the power of an endless life for evil in men's lives to which the Roman Church can lay no special claim. For Protestantism equally with Romanism it has been a power of "other worldliness," of temptation to withdraw the interest and noble passion of men's lives from earthly duties and responsibilities to dreams of an imagined bliss. or fears of an imagined pain. It would seem that every thoughtful person must at one time or another, in these later times, have thought with painful earnestness how different might have been this earth-bound world if all, or even half, of the intellectual and emotional energy that has been spent upon another life had been spent on this. Why, in that case, we should have had a very real heaven here! The grass could not have been more green, the trees more beautiful in their various forms and leafage, the sea more glorious, the mountains more magnificent, the sky more blue, o'erarching all the rest; but, in that case, we should have brought our eyes up to their style, we should have made our lives more worthy of their wonderful environment of earth and air, and more responsive to the invitation of "the spiritual stars which rising nightly shed their private beam into each separate heart."

"The power of an endless life," the power of the idea of this life upon the life which now is,—can there be any goodness in it, any future for it, clogged as it has been in the past with so many miserable associations, coming to us, as it does, down the long corridors of history with the smell of fire (eternal fire) upon its garments, its hands red with the blood of thousands and callous with such cruelties as we can hardly think upon and live, its forehead seamed with lines of sordid care, its lips denouncing death on all the larger liberties of thought and life, alike its terrors and its blandishments persuading men to the neglect of simple, human, mundane cares and duties and delights? Can any good come from this Nazareth, this Babylon, which was so long a fount of terror, the energizing force of persecution, the hot-bed of the most intolerable ecclesiastical pretensions and rapacities that have ever preyed upon the vitals of the world? To these questions, without the slightest hesitation or equivocation, I answer most emphatically, Yes. And I do not believe that the accusation I have brought against the doctrine of immortality in the past as an ideal power exhausts the sum of its contents. For those who think it does, I cannot wonder much that they are hopeless in their condemnation of the whole miserable business; that to cure men of their belief in or their hope of immortality seems the first step toward the deliverance of mankind from the bondage of corruption into the glorious liberty of the children of God.

But I am convinced that he would be only a careless student of Christian history who in the power of this conception, while finding all the shameful and the doubtful elements that I have named, found only these. These have been the ecclesiastical elements. But the ecclesiastical elements of Christianity have never been exhaustive of its best of moral and spiritual life. These have been the work of men whose unconscious ambition has been, apparently, to devise a scheme of doctrine and observance as widely different as possible from the life and teachings of Jesus of Nazareth. Meantime, in many leafy coverts of the world, remote from the white dust and glare of the ecclesiastical highway, in huts where poor men wrought and patient mothers bent above their babes, in students' pensive citadels, in scenes of mortal struggle with the powers that sometimes league against the struggling will, in moments of great agony when no device of skill or love or prayer could stay the fleeting breath of husband, wife, or child, and in ten thousand other situations possible in the boundless multiformity of human life, the power of an endless life, the hope of it, the strong assurance, has been a power of perfect blessing and of nameless peace. And, in the future, which, with its stupendous possibilities, awaits the patience of men's thought, the ardor of their wills, it needs no prophet's eye to see that this power of an endless life, divesting itself of all the gross and cluttering integuments

which have hindered its free motion in the past, shall rein-
vest itself in garments of a heavenly brightness and a clean-
ness without stain, and shall go forth, never again, it may be,
with such dominance as it formerly enjoyed, but gently and
sweetly blending its legitimate and noble uses with every
other noble and legitimate use that makes for the enlighten-
ment and expansion of our common life.

For him whose heart-strings, sounding in unison, never
give out this mystic tone, we have no word of blame. To
deny such a one our fellowship, if it had any attraction for
him, would be not less absurd than to deny it to one who
should not find in himself any response to the reality that is
connoted by that least and greatest of all monosyllables,
which says so little and which means so much,— dare I to
speak it? — God. These are the very people that we want
with us, if, haply, we can make them sharers of our joy. At
no time, to my consciousness, has there been granted any
audible or visible sign to which I might appeal for evidence
of things that lie beyond the veil. What power of comfort,
peace, and satisfaction is and abides with those who can
but think themselves more fortunate I can but dimly guess.
But I am glad that for a great and growing company, who
have broken with the traditions of the past, to whom the
resurrection of Jesus would prove nothing satisfying if it had
any evidence for itself, and who have not attained to the
assurance of the Spiritualist faith, the tendencies of science,
the voices of the heart, the aspirations of the intellect and
moral will, combine to make a life beyond this life appear
as rational a hope and expectation as the coming autumn's
bounty after the summer's ripening of the immeasurable
promise of the spring. For such what is the power of the
idea of an immortal life?

It is a power of intellectual prophecy. As such, it cannot
be the same for all. There are those who are incurious to
all material and spiritual things. So long as they have
enough to eat and drink, and are comfortably housed and
clothed, what do they care for all the wonder and the mystery

of the world ?   But all have not this dulness and this density
of heart and mind.   Some have gone a little way, some have
gone far, some very far indeed, upon the road of study and
interpretation of the meaning of the world.   And the further
they have gone, the further do they wish to go.   To cease
from their pursuit of knowledge, having gathered their few
shells and pebbles on the shore of truth's illimitable sea, to
go home and go to sleep and never wake again,— that course
and end may cause no pang for .those who do not think.
For those who do it almost stops the heart.   And corre-
spondingly for those who do, and in the measure of their
thoughtfulness, their penetration into the deep things of
God, with the glad confidence of an immortal life there
comes "the trumpet of a prophecy," — that the great search
shall go on, that new secrets of the world shall be discovered,
that new territories of knowledge shall be annexed to our
present narrow state, that the fragments of our knowledge
shall be pieced together into some hint of the immeasurable
unity of things.   That is worth hoping for; that is worth
living for; that is worth dying for.   Those who never speak
of immortality without disrespect, for whom it has no implications that are not selfish, mean, and low, have never, you
may be sure, seen "the bright countenance of truth in the
quiet and still air of delightful studies "; they are not like
him

> " Who, through long days of labor,
>   And nights devoid of ease,
>   Still heard in his soul the music
>   Of wonderful melodies, "—

the melodies of the inviolable order of the world.   For else

> " Seeking through all they felt or saw
>   The springs of life, the depths of awe,
>   To find the law within the law,"

they would have known that in the desire and passion to
continue in this way there is nothing selfish, mean, or low.
A man knows well enough the better and the worse in his

own life, he knows when he is greatly stirred, and no opinion
of another can convince the man or woman who has once
conceived a passion for some large and splendid knowledge
of God's universe that he is comforting himself ignobly when
his heart thrills with gratitude that beyond the confines of
this present life there stretches out for him an immeasurable
opportunity for the enlargement of his vision of the majestic
wonder of the world.

Time was when science was for a few only. But the
printing-press has abolished the monopoly of science. And
still the number of those who think is small compared with
that of those who feel. The great men of science are but
few, and those who range their many-gated Thebes of knowledge with a grateful mind are not a countless multitude. But
no man can number those who love and those who mourn
for loved ones and companions "hid in Death's dateless
night." And for all these the idea and assurance of an immortal life is a power of consolation. It could not well be
that, while the old dogma raged without hindrance up and
down the world. There was the awful possibility for each
and every one that he might be of the reprobate, and not
of the elect; for the signs that differentiated these from those
were made out with difficulty. And then, if one was perfectly
sure of his own salvation, there was the chance that some
dear friend might not be sure of his; and, though Jonathan
Edwards argued very ably that the saints in heaven would
rejoice to witness the just punishment of their friends and
kindred in the lowest deep, it may be doubted whether many
were convinced it would be really so. But in our time, outside the Roman Catholic enclosure, the old penal theology
has been so broken through in many places that it seems
only a question of time, and that the shortest, whether it
shall any longer vex the human heart. The dogmatism of
the creeds has been shown to have but little warrant in New
Testament phrases, and these, generally anonymous, to have
no slightest claim on our acceptance over and above their intrinsic rationality. At length, then, it is safe for men to hope

for immortality and to believe in its reality. At length the power of an endless life is a power of comfort and of consolation for all sorrowful and mourning hearts. It means reunion with the dear ones we have loved and who have vanished from our sight. It means this, I cannot but think, if it means anything. For heaven were not heaven if there we should forever miss the friends who seemed to make this life a foretaste of its joy. It can have no spaces wide enough to forever isolate from one another those for whose hearts there has been only one beat of joy and sorrow here. By what divine telegraphy I know not, we shall find each other out, and again "know ourselves into one." And here, again, we can with perfect frankness and sincerity receive the challenge of all those who flout the hope of an immortal life, as selfish, mean, and low. It is as selfish, mean, and low as the love which glorifies our human life, which dares and suffers everything for the beloved one. No: it is not where love is most considerate of self, but where its self-abandonment and sacrifice is most, that its demand is most impassioned for its own. Those that love, loving only, or being loved, may indeed comfort themselves without the hope of a renewed and glorified affection. Not so can they who love, not merely loving, not merely being loved, but their friend, father or mother, brother or sister, husband or wife or child, with a great passion of self-sacrificing tenderness and holy trust. Take such a love as that of Lucy Smith in the story of her life which Mr. Merriam has written. Its full meaning cannot be for those of you who are not women, or men, of sorrows and acquainted with grief. But that any one could read of such a love and such a longing as was hers, and not feel that nothing could be higher, sweeter, nobler, better in this world of many high and sweet and good and noble things, I am myself unable to conceive.

"Such a love and longing as was hers." And in saying that I pass to my last word. For her love and longing were a consecration to all best and highest things.

"What should she do with all the days and hours
That must be counted ere she saw his face?
How should she charm the interval that lowered
Between this time and that sweet time of grace?"

She would lay hold of all things excellent in thought and deed. She would make herself worthy of his nobleness. She would grow here as he was growing there. Even as the heavens globe themselves in a drop of dew, so in one clear, transparent personal experience globes itself the universal law of souls. "Every man that hath this hope purifieth himself." That is the highest and the deepest, the strongest and the purest power of an endless life, of its persuasive influence on our earthly lives,— the power of moral instigation and of moral consecration. "For their sakes I consecrate myself," says the Fourth Gospel,— Christ-words, simple and sweet enough for the real Jesus to have uttered them. He said it of the living. We say it of the dead. Were we to be alone in heaven, alone with our whole past, the power of this idea must, it would seem, be something wonderful for those with whom it is a real thing. How can we help questioning whether it *is* a real thing for those who go on doing mean and selfish, coarse and brutal things, very much as if they expected "to fall head foremost in the jaws of vacant darkness and to cease"? Do they expect to be themselves in everything but memory in that other world,— to have no memory there? If not, how can they go on, as they often do, committing crimes and harboring thoughts and tolerating dispositions which, remembered in the heart of heaven, would make even there a momentary hell? The other day I spoke into that marvellous instrument, the phonograph, the latest triumph of man's audacious ingenuity, a bit of verse of my own making. In another moment I became the auditor, and the instrument spoke back to me my poem, word for word, as I had uttered it. But, alas! I had made two mistakes; and these came back to me, and they could not be recalled! *They could not be recalled!* What a phonograph is this memory of ours! and how we talk away to it, mindless of our mistakes!

And what is true of man's phonograph is true of God's, called memory, of the mistakes we make with it. *They cannot be recalled.* With what discords will they smite our ears some day! How will the cruel and the unjust words come back!— the words we knew, when we were saying them, were cruel and unjust— ay, and perhaps the sound of falling tears close following, and of quick sobs as of a broken heart. Do we believe in immortality? Do we believe that memory will survive the shock of death, and yet go saying and doing things whose faintest recollection will abash us in the presence of the holy ones of heaven,— nay, in the presence of our own better selves, and fill us with unutterable pain?

" Every man that hath this hope purifieth himself." Yes, and not only because of his own eyes turned inward on his heart, but because of eyes in which the love-light danced for us of yore, and which are now, as they were then, too pure to look upon uncleanness. Do men really believe in immortality, do they really hope for it, do they really think that they shall meet with their lost friends again, with those to whom they have given bonds of mute farewells and floods of secret tears to be in all things worthy of their love, while yet they do continually the things the consciousness of which would spoil the joy of their reunion with them in the heavenly places, turning it to grief and shame? And this personal aspect is not all. What grief and shame to stand upon the threshold of another life, and be obliged to think of all the glorious opportunity of this as wasted or but half improved! Such faith have I in the stupendous possibilities of God that I can well believe that, in the life to come, he will show to us more wonderful things out of his love than we have dreamed of here. Such knowledge have I of the actual blessedness and wonder of this present life that I believe there are some good things here which, if we do not take them now, in all the ranges of existence we shall have no opportunity to find again what we have carelessly let slip.

The Power of an Endless Life, the power of its ideal

beauty and persuasion on our mortal state! I have not begun to tell what I have felt and known of this in favored hours, what *you* have felt and known. But, if I have not wholly failed to put in words what sometimes fills the spaces of my heart with an unutterable joy, I have made some things clear, some things that will grow clearer to you as you take them home and think of them in that deep inward silence where the voice of God is ever heard most clearly, as if he walked *our* garden with us in the coolness of the day. God grant that this idea and this hope and this assurance may be so real to us, so genuine, so true, a fact so perfectly substantial and inexpugnable in our lives, that it shall be for each and every one of us a power of intellectual prophecy, of comfort in our sorrow, of moral consecration that shall lift our lives up to a higher level and a clearer light, making all present things more beautiful, and from our thought of death removing every fear.

> "Twilight and evening bell,
>   And after that the dark!
> And may there be no sadness of farewel'
>   When I embark.
>
> "Sunset and evening star,
>   And one clear call for me;
> And may there be no moaning of the bar
>   When I put out to sea,
>
> "But such a tide as moving seems asleep,
>   Too full for sound and foam,
> When that which drew from out the boundless deep
>   Turns again home."

WHY I AM A UNITARIAN.*

As a matter of fact, it is very possible that I am a Unitarian because I was to the Unitarian manner born and reared, my parents attending the Unitarian church in the old sea-girt town of Marblehead, and I following their example. But I am bound to say that, though two better people never lived, for all their simple trust in the eternal goodness and their absolute fidelity in every calling to which they were called, they had "no religion, to speak of." They were not formally religious, not church members. They held no ' definite creed, and they took no pains to fashion one for me. But, as a boy and youth, I went to the Unitarian church, and heard the exposition of its doctrinal position, but for which it is possible my opinions may have taken another turn; for the unconscious influences of youth are powerful both for evil and for good. If it was the environment of my boyhood and my youth that made me a Unitarian, then I am more glad than I can say that it was a Unitarian environment; for the principles and beliefs of Unitarians are now so precious to my mind, and its traditions are so inspiring to my heart, that I am compelled to feel that without them my life would have been far less joyous and serene and satisfactory than it has been so far.

But what is wanted of me in this series of confessions is

* Although this number of our series preserves the usual form upon the title-page, it is not a sermon, as the reader will easily discover. It is an article that appeared in the New York *Press* of Dec. 21, 1890, one of a series by different preachers, giving reasons for the faith that is in them. It is reprinted here, with the permission of the publishers to whom it belongs, by the advice of friends, who think its close resemblance to my Unity Tract, "What do Unitarians believe?" will not prevent its serving a good turn.

not, I suspect, the historical genesis of my Unitarian belief, but the conscious and deliberate reasons that I give myself and others for holding it so confidently and contentedly as I. do. These reasons are such that it seems to me that, if I had been born a Mohammedan or a Buddhist, an Episcopalian or Presbyterian, I should have been as convinced a Unitarian as I am. For, in my conscious and deliberate thinking, I am a Unitarian because its principles and its beliefs commend themselves to me as the most rational that I am able to conceive, with the help of all the creeds of Christendom and those beyond, and the most satisfactory imaginable to my mind and heart. I know that there are those who will imagine that I thus confess a fatal error at the start, — the making of reason, and not revelation, the basis of my belief. But, in doing this frankly and openly, I only do what others are obliged to do secretly and clandestinely. They reckon ill who think they can leave reason out or assign to it a less than fundamental place. Without this theirs is the fabled world which rested on an elephant, and the elephant on four tortoises, and so on. Must not the Protestant who accepts the Bible as an authoritative revelation have a reason for accepting it as such? and must not the Roman Catholic who accepts the Church as the treasury of tradition and the interpreter of the Bible, and hence the source of his authoritative revelation, have a reason for accepting it as such? Thus fundamentally, in my reliance upon reason, I am conditioned precisely as my Presbyterian or Roman Catholic friend. The difference is that they do not feel at liberty to question the contents of Church or Bible, while I do. But does it not stand to reason — there is no avoiding this appeal — that, if reason is sufficient to settle the claims of a revelation to be considered such, it is also equal to the rational criticism of its contents. And, however it may have been in past times, it is certain that in our own the Roman Catholic and orthodox Protestant alike endeavor to establish the reasonableness not only of their general claim, but of the contents of their revelation of the Church or Book. Cardinal Manning says that, when doctrines are approved by reason, they cease to be doctrines of revelation, and that the first step toward infidelity is to attempt to rationalize dogma. If this be so, then Cardinal Newman took many steps that way, and did his best to deprive the doctrines of the Church of their character of revelation, because he did his best to give them a reasonable appearance and win for them a rational assent.

I am a Unitarian because I am rationally convinced of the soundness of those principles for which Unitarianism stands, and those beliefs which have been pre-eminently characteristic of its development. Its principles are three, and they are: (1) The right and duty of every man to exercise his freest thought upon the highest themes; (2) The right and duty of making reasonableness, or rationality, the final test of truth; (3) The superiority of character to creed, of conduct to belief. Concerning these principles there is among Unitarians entire agreement, though not always perfect courage in their application to practical exigencies that arise in our denominational life. An obvious corollary of the first of these three principles is the right of every man to fashion his own creed. From first to last there have been various small attempts to overrule this right, and formulate a creed which should be used as a limitation or test of fellowship. Such an attempt was made in 1865, when our National Conference was organized, and again a few years later. But the attempt, whenever made and seconded by whatever earnestness or ability, has always failed, or the creed devised has straightway lapsed into "innocuous desuetude." Even when the creed-making clique has deceived itself and a few others with the assurance that what it wanted was not a creed, but "a statement of purpose," but little headway has been made. Moreover, no creed, however unanimously accepted by a general Unitarian body, would have any authority for our Unitarian churches. The system of these churches is without exception purely Congregational. Not one of them acknowledges in any least degree the authority of any central

or superior organization. And the acknowledged Unitarianism of individual men has not been affected by their relations to collective organizations. Dr. Bellows, who was
never happy when he was not organizing something or somebody, and Dr. Furness, to whom all organization was intolerable, were equal in their Unitarian standing. If at any
time the American Unitarian Association of the National
Conference should adopt a statement of belief, those Unitarians who could not accept such a statement would be just
as good Unitarians as they are now, and better than their
statement-making friends. The most of a creed attempted
of late years is the expression " Lord and Master, Jesus
Christ," in the preamble to the National Conference adopted
in 1865. But even so much is declared by an article of the
constitution to express only the views of the majority who
placed it there, the most of whom are now in heaven. The
most simple and straightforward statement of our Unitarian
position is that of the Western Unitarian Conference, which
welcomes to its fellowship all who desire to work with it for
righteousness and truth and love, and then publishes a statement of " things commonly believed among us," without any
pretence that they are equally believed by all. This is precisely the position of the National Conference, but that the
latter puts the cart before the horse,— the doctrine (and not
much of that) before the principle. This freedom of the
churches and of individual belief is, of course, uneqally at-
tractive to different men; but, with occasional grumblings
and protestations, it is the characteristic freedom of the Unitarian body. In this article I speak only for myself; and
this freedom is a reason, equal, if not superior, to any other
why I am a Unitarian, for this makes all the other good
things possible.

Our second principle is very like the first, being the right
and duty of making reasonableness the final test of truth.
Sixty or seventy years ago there were Unitarians who contended that in any conflict of reason and revelation we
should follow the written word. But Channing said,— and

no words he spoke have been more formative and impressive, — "The truth is — and it ought not to be disguised — that our ultimate reliance is and must be upon our own reason." From Channing's time till now this understanding has increased, and it is now universal in the Unitarian camp. There is still much difference as to what is reasonable, and, therefore, to be believed; but there is entire agreement that what is not reasonable is not to be believed wherever or by whomsoever taught. In 1840 there were those who would have denied Theodore Parker the Unitarian or Christian name because of his opinions about miracles and other matters. Now the conservatives claim him as their own; and the Unitarian Association publishes his sermons, and hangs his portrait in its noble Channing Hall.

The third principle which makes me glad to be a Unitarian is the superiority of character to creed, of conduct to belief. This principle should have been, perhaps, my first and foremost. For this implies the freedom of the intellect. This implies that "we are not," as Thomas Jefferson so wisely said, "responsible for the rightfulness, but for the righteousness of our opinions"; that we had better hold mistaken opinions with a fair and open mind than the most orthodox or true while seeking our own will or any mere conformity. But to say that character is more than creed, conduct more than opinion, is not to say that opinion is of no importance, that it makes no difference what a man believes. We all believe that it makes a great deal of difference what a man believes, — that the man's life whose thoughts of God and nature and humanity are grand and elevated must be more right than one's whose thoughts of these things are poor and mean. High thinking is an absolute good; but, whatever its importance, it is no deduction from the soundness of the principle. Character is more than creed. It would be impossible to find a Unitarian denying this, and such community of inspiring thought and feeling makes my gladness that I am a Unitarian continually more abound.

Seeing that Unitarians have no general statement of belief and no general body capable of imposing one on individuals or churches, and seeing that they believe not only in the right, but in the duty of private judgment, it will not be expected that all Unitarians should believe alike; and they do not. And this is a particular in which they much resemble other, especially the Protestant, sects. There is to-day very little unanimity of belief in any one of these. Episcopalians, Congregationalists, Presbyterians, witness the truth of this. The difference between Unitarians and these orthodox sects is that the latter pretend to unanimity and do not have it, while the former do not pretend to it and do not have it. But they have quite as much of it as their evangelical critics, if they have not a little more.

We are indebted to Cardinal Newman for the delightful paradox that the Roman Catholic Church has been the principal abettor of free thought, because it has forbidden it; for men will always have forbidden things. There is much truth in this, though I should credit the result to human nature rather than to the Church. On the other hand, with perfect intellectual freedom there at once arises a tendency to intellectual agreement. And so it happens that, although Unitarians do not all believe alike, there is among them much more agreement in 1890 than in 1840 or 1820, and there are some things so commonly believed among them that the belief might safely be set down as universal.

Among these things are the principles I have already named. And there are also several beliefs of first-rate importance, each one of which in turn is a fresh reason why I am a Unitarian. Naturally, I name the unity of the Divine Being first of all; for it is this belief which gives to Unitarians their distinctive name, and, as time has gone on, there has not been the slightest inclination to recede from its most definite expression. If any have derived a contrary impression from the fact that, as between Arius and Athanasius in the early church, many more Unitarians now incline to Athanasius than formerly, they have been much deceived.

The utter incongruity of the Arian doctrine with the human-ity of Jesus, on which Athanasius insisted no less than on his godhead, has done much to bring it into disrepute ; while the perception that every man is "of one substance" with the Father has made the Athanasian claim for Jesus less false than partial. In every way, the Unitarian belief in the divine unity resumes to-day a much greater wealth of meaning than it did as first conceived among us. Even at first, the belief was much less numerical than is commonly supposed. That Calvinism had three gods instead of one was less objectionable than its dualism of love and justice in the divine nature. With our early Unitarians, as with the reforming Presbyterians, the moral atrociousness was what most repelled. But, from Channing's time till ours, Unita-rianism as "a movement of reason in sympathy with science" has found new reasons every day for believing that there is one God and Father of all,— one, and one only. Science is but another name for the discovered unity and harmony of the world. The revelations of the spectroscope, of natural selection, of the correlation and conservation of forces, of comparative physiology, philology, mythology, politics, relig-ion, are revelations of an all-pervading unity. And because these revelations of the different sciences are a delight to my imagination, and not merely satisfactory to my under-standing, their splendid confirmation of the central Unita-rian doctrine confirms my Unitarianism steadily with every fresh advance.

But, if any one contended that the doctrine of the dignity of human nature had been even more characteristic of Uni-tarianism in its historic course than any other, I should yield the point at once. Certainly, Channing's greatest thought was this, while Dewey's was the dignity of human life. Channing said, " My one sublime idea which has given me unity of mind is the greatness, the divinity, of the soul." This was the fountain from which all his other thought came streaming forth. With him, as it had been with Jesus, the goodness of God was an inference from human goodness.

How strange that, when this inference is neither here nor
there, but everywhere, in the teachings of Jesus, the doctrine
of total depravity should ever have been a part of Christianity. " Forgive us our trespasses, as we forgive those who
trespass against us," — that is the key-note of Jesus' argument from man to God.

But, when Unitarianism found itself confronted with the
Darwinian theory of human origin, what did it do? Its
persuasion of the dignity of human nature would seem to
be an insuperable bar to its acceptance of that theory,
though all the other sects should fall into line. But it was
not so. It was the first of all the sects to give Darwin
calm attention and then clear assent. And great has been
its reward; for, while accepting the theory on scientific
grounds, it has found in the rise of man from brute conditions a further reason for believing in his essential dignity
and worth. The long way he has come from his primeval
state argues what splendid stuff was in his grain, and prophe-
sies the long way he has to go, the heights, undreamed of
yet, whence his " Excelsior! " shall sound.

With the Unitarian belief in the dignity of human nature
goes along the belief in the dignity of human life, which
means the excellence and glory of the life that now is, whatever promise there may be of that which is to come. For
this aspect of our faith, ·we are indebted to Orville Dewey as
to no other man. That it is "good for us to be here " is a
persuasion that is abated by no painful elements of our experience. If many things are miserable to see or to endure,
what have we here but further opportunity to approve our
manhood and our womanhood by abolishing the misery and
enduring what must be endured with a courageous heart?

Now, it is not denied that there are points of belief on
which Unitarians are less completely agreed than on those
I have already named. So far as these are concerned, I am
a Unitarian because in the breadth of its inclusion the denomination presents me with opinions that appeal to me as
rational and just, while the average tendency of the denom-

ination is to such opinions. For example, time was when Christianity was universally regarded by Unitarians as a supernatural revelation, attested by signs and wonders, promulgated by one who, even if purely human, was endowed with certain supernatural gifts, and perpetuated in a literature — the New Testament — whose writers were miraculously restrained from all erroneous statements, whether of doctrine or fact. These views are no longer held in their entirety by any Unitarians. Many, who still think and speak of Christianity as supernatural, and of Jesus as a worker of miracles, regard the New Testament, and the Bible as a whole, as a purely human composition, subject to inaccuracy and error, as all human things must be. But there are many more who do not regard Christianity as a supernatural religion. It is one of the great religions of the world, differing from the others not in kind, but in degree, its general superiority not precluding inferiority of particular precepts, tendencies, ideas, and ideals. Moreover, there are to-day few Unitarians, if any, who believe in any of the New Testament miracles, from the birth of Jesus to his resurrection, inclusively, in the proper sense of the word "miracles," — violations of natural law. And it is only as violations of natural law that miracles can prove a supernatural revelation. On the other hand, there are few who would set aside all the miraculous stories of the New Testament as devoid of any fact foundation. These stories are supposed to have been fed by many streams of popular thought and life. To a little fact, a very little, there were added increments of spontaneous exaggeration, reflections from Messianic expectations, changes of words into things, parables into events, and so on. There are those among us — looking to Dr. Furness as the author and finisher of their faith in this respect — who think that Jesus' wonder-working was the exponent of his moral excellence. Others object that approximate excellence should give approximate power, and there is no sign that it does. This variety of belief concerning miracles, with an increasing tendency to broader and more rational views, is another reason why I am a Unitarian.

And still another is the belief in immortality among us, not because of Jesus' resurrection, but because of its answer to the intellectual and moral and affectional demands of mortal imperfection. A living hope seems to me better every way than a "dead certainty." Again, I am a Unitarian because Unitarianism has been delivered from its old doctrine of probation,—as if this bit of mortal life could determine an eternity of weal or woe,—and has attained to the conviction that for the best and worst who enter on another life there is "the glory of going on," and no mere settling down to the enjoyment or the suffering of a condition wholly determined by our conduct here on earth.

Once more, I am a Unitarian because of the increasing rationality of the Unitarian belief concerning the life and character of Jesus and his relation to the religious life of men. To-day the majority of Unitarians hold to a purely human view of Jesus. Those who do not, regard him as much more akin to man than to God. The elevation of any human being into equality with the Infinite and Eternal God is to me a thing so monstrously irreverent that I cannot but be glad that any approach to such a view has less and less currency among us as the years go by. Meantime, the doctrine of the deity of Jesus is utterly discredited by the history of its growth as we trace it in the New Testament and the early church. The Unitarian doctrine of the atonement is another doctrine that commands my rational assent. It is that "God was in Christ reconciling the world unto himself," as he is now and always has been in good men and women, willing to suffer, and to die, if need be, for their fellow-men.

The Unitarian doctrine of the Bible commends itself to me because it is more rational than any other, or was until it won the gradual acceptance of many thousands in the other Christian sects. It is that its various books have drifted together in obedience to various tides of theory and sentiment. That, in the struggle for existence, there was generally a survival of the fittest seems extremely probable, but "generally" is not "always," and the fittest had as little claim to any supernatural origin as the unfittest. At length the purely human character of the Bible may be regarded as the quite unanimous opinion of our folk. The most conservative allow that the separate books "differ greatly from one another both in character and practical value" (Dr. A. P. Peabody), and deprecate the putting of them all on one high level. The most radical find in the Old Testament and New the most wonderful and admirable collection of sacred scriptures that any people has preserved. With our present knowledge, and still more our present ignorance, of the origins of the various parts of the Bible, it seems to us hardly less than wicked for any educated person to speak of it as a supernatural book or as one written by any other inspiration than the love of God and man. That some parts of it had a less lofty inspiration it would be foolish to deny.

Last, but not least, I am a Unitarian because Unitarianism makes the most exigent demands upon men's moral will, and in the example of Jesus and all other great and noble souls offers the best encouragement and inspiration for doing what is right. What man has done man may do, but not what God has done or any superhuman being. There is little moral inspiration in a divine or superhuman Christ,— only such as would reside in an impersonal moral ideal. It is the goodness of a man struggling with temptation that helps us to be good; if getting thrown sometimes, so much the better.

While I am a Unitarian mainly for the reasons that I have already named, I am made proud and happy in my allegiance by the traditions of nobility that adorn our history, by the great names of Channing and Parker and Ware and Dewey and Bellows and Hedge and Clarke and many others; by the presence with us of such living men as Martineau and Furness; by the contribution we have made to literature in the persons of Bancroft and Prescott and Motley and Parkman and Emerson and Longfellow and Lowell and Bryant and Hawthorne and Holmes; by our tradition of thought in sympathy with science ever since Priestley studied theology and science with an equal mind; by our tradition of public spirit in sympathy with reform and that "divine right of bolting" which had in Freeman Clarke its brave exponent; by the genial fellowship of men to work with whom is a continual incitement to "the best and honorablest things." A lover of literature, the openness of Unitarianism on the side of literature has been to me a perennial delight. A lover of poetry, I have been glad that of our six major poets five were of our household of faith, and the sixth — Whittier — in full agreement with our tendencies of thought and life; for this has seemed to me a confirmation of my opinion that, were only men poetical enough, they would find no lack of poetry in our views of man, the universe, and God. "She is a little college," Webster said of Dartmouth, "but there are those who love her." The Unitarian body, though steadily increasing, is comparatively small; but there are those who love it none the less on this account, and who, while rejoicing in its growth, rejoice still more that its characteristic doctrines are being welcomed by so many in the other sects that they will not continue to be specially characteristic of us for many years.

> " What matter we or they,
> Ours or another's day,
> So the right word be said,
> And life the sweeter made ? "

"AND BUT FOR YOU."

ON the eastern shore of the Dead Sea, not many miles away from where the Jordan enters it, near certain hot baths of Callirhoe, there is a deep ravine through which pours itself a rapid mountain stream, fretted and maddened by great blocks of trap and tufa that have fallen from the overhanging cliffs. Where these are most precipitous, their overhanging crest has still the monstrous ruins of a fortress, which was a palace also, of King Herod Antipas, to whose rule Jesus of Nazareth was subject for the greater part of his eventful life. It was to this castle of Machærus that John the Baptist, the scene of whose preaching was near at hand, was taken for imprisonment when he was arrested for his opposition to the course of Antipas in appropriating the wife of his brother, Herod Boethus, when he had one already of his own. It was here in some splendid hall (for Herod Antipas inherited old Herod's passion for architectural display and lavish ornament) that Salome, the daughter of the stolen wife, danced so delightfully that the tetrarch promised her anything she asked; and she asked the head of John the Baptist in a dish, and got what she desired, to please her mother's wicked heart. There is a representation of that dancing, which I well remember, in the tympanum of the northern portal in the west front of Rouen Cathedral. Salome, in high relief, is represented with her hands upon the floor, her heels high up in the air; and in the crumbling stone the happy tetrarch has not ceased to smile. It may well be doubted whether the dancing of Salome was such as that. That was the kind the pious sculptor of the thirteenth century would have rewarded well, had he been

Antipas. Whatever its peculiar grace or antic gayety, it was the price of blood. The criticism of royal marriages has been a dangerous business for prophets from that day to this; but it has been generally only the official head which has been taken off,— as Wolsey's, for example, when he objected to Henry Eighth's establishing the Church of England by putting Katherine of Aragon away and taking Anne Boleyn.

There is every reason to believe that the death of John the Baptist made a deep and wide impression throughout Palestine, as his teaching had already done. Far into the second century its echoes still went sounding on, and there were companies of believers gathered in his name. For two or three generations after his death his legend was more widely known than that of Jesus, and his influence appeared to have the promise of a greater permanence. That he made a much deeper contemporary impression than Jesus does not admit of any doubt. Among those who came to his baptism of repentance was Jesus; but whether after his baptism he lingered with him by the Jordan's side or went back to his carpentry at Nazareth, it is impossible for us to know. What seems most likely, balancing the probabilities, is that he went back to Nazareth (such return to their habitual work was the general way with John's disciples), and that there the news of John's imprisonment, which had gone far and wide, came to him also at his manful toil, until, like another of old time, the word of the Lord in his heart was like a fire shut up in his bones; he was weary with forbearing and he could not stay. He did not wait to hear what would become of John. Enough that his voice crying in the wilderness had ceased to cry; that there was silence and a void where there had been a splendid blasting of iniquity and a glorious summons to the righteous way. How often from his mother's lips or in the synagogue had he heard the story of Amos, the shepherd of Tekoa,— how on the lonely hillside, husbanding the sycamore fruit, he learned how the Syrians had threshed Israel with threshing-wains of iron, and how the Tyrians had sold Israel's sons to Edom, until it seemed to him he heard Jehovah roaring out of Zion and thundering from Jerusalem, and left his fruit and herds, that he might go and speak the word of prophecy and be a shepherd to the people who were like sheep gone astray and lost! Had *he* waited to see if some one else would not, perchance, hear what he had heard or go in before him to the breach and take into his breast the sheaf of spears, so that there might be no need of him? Indeed, he had not done so. Why any more should Jesus, then, wait for another? Was not the crying need the call of God? Should he not heed it, and obey? And so good-by to saw and plane, to tranquil work, to lonely brooding on the hills behind the town that showed him Hermon and the sea! Welcome the wandering life, the oppressor's scorn, the proud man's contumely, the doubts and fears of neighbors, relatives, and friends, who didn't see what call he had to preach, and all the vague, uncertain possibilities of suffering and death that such a rôle as that of John suggested to an imaginative mind! But unlike John, who went into the wilderness, and bade men come to him, he would go and find them where they were,—the more of them, the better; and so it was that in Capernaum, at the head of Lake Genesareth, a busy, stirring place, he first began to speak those words whose echoes linger and beseech us still, and will not die until humanity's great heart has ceased to beat.

And now if there was anything enigmatical in the title of my discourse, "And but for you," you see plainly enough the meaning of those monosyllables. You would see it plainly enough, if I had not quoted once again those favorite stanzas,* and even if you had not remembered them as a part of those stanzas.

> * " Say not, the struggle naught availeth,
> The labor and the wounds are vain,
> The enemy faints not, nor faileth,
> And as things have been they remain.
>
> " If hopes were dupes, fears may be liars;
> It may be, in yon smoke concealed,
> Your comrades chase e'en now the fliers,
> And, but for you, possess the field."

Arthur Hugh Clough.

It is only forty-two years since Clough wrote those stanzas in 1849, but something like them must have shaped itself
within the mind and heart of Jesus eighteen hundred and
ten or twelve years before, when the news of John's imprisonment came up to Nazareth from the south. "One more
disappointment!" sighed the sick heart of this or that one
who had gone with Jesus to receive the baptism to repentance, as he settled back into the old routine. What was
the use of hoping for a better time? But for one poor mechanic, the gap made by John's imprisonment was *a gap to
fill*. The void was clamorous and eloquent for him to come
and fill it with his voice, his heart, his life. And he obeyed
the voice. He was not disobedient to the heavenly vision.

Wherein he was like many others of the sons of God.
There are those who are never happy unless they are assign-
ing to Jesus some trait or quality wholly peculiar to himself;
but, for my part, whenever he is at his best, I find him the
interpreter of humanity. I like to find as good or better
than he taught in Epictetus or some other teacher of the
ancient world. If his teaching had been singular, I should
suspect its truth; but when deep answers unto deep, one
soul to another across many leagues and lands, then God's
voice seems to make itself a part of theirs. I do not even
care to show that his degree of excellence was without a
parallel in other lives. It is a question that assumes divine
omniscience in the answerer; and, if that were possible, such
yard-stick rivalries are, of all things, least edifying to the
spiritual man. So I am glad that, when a fallen prophet
summoned Jesus to rise up, and he obeyed, he only did what
hundreds and thousands had done before him in the world,
— hundreds and thousands have done from his day to ours.
Why not? The glory of humanity is more than that of any
individual man. His honor is not less because it is so
widely shared. The glory of righteousness stands not in
any personal comparison, but in obedience to ideal ends and
helpfulness for pressing human needs.

The men who have answered, "Here am I, for Thou *didst*

call me," when some trusted leader has been stricken down, when some line of battle against odds has seemed to waver and to break, some glorious banner has been trailed in dust, to whom the need for one more man has been the call of God,—these pass the torch from hand to hand all down the rugged ways of history, leaving no darkness without some irradiation of celestial light. There have been, and there are, I know, men — and their name is legion — of quite another sort : such as always go with the majority. The strong cause is their cause. Nothing succeeds with them like success. The church or party that is booming is the party or the church for them. On the eve of a political election they are on hand, for sale, to let, "in blocks of five," by hundreds, and alone. All that they want to know is which side is going to win. That is their side. If free coinage is looking up, they are for free coinage ; if sound money, then for sound money. Such men can never understand how certain senators and representatives at Washington can fight so desperately for a public measure, which has in it no political advantage, which has already helped to bring defeat upon their party at the polls. But there are also those who, though they may have no confidence in the public measure, cannot escape a kind of admiration for the men who, like Antæus, gather strength from every fall ; who yield not their opinion of the right way to any opposition, though it should sweep them and their party from the place of power into oblivion and contempt. Wrong-headed and mistaken such may be, no doubt ; but for their country's peace and righteousness any one of them is worth a score of those of either party whose hand is always on the popular pulse, and who are never marshalled, if they know it, any way but that in which the crowd is going. These are a multitude in every age and land. They attach themselves to the successful party, church, or individual. They are for that which goes and pays. And they are " the sewerage of history," and the pestilential rottenness that breeds the sickness of communities and consummates the ruin of the State.

But there never was a time when a forlorn hope did not pique the courage of brave soldiers in the enemy's front, marching, over the bodies of their friends who tried and failed, to victory or death. Did ever sinking ship or perilous adventure cry in vain for men to man the life-boat or go sounding on some dim and perilous way? Thank God for men whom any perilous cause invites and fascinates till they are weary with forbearing and they cannot stay. When Sumner was struck down in 1856, how many were raised up!. — a thousand not too many to fill up the gap his glorious bulk had filled. Wendell Phillips stood on a street corner in Boston, near the old State House, when a mob of "gentlemen of property and standing" dragged Garrison along and over ground which was not ignorant of heroic blood. Henceforth he, Wendell Phillips, was an abolitionist. They that had put a rope round Garrison's body, itching to put it round his neck, — they did not know that they were also tugging at a young man's heart, and dragging him from all the proud associations of his youth to be the matchless orator of the cause which seemed so crushed and ruined that October day.

> "He stood upon the world's broad threshold: wide
>   The din of battle and of slaughter rose;
> He saw God stand upon the weaker side,
>   That sank in seeming loss before its foes;
> Many there were who made great haste and sold
>   Unto the cunning enemy their swords.
> He scorned their gifts of fame, and power, and gold,
>   And, underneath their soft and flowery words,
> Heard the cold serpent hiss. Therefore, he went
>   And humbly joined him to the weaker part,
> Fanatic named, and fool, yet well content,
>   So he could be the nearer to God's heart,
> And feel its solemn pulses sending blood
>   Through all the wide-spread veins of endless good."

How hard it is for some men to conceive that any man should be attracted to a cause by danger and despite or by its very humbleness! yet men have been attracted in this way to many lost or weak and struggling causes since Jesus heard of John's imprisonment and made haste to fling himself into the empty space. " If the Unitarians," said Channing, " were not few and despised, I would not call myself a Unitarian." Oh, logic hard to understand for the majority of men ! These are the very reasons that to-day *warn off* hundreds and thousands who are persuaded that the Unitarian cause is just. It is not now despised as it was once. Too largely have its doctrines been appropriated by the other sects for that. That we are comparatively few is quite sufficient reason for these crowd-following cowards to stand aloof. And they are no great loss. It is true that, if all who agree with us in thought should make a good confession, should come and range themselves with us as honesty requires, our churches could not hold the thronging multitudes. But the gain in numbers would be a loss of moral energy, save as their coming signified that they had put off the old man of cowardice and double-dealing, and put on the new man of courage and straightforwardness.

Opportunism is a comparatively new *word* in our politics ; but it is not a new *thing* in them or in any, nor in the general course of human things. And there is an opportunism which is not so bad, which is indeed very admirable and excellent, — the kind ascribed by Tennyson to the statesmen of Victoria's reign : —

> " And statesmen at her council met
> Who knew the seasons, when to take
> Occasion by the hand and make
> The bounds of freedom wider yet."

But that is a miserable opportunism which only follows, never leads, the popular sentiment and thought and will ; and that is the most miserable of all which is for any meas· ure that will make for victory at the polls. Of all creatures, the most despicable are those politicians who would wipe out the whole party program and begin anew, immediately they are defeated at the polls. I like the pluck, albeit the fatuity, of those who hold not their opinions subject to any breath of popular approval or disdain. But there is an opportunism which as yet I have not named. It is that which finds in others' chances thrown away the means of victory. "The brave man's hope is the coward's excuse." All stories of great deeds and high adventures illustrate this proverb, and its converse truth no less. Opportunity,— it is the brave man's use of what the coward throws away,— a lesson never taught in words more grandly than in a poem of that true poet, Edward Rowland Sill, as if the name he bore had made his verse a sword. See if it does not flash and cleave like Roland's Durandal : —

> "This I beheld, or dreamed it in a dream :
> There spread a cloud of dust along a plain;
> And underneath the cloud, or in it, raged
> A furious battle, and men yelled, and swords
> Shocked upon swords and shields. A prince's banner
> Wavered, then staggered backward, hemmed by foes.
> A craven hung along the battle's edge,
> And thought, ' Had I a sword of keener steel —
> That blue blade that the king's son bears,— but this
> Blunt thing ! ' — he snapt and flung it from his hand,
> And lowering crept away and left the field.
> Then came the king's son, wounded, sore bestead,
> And weaponless, and saw the broken sword,
> Hilt-buried in the dry and trodden sand,
> And ran and snatched it, and, with battle-shout
> Lifted afresh, he hewed his enemy down,
> And saved a great cause that heroic day."

The name of this king's son ? O friends ! he has had, and he has, a thousand names ; for I could safely say that no good thing has yet been done for humankind which at some stage has not involved this situation : the desperate cause, *as such*, so stimulating to some brave man's heart that he has put forth all his strength, and turned the sorrow into joy, the defeat, already consummated but for him, into a victory certain and complete. "When the tale of bricks is doubled, then Moses comes "; or, if not Moses, then Jesus or Luther or Cromwell or Washington or Garrison or Lincoln or Cobden or Bright or Faust or Gutenberg or Columbus or Cabot or Watt or Stephenson or Channing or Parker, or any one of hundreds who have left no memorial, but whom the desperate cause of invention or discovery or truth or freedom so inspired that, so help them God, they could no otherwise than go wherever it might lead.

It is a far cry, perhaps you think, from such great things as these, world-famous things, to common, every-day affairs. Easier, perhaps you think, to do great things than to do small things greatly. There, there is great inspiration,—the applause of listening senates, the great common impulse making many hearts as one, the sublime self-consciousness of doing memorable things, the sustenance and bracing of a great idea. Put you, perhaps you think, where great ones were, and you, too, might have been great, making the brave choice, leading the forlorn hope, heeding the crying need, and answering, "Here am I." Nay! but how often need we to be told that, even as the movements and attractions of the planets and the mightiest stars find equal illustration in the particles and atoms of the world, and, as the geologic changes that have shaped the continents repeat themselves in every tiny rivulet and roadside pool left by the summer rain, so all the grandeurs of the moral life have illustration of their laws in humblest tasks that human hands can do? Not only so, but the great things of history are never great in lonely isolation.

"Never, believe me, appear the immortals,
   Never, alone.

Schiller meant by that that great men always come in groups or pairs. It is Columbus and Diaz and Vespucci, Shakspere and Bacon and Spenser, Locke and Newton, Voltaire and Rousseau and D'Alembert, Darwin and Wallace, Goethe and Schiller, Luther and Erasmus, Washington and Franklin and Adams and Jefferson, Webster, Calhoun, and Clay, Garrison and Phillips, Sumner and Lincoln and Chase, Grant and Farragut and Sherman, and so on. But there is higher truth than this in the assertion. Even in literature and science, the great man never is a wholly isolated product. Shakspere would not have written his immortal plays if

he had not fallen on a great play-writing time. Nor would
Columbus have discovered America if his time had not been
reaching out on every side, impatient for new lands, new
pathways to its riches in the East. The histories of great
discoveries and inventions always show a multitude of men
feeling after God, if haply they may find him in the
printing-press or the electric telegraph· or in the heart of
Africa or some frozen sea. Always about the statues of the
great inventors and discoverers I see a multitude like that
which Kaulbach painted around Luther, near and far, in his
great " Era of the Reformation." Until quite recently, the
theological imagination has pleased itself with representing
Jesus as the most isolated of human products,— nay, not
human, but supernatural and divine, because so isolated.
What do our latest studies show but that no man was
ever less isolated, no man ever came more obviously in the
fulness of time, no man ever came more truly to his own or
was received by them more cordially? Judea, Greece, and
Alexandria, and Rome were all alive with germs kindred to
that which burst the Galilean soil and held up its flower of
noble purity for men to love and bless. And, if these things
are so in the spheres of literature and science and religion,
they are much more obviously so in the spheres of practical
activity. Take Grant and Sherman — the last great hero of
the glorious contest he, not used to bringing up the rear —
and Sheridan and Hancock and Hooker, and the rest of their
great company of leaders in the war for union and emancipation. We build their monuments, we have great civic
banquets in their honor, and we are in constant danger of
thinking that the whole business was accomplished by the
splendor of their genius. A moment's thought rings out the
passing knell of that illusion. What could these men have
done without the millions of brave, simple folk, the common
soldiers of the war, making their breasts a shield for freedom's mighty heart? In vain the strategy of Grant pushing
on to Richmond, of Sherman marching to the sea, if, upon
the sentinel's beat, and in the " flying hell of horse and foot

and guns," these had not done what for the moment was the hard, the perilous thing,— strengthened the wavering line, answered the crying need. If their young lives rebelled a moment at the thought of shattered limbs or sudden death, they heard,— sung by the poet in their hearts, great Conscience, the incarnate God,—

> " It may be, in yon smoke concealed,
> Your comrades chase e'en now the fliers,
> *And, but for you*, possess the field."

And still all this were hardly worth the while if life everywhere and always were not a war for union and emancipation,— for union ; for the breaking down of barriers of race and caste and creed ; for emancipation from the bonds of ignorance and superstition, and base greed and filthy lust. And in this war, as in the little one, comparatively, that our national heroes fought, there is the same order and gradation, the same dependence of the greatest on the least. Let the great saints and heroes do their best, the good cause will not conquer unless in every rank and all along the line, in " moments to which Heaven has joined great issues," in some imminent breach or where in silent darkness the sentinel keeps lonely watch upon the insidious foe, there are millions upon millions of fidelities to the one duty of the hour. So that the heroes of Carlyle be truly heroes, let us join with him in all the admiration for them he demands. But let us not forget that there are others equally worthy of our admiration : —

> " The bravely dumb that did their deed,
> And scorned to blot it with a name."

I have read more biography than all other things together, the biography of greatness in every sphere of its wide manifestation ; and, the more I have read, the more I have been convinced that, with all honor to the great and greatest as it is rightly due, it is not by these pre-eminently that the state of the world is maintained, but by the multitudes that no man can number, who, according to the light that is given them, do out their duty with a patient heart and mind.

As it is written in the Scripture, "there is no discharge in that war." For Nelson's "England," etc., write "God expects every man to do his duty." A lovely poem that of Browning's where the lute-string breaks, and a cicada comes and perches on the lute, and sounds the missing note. Lute-strings, heart-strings, are always breaking in life's passionate symphony of joy and pain. Less than cicada will you be to come and sound the missing note and make the music whole? No poem that Longfellow ever wrote is to me so sweet a poem as his answer to some one who wondered at his patient endurance of an intolerable Cambridge bore: "If I were not kind to him, who would be?" In the social circle, at the crowded reception, or the ball, where feet go twinkling to the music's sensuous charm, there is always opportunity for the exercise of that noble disposition. So there is always opportunity for special service in the ways of social help. Of these, as of the individual, it is true that to them that have shall be given, and from them that have not shall be taken away the little that they have. The great, showy charities can always get enough money, enough personal service. There are others not so showy, which go struggling on from year to year, hard pressed for means to do their better work. You crave an instance. Take the "Wayside Home," which, if it only gave to the poor women whom it gathers to its tender breast a few sober, decent hours, would amply justify itself. But it does a great deal more than that; and the noble women who have given to it years of anxious thought and care are now trembling with anxiety lest they should have to give it up, and say to the poor creatures coming out of jail or from the street, "Go back again: we cannot help you any more." *There* is a crying need; and who will answer to its cry? Is it another instance that you want? Well, take our "Brooklyn Guild,"—no charity, but the purest social help, and capable, I certainly believe, of bringing larger returns for the money spent on it than any other enterprise of social help in this great city. It has helpers, men and women, who give to it the time-equivalent of many hundred dollars, individually, every year, and have great satisfaction in so doing. There should be ten of these where there is one. But there is need of money, too; of three or four thousand dollars, right away, to pay for the building and the repairs that have been made upon it, after which it might be easy enough to meet the running expenses by a subscription that would go alone. If this were a great, showy charity of the pauperizing kind, our wealthy men would tread upon each other in the race to give it all it needs. But there is nothing showy about it. It is "an infant crying in the night, and with no language but a cry," which yet may be a man strong-armed for wide beneficence, if its exposure on the chilly mountains of indifference is not too much prolonged.

A great come-down, perhaps you may be thinking, from the glittering generalities of the former part of my discourse to these extremely practical matters. Nay, but my sermon is not worth the paper it is written on,— it has spoiled it all for naught,— unless it does come down, and bring you with it, to a hundred things just as concrete and practical as these. In your social life, in your political, in your matters of business, in your home duties, in your relations to each other as members of the same family, as neighbors and as friends, hardly a day shall pass, and there not be some gap to fill, some want to meet, which shall be just as much God's call to you, as John's imprisonment and death were to the peasant-carpenter of Nazareth, to lift up the fallen banner and sustain the wavering line.

> "Then in such hour of need
> Do ye like angels appear,—
> Radiant with ardor divine,
> Languor not in your heart,
> Weakness not in your word,
> Weariness not on your brow.
> Move through the ranks and recall
> The stragglers, refresh the outworn,
> Fill up the gaps in the files,
> Stablish, continue the march,
> On to the bound of the waste,
> On to the city of God." *

* Adapted from Matthew Arnold's " Rugby Chapel."

WORDS FITLY SPOKEN.*

"How GOOD they are!" said the wise Solomon, the imaginary Solomon of the Book of Proverbs. But this consideration I shall reserve for the middle part and end of my
discourse, asking you, first of all, to consider with me the
subject of words in a more general way. "Words, words,
words"! So men express contempt for them in their daily
speech; and you may think that this time, most certainly, I
have failed to act on Dr. Channing's principle,— never to
choose any but great subjects. Nay, but I have chosen one
of the greatest subjects possible! That words are not matters
of great importance is certainly not the opinion of the corps of
scholars who are bringing out the Century Dictionary in six
splendid volumes, nor of that other corps of scholars who
are bringing out the New English Dictionary in as many volumes more, nor of the third corps who have just remade Webster's Unabridged into the International by many valuable
changes and additions. But the making of these great dictionaries is not merely an enterprise of scholarship, it is also
an enterprise of business; for there must be publishers as
well as scholars, and there must be purchasers of these costly
books by hundreds and thousands to justify the expense of
their production. As the fortunate possessor of both the
Century and the New English, so far as they are out, and
meaning to have the International, you will not expect me to
set a low opinion upon words; and it stands to reason that
none of the publishers or patrons of these enterprises of

* I am obliged to ask my gentle readers not to be discouraged by the fore part of this
sermon. It gets more serious as it goes on; but I like the fore part, too, and hope that
they will read it all.

scholarship do so, though it may well be that our conviction of their value is less absolute than that of the scholars who have made the millions of references and quotations and examinations necessary to their colossal work.

There is something marvellous in the scope of words, though from the multitudinous richness of our own language we cannot infer that of every other. There will be two hundred and twenty thousand words in the Century Dictionary; and there are more than a thousand living languages, no one of which is intelligible to the speakers of the others. But few others, if any, of these languages have the variety of our own; and some of them have a very small vocabulary. Even a people so highly civilized as the Chinese have but 500 words, all monosyllables, which can be made 1,500 by significant intonations. Perhaps the thing to be most thankful for is not that, with the words it has naturalized, the English language has so many, but that so much can be accomplished with so few of these. A few hundreds serve us for our ordinary speech. Shakspere got along with 15,000, Milton with 8,000, while yet Milton's diction was more habitually varied than Shakspere's, the former having 100 different words to every 135, the latter 100 to every 164, while the King James Bible has 100 to every 531. With such a practically unlimited vocabulary to draw upon, it seems strange, at first glance, that men do not succeed better in making their meaning plain. "Half the controversies of the world are verbal ones," said Cardinal Newman; "and, if they could be brought to a plain issue, they would be brought to a prompt termination." But to bring them to a plain issue,— that is the difficult thing; and why it is so is the great moral lesson of the New English Dictionary, which is pre-eminently a history of words, giving all the changes they have undergone in their spelling and their meaning. And the worst of it is that, as time goes on, each word gets new and newer meanings instead of getting more and more limited in its use. This is the tendency, with exceptions here and there. Take, for example, the word which has recurred most frequently in

some reading that I have been doing recently, the word
"style." It comes from the word *stilus*, the metal-pointed
instrument with which the Romans did their writing upon
waxen tablets. *Now*, it nowhere means that, but it means a
dozen other things. We speak of an author's style, of styles
of architecture ; we say that a lady has no style, and so on.
But this word is only one of thousands that have suffered a
sea-change for worse or better. Hence the absurdity of the
endeavor, which we often see, to hold people to the original
meaning of a word, as if that determined its meaning for all
time. Whether religion is from *religo*, to bind back, or *re-
lego*, to reread,— what reams of paper have been written
over about this ! and it is an interesting question in philology ; but it no more decides the present meaning of religion
than the original meaning of the word "style" decides our
meaning when we say that Grote had none at all and that
Ruskin's is "musical, impressional." We certainly do not
mean that Grote had no Roman *stilus*, and that Ruskin has
one which is at the same time a tuning-fork.

The fact that all our abstract terms of thought and feeling
run back into some root of sense-perception has done much
to confuse their meaning, and to create the differences of
philosophers, too often making good the malicious saying
of Talleyrand,—"The use of language is to conceal our
thoughts." In the sphere of political economy, how magnificent would be the gain if there could be a general agreement in the use of terms ; if rent, capital, value, and so on,
meant the same thing to all. In fact, they mean almost as
many different things as there are different economists, with
that result of "infinite confusion in the world" which we
should have (said some wise theologian) if the moments of
time, instead of coming successively, as they now do, came
simultaneously and together.

One could do much worse than the Scotchman who, kept
waiting a long time, relieved the tedium by reading in the
dictionary. Upon inquiry how he liked it, he made answer
that the stories were written in good language, but they were

dreadful short. He builded better than he knew or those who laughed at him. For, in truth, the dictionary is full of stories,—some one has said of fossil histories, but many of them are too much alive for that to be the happiest designation. What Emerson said — I never thought quite truly — of the words of Swedenborg, "These words are vascular: cut them, and they will bleed," is true of many hundred, many thousand words, just as they stand unrelated in the dictionaries,— unrelated to each other, but related to as many aspects of the world's past life for many generations. The life-blood of humanity is in them. They are living organisms; and that is why I cannot bear the doctrine of these *verbicides* who go in for phonetic spelling,— that is, for making words so many arbitrary signs. "As good almost kill a man," said Milton, "as kill a good book," which is "the precious life-blood of a master-spirit." But a language which is the growth of centuries has in it the life-blood of many master-spirits, and the life-blood of lesser folk innumerable. It abounds in ancient histories and old mythologies and superstitions; it is a museum of the manners and the customs of the past; it reports the germs and transformations of ten thousand processes of thought and feeling, so that if we are men, and nothing human is foreign to us, all of this verbal multiplicity is of our family stock. Of chapters in evolution, that of language is not the least remarkable. Wonderful and beautiful has been the evolution of many special words, while hardly does the evolution of a man from the human ovum or the ascidian impress us more than the evolution of 220,000 English words from 121 Sanskrit roots, as Max Müller has provisionally reckoned, anticipating the reduction of these to a yet smaller number at no distant day.

So much, in a general way, for the wonder and the mystery of words. How good they are, even in their mass and disconnection, or "marching single in an endless file," there is in them such possibility of communication man with man, of entering into the thought of great writers and of mighty poets, of reading clear the branching of the races from their parent stock, of telling one another something of our hopes and fears, and winging them with messages of love! Fitly spoken, how good they are, and fitly written, too! Doctor Hedge contended that it was the choice of the best, the happiest word imaginable to express his meaning that made Emerson our prince of poets, and that always the poet's finest art was in his choice of words, and his use of them in some fresh original way. Ruskin explains the secret of his matchless style to be his refusal over and over again of words that are to bear up the weight of his meaning until he gets the best, and there is much agreement of the competent that this is the most important thing in writing well. But there are other things that serve,— the arrangement of words in the clause and of the clauses in the sentence, so that they shall mutually support each other and contribute to a general harmony. When all is done that can be done, how excellent is the result, whether the form be poetry or prose! I often think the latter has its reaches of perfection to which the former cannot quite attain. I find no poetry quite so heart-moving and exalting as the prose of Thackeray and Emerson and Taylor and Milton and Burke and Webster and Newman and Hedge, when these are at their best.

Do not imagine that we have here a superficial business. True, there are those who teach that a good style is possible where there is nothing to be said, where there is no intellect, no earnestness; but they cannot walk the line of this absurdity for half a page. They are continually affording evidence that it is not so. And, were it otherwise, we should appeal from them to others of more serious temper who maintain a different creed. "No man is worth reading to form your style," says Ruskin, "who does not mean what he says; nor was any great style ever intended but by some man who meant what he said. . . . And of yet greater importance is it to know that every beauty possessed by the language of a nation is significant of the innermost laws of its being. Keep the temper of a people stern and manly,

make their associations grave, courteous, and for worthy
objects, occupy them in just deeds, and their tongue must
needs be a grand one. Nor is it possible, therefore, that
any tongue should be a noble one of which the words are
not so many trumpet-calls to action. All great languages
invariably utter great things and command them; they
cannot be mimicked but by obedience; the breath of them
is inspiration, because it is not only vocal, but vital; and
you can only learn to speak as these men spoke by becoming
what these men were."

Swedenborg teaches that in the heavenly world the soul
will make a body corresponding to itself, as, in fact, it does
here by slow degrees; for than the saying, "Beauty is only
skin deep," a falser never was. It is as deep as mind and
soul. Now, thought is the soul of speech; and it makes
itself "a body as it hath pleased him," — a body corresponding to itself. "The style," said Buffon, "is the man." And
for every man who has anything to say there is a door of
utterance. There never was a "mute, inglorious Milton"
since the world began. A Milton could not be inglorious,
could not be mute. Somehow, his song and speech would
out. "I know it, but I can't say it," expostulates the boy
at school; and the wise teacher makes reply, "If you knew
it, you *could* say it." It is just as true of the preacher, the
philosopher, the man of science. If they knew it, they could
say it,— the lesson they would fain recite. Where there is
imperfect utterance, you may be sure there is imperfect
knowledge. A lack of clearness in the style argues a lack
of clearness in the thought.

The written thought is good, but the spoken thought is
better. A word fitly spoken, how good it is! Many legends
and stories have endeavored to report or symbolize this
charm, the best of them, the most extravagant, falling short
of the reality, unless it be there in the Old Testament where
God *said*, "Let there be light, and there was light," — a
glorious tribute to that Word which is personified in the
proem to the Fourth Gospel: "In the beginning was the

Word, and the Word was with God, and the Word was God."
How many God-like men, from first to last, have spoken
words at which, for those who sat in darkness, light has
sprung up, and new creations of the intellectual world have
shaped themselves in orderly array! And what man or
woman, who is not merely brutish, does not account among
life's grandest moments, its most favored hours, those when
they listened, with a joy so keen that it was almost pain, to
the words of some great master-spirit, speaking, as Melanch-
thon said of Luther, "with words born, not on his lips, but in
his soul"? You know the kind of speech I mean,— the kind
which made the Athenians say, not "What a fine oration!"
but "Let us fight Philip," and made Philip say of Demos-
thenes, "Had I been there, he would have persuaded me to
take up arms against myself." Such speech was Sumner's
when he thundered, "Let my people go!" and, many a time,
that of some member of the glorious company of whom Phillips said: "What world-wide benefactors these imprudent
men are,— the Lovejoys, the Browns, the Garrisons, the
saints, and the martyrs! How prudently most men slip away
into nameless graves, while now and then one or two forget
themselves into immortality!" We often make a broad distinction between deeds and words, much to the latter's disad-
vantage. But it ought not to be forgotten that words are
sometimes themselves deeds of the largest import, the most
concrete significance; that they evince a courage as invinci-
ble as any shown upon a war-ship's shattered deck or at the
cannon's roaring mouth. If Luther's words were, as Novalis
said, half-battles, in this he does not stand alone. There
have been words on which, as upon golden hinges or grating
harsh thunder, the gates of life have swung wide open to
mankind, making it welcome to some better thought, some
larger privilege, some higher aspiration, than it knew before.
Such were the words that Jesus spoke by the lakeside and at
the mountain's foot; such were Paul's, that, like a battering-
ram, went crashing through the temple-wall that kept the
nations out of Christianity, and set them streaming in; such

were Luther's "Here I stand: I can no otherwise"; such the opening sentences of our own Declaration of Independence, which Rufus Choate called "glittering generalities," and Wendell Phillips, with more penetration, "blazing ubiquities"; such Garrison's prophetic utterance, as he flung the standard of the *Liberator* to the breeze; such Lincoln's words at Gettysburg and in his last inaugural address, when already the foul plot was gendered that was to rob us of his glorious innocency, and set up a drunken satyr in his place.

All proverbs hint more than they state a truth, and none of them more obviously than that which says that speech is silver, silence is golden. If there were any general acceptance of the saying, men and women would not be so "friendly to silver" as they are. Carlyle was always clamoring for silence. Mr. John Morley says he "preached the gospel of silence in thirty volumes octavo," thus showing that he had no real faith in what he preached; and few have any more. Insatiable is men's greed for talk in these last days. Hundreds and thousands of people, excellent and intelligent, prefer the talk of an indifferent speaker to the page of the most wise and learned and discriminating book. Few things are sadder in our modern life than the lapse away from it of that meditative habit of the mind which has been productive of so many of the best and most enduring things of literature in the past. A dreadful blight has fallen on that

> "harvest of a quiet eye
> Which broods, and sleeps on its own heart."

And, as there is room and call for more of brooding silence and communion with ourselves and with the brooding minds of literature, so is there room and call for more of reticence and silence in our dealings with our fellow-men. There are times when each must

> "hold with each, in unvoiced sympathy,
> The sweet commune of friends, and come to know
> The golden speech of silence."

There are times when no word can be fitly spoken, when silence is our sacrament, and to breathe a syllable would be to profane it. This is a secret every lover knows,—every lover of things beautiful in nature or in art, and every lover of things personal in man or maid. Only less trying and impertinent than the advertisements on cliff and scar are the exclamatory admirations of the tourist who is fierce against their blasphemy. "Still as the hour-glass" is often love's best speech, when hearts are overfull with heavenly joy; and, when they are full of sorrow, it is much the same. It is when we think that we must *say something* to the stricken and bereaved that we deserve the terrible rebuke of Lowell to the talkative consoler,—

"Console, if you will: I can bear it."

I have heard it told of Dr. Bartol that he once went to see a lady of his congregation who was in great sorrow; that he sat an hour with her in perfect mutual silence, and then went away. Many have done worse than that: and you will remember that he had a very noble precedent in the conduct of Job's friends, who "sat down with him upon the ground seven days and seven nights, and none spake a word to him, for they saw that his grief was very great." When they began to talk, it proved that they had nothing fit to say.

These negative aspects must not detain us over-long; but it is impossible to think of words fitly spoken and not think of those which are quite otherwise than so. Such are too frequently the words by which our casual meetings are dis-honored and defiled,—words of mere gossip, degenerating into scandal at an easy pace, which, whether or not they in-jure those whose real or imaginary failures are the matter of exchange, are an undoubted injury to those who deal in these currencies — too often counterfeit — as if they were lawful coin. The Psalmist might well pray, "O Lord, set a watch at the door of my lips!" But happiest they who do this for themselves: words are such living forces, they react with such tremendous energy on the man who utters them. How clearly Jesus was persuaded of these things we know by his saying, "That which cometh out of a man defileth him"; and, again, "By thy words shalt thou be justified, and by thy words shalt thou be condemned." *Fama crescit eundo,*— "Rumor grows in going"; and we all know something of the increments by which it grows. We like to tell a story well. There is a Robinson Crusoe, a Scheherezade, in every one of us, more or less developed, who touches up the flying rumor here and there until at length the truth to the exaggeration is as one to ten, one to a hundred,— yes, to a thousand frequently. Then, too, with what exaggerating ears we hear words that belittle or defame the person against whom, for some doubtful, vain, or envious reason, we have taken a brief in that court of the imagination which is the supreme court for many in their judgments of their fellowmen. No words are more unfit for currency than those we get after this fashion, not merely unassayed, but full of the alloy of our own selfish predilection, rejoicing in iniquity, not in the truth and goodness of a fellow-man. Again, of words unfitly spoken, few are more hurtful to our social, friendly, and domestic life than those unreal words which we permit ourselves in the heat of argument or passionate recrimination, when we say things we do not really mean, things which are false to our own hearts, just for effect, just for the pain that they will give,— things that we hate ourselves for saying in advance. These are no idle words: they are too conscious and deliberate for that; but, all the same, we must give an account of them in the day of judgment, which is every day that shines. By such unreal words not taken back, but proudly left to fester in a wounded heart, the life of love has frequently been quenched outright. There are no words more fitly spoken than those which hasten with repentant sorrow and confession to redeem the cruel loss the others have incurred.

A word fitly spoken, how good it is! And what one of us has not made proof of this, not merely in ten thousand unremembered ways, but in moments which we never can forget, which ever and anon come back to us out of the irrevocable past, and are like a cooling palm upon our foreheads or a strengthening hand struck into ours! It will make little difference what I say for the next few minutes because you will all be busy with such moments coming back to you; so that, if my tone waxes too personal and intimate, I shall escape your censure, you will pay so little heed. I remember that one pleasant autumn evening, about forty years ago, when my father was at sea, my mother told me, as she went away upon some kindly errand or to do a little neighboring, that a cord of wood left in the yard must be put under cover before dark. But the games were so jolly nice that evening that the hours slipped by unheeded, till at length, in the darkness of the evening's end, my mother, coming back, found that my work was still undone. Although of gentle heart, she said that I must straightway go about it,— said it so firmly that I knew there would be no reprieve. And for an hour or more I pulled and hauled at the big logs, hotter with inward rage than with my work, till it was finished, and I went off to bed, omitting my good-night. And there I lay, tossing upon a troubled heart, planning the direst things. I would run away. No, I would stay, but I would never speak to her again. Waking the next morning in the same bitter frame, I went down to initiate the *régime* of silence. But, as I came into the room, she greeted me in such a sweet and kindly way that all my hateful resolutions vanished like the late April snow before the warm south wind. Had she forgotten all about "the late unpleasantness"? I do not know unto this day. What did she say? That I have clean forgotten. Enough that it was some word fitly spoken. And how good it was, melting at once the hardness of my heart! and, as her blessed face shines on me out of heaven, it is oftenest with the look it wore that autumn morning.

The heart of a young man or maid is fruitful soil in which to drop these fitly spoken words. All unconsciously they fall from the lips of parents, teachers, and employers, and after that they have a sworn defender in the child, the youth, the maiden, upon whom their benediction has been shed. Youth is the time when it is so good to be trusted; when almost anything that is asked in faith, nothing wavering, we can perform. All things are possible *for* him that believeth in us then. Blessed are those parents who are not sceptical, who are not cynical about the ambitions and the aspirations which their children cherish, who can treat the most chimerical of their plans and expectations without any touch of scorn! Such generous consideration is more endearing to their children's hearts than all the care and trouble of the earlier years. I can remember how my heart rushed out to meet my father, how I laid my fealty at his feet as I had never done before, when, after two years of schooling difficult to manage in the hard times of 1857 and 1858, I went to him after he had gone to bed, and he, apprised of something new by the untimely visitation, said, "Well, what next?" And I told him that I hoped it might be five years more of study, which meant five years of hard-earned money going out and nothing coming in. I remember how I braced myself to say it, feeling sure that it would hurt, and how quickly I was reassured and comforted by his reply, which was that I must go ahead, and he would do his best to make the crooked places straight and the rough places plain. And never was a promise better kept.

And how many of us can recall words spoken to us in our young manhood or our early womanhood which gave a new direction to our energies and opened wide for us the doors of a new world! I remember well a day, some thirty years ago, when I went to see two very different men about the plans that I had laid for entering the ministry. One of them was a merchant of great sense and probity, who read Blair's Sermons with perennial delight, but who conceived rightly that mine would be very different from Blair's, but also that, if good for anything, they would be of less worth and furnish me less satisfaction than almost any other occupation. From him I went to see James Freeman Clarke, and in his presence I warmed myself, as I had great need of doing after the chilly drench to which I had submitted just before. His words were few; but they convinced me that I had been following no deceitful light. He did not disguise the hindrances and limitations of the preacher's work, the desire of many to hear only the echoes of their own voices, to see in the preacher's thought only an admirable reflection of their own, the petty criticism and annoyance that would be sure to come; but he set before me, in such a glowing light, the satisfactions that would await my industry and faithfulness that I went upon my way with a rejoicing heart. Nor have I found the years discrediting the hope which he aroused that morning in my breast.

But many of you here, I have no doubt, could furnish better illustrations from your personal experience than these of mine. All life and literature are full of them. To some men it seems to be given without measure to say the kind, the just, the timely, helpful word to some one in great need of it. Every little while we have some fresh testimony to this quality in Samuel J. May. Theodore Parker had it. How many pages of the biography of Louisa Alcott that power of his illuminates with its cheerful ray! He was to many what he was to her, bringing to them a vital sympathy and prudent counsel that strengthened the weak hands and confirmed the feeble knees. All praise and honor, too, for those who, *just because they love us*, do not like our faults, and who withstand us to the face because we ought to be blamed when we have acted shamefully, yet with such generous expectation mingled with their blame that we feel their virtue passing into us and cleansing us of our iniquity. The word fitly spoken, how good it is in poetry, in the great masters of prose, in oratory, in brilliant repartee; but it is nowhere else *so* good as where it turns the hearts of many or the heart of one from things that ruin or debase to things that make for righteousness and truth and love.

One closing word: Out of the abundance of the heart the mouth speaketh. In the exigencies of our personal and social life we cannot pause to weigh our words, as can the poet or the essayist with pen in hand. It is, Stand and deliver, right away. There is, then, for us no resource but to make ourselves whole ; to see to it that our lives are of such even substance that, whatever we may say or do, it shall be dominated by their central truth, it shall express their total sanity. Keep thine heart with all diligence; for out of thine heart are the issues, not of life alone, but of death also. That they may be those of life, that our words may all be fitly spoken and our deeds may all be fitly done, we have great need to "still suspect and still revere ourselves in lowliness of heart."

THE TWILIGHT OF THE GODS.

In the wide range of Norse mythology there is no other fancy so impressive as that of Ragnarok, or Götterdämmerung, the Twilight of the Gods. In Wagner's brain it turned to music; and, interpreted by his genius, it has become domesticated in ten thousand minds and hearts to which it was a stranger in its archaic form, or in the scholar's cumbrous dress. This fancy, as elaborated in the Younger Edda, is a matter of so much detail that, should I attempt to follow it through all its ramifications, the twilight of the day would deepen ere I made an end. Suffice it that there came a time in Asgard when a subtile change infected all the gods; while upon earth the summer sunshine paled, and warmed men's hearts no better than the moon. Then came a winter of such bitter cold that the wild beasts were frozen in their caves, which had aforetime been so comfortably warm; rivers were frozen to one solid mass; and, even in Asgard, Thor and Odin and their divine companions shivered upon their thrones. Only in Jotunheim was there great joy; for there the great Frost Giants hugged themselves, and cried, "The Fimbul Winter has come at last!" Now, the Fimbul winter had been long foretold; and it was a winter that the gods could not survive. Three years it lasted, and killed every living thing upon the earth; and then the sun was snatched from out the heavens by a monster beast, the moon quickly by another, and from the under-world the Fenris Wolf that had been long in leash broke loose, and the Midgard Serpent wallowed forth, and all the hosts of Helheim and Jotunheim and Muspelheim, giants of wickedness and frost and fire, went forth to battle

with the gods, whom Heimdal, standing on the Rainbow
Bridge, summoned to come from Asgard and join battle
with their foes. Straight Odin rode to Mimir's fountain,
which was at the root of the tree Ygdrasil; and there the
Norns sat veiled and silent,— those ancient mothers, with
no words to say,— and what Mimir said to Odin no man
knows. But Odin went forth to battle, and he fell fighting
the Fenris Wolf; and Thor, also, fighting the Midgard Serpent; and Loke, the calumniator of the gods, and Heimdal,
keeper of their house, fell, slain by mutual blows. Then
Surt, chief of the fiery host from Muspelheim, flung a flaming brand into the midst; and straightway there was "a
breathless hush, a sudden rush of air," and then a roaring
flame filled all space and devoured all worlds. Ygdrasil fell
in ashes, and the earth sank beneath the sea. "No sun, no
moon, no stars, no Asgard, no Hel, no Jotunheim; gods,
giants, monsters, men,— all dead! Nothing remained but
a vast abyss, filled with the moaning seas and brooded over
by a pale, colorless light. Ragnarok, the end of all things,
the Twilight of the Gods, had come."

Why do I conjure up this dream which scared our Scan-
dinavian progenitors in their heavy sleep and dimmed for
them the joy of battle? Certainly not with any thought of
trying to unravel what it meant to them,— how much of it
was their natural philosophy and how much the poet's free
addition to the original base; and just as certainly with as
little thought of finding, part for part, a parallel to this
awful fancy in our modern world. Only for us, too, there
has been deepening for some time past a "Twilight of the
Gods." We, too, have a mythology. A theology we call
it, but it is essentially as mythological as the mythology
which it displaced in Northern Europe ten or twelve centuries ago. It has its survivals of a barbarism not a whit less
gross and superstitious than that of the people whose mythology is preserved to us in the Elder and the Younger
Eddas. And of late the gods of this mythology have been
shivering upon their thrones. The natural history of the

Bible and the Church and the natural history of Christian dogma have been to them what the icy wind of Jotunheim was to Thor and Odin, sitting high in Asgard, in the wonderfully strange and beautiful old story on which I have so largely drawn. It has made them stare at one another with a wild surmise, much wondering what is coming next. What Norns, what ancient mothers, shall they seek, what Mimir's well, to know the secret of the coming days? After the ice-bound years, the battle and darkness, will there be a new and better time?

But, lest our metaphor obscure the meaning I would fain develop into clearest visibility, let us at once part company with its details, if haply we may thus hold fast to the general idea with a firmer hand,—the Twilight of the Gods; the twilight of the traditional Christianity of the churches and the creeds. The metaphor, the symbol, is, I think, a very apt description of the actually prevailing state of things. There are individuals enough who do not see men as trees walking nor trees as men walking. They see trees as trees and men as men, outlined as distinctly as the men and women in the sketches of Millet, with their thick, dark, circumscribing lines. There are men of various circumstance and mental quality who have this clearness, this positivity. The dogmatists of the churches have it : never a doubt have they that they have the whole story in their creeds and articles. And the dogmatic liberals have it: never a doubt have they that they have the whole story in their liberal magazines and books. They deny the infallibility of the Bible and the Church ; but they believe in their own personal infallibility, and in that of Thomas Paine and Robert Ingersoll, as implicitly as the average man believes in the infallibility of his daily paper, or the Roman Catholic in the infallibility of the pope. There is, too, the noble confidence and certainty of the scientific man and of the critical and historical scholar, who has earned his confidence by lavishing his life's best oil to find the truth of things. But such individual or sporadic exhibitions of the

dogmatic temper, or of a noble confidence,—words shaped
upon the thought as closely as may be,—do not bring the
daylight back,—do not alter the fact that there is a twilight
in theology, a dim and formless time, foreboding general
catastrophe and wreck, whatever may emerge thereafter into
heaven's light.   Doubtless there are hundreds of ministers
in the pulpits, thousands of people in the pews, who do not
know that anything serious is going on.   Thoreau would
not go round the corner to see the universe blow up ; and
there are many who, in that event, would not appreciate that
anything had happened.   The real thinking of the world is
done by a comparatively small number of people, but unto
them is given to determine the state of the world.   And
wherever in the theological world real thinking is going on
there are the signs of such disintegration, change, collapse
of old ideas, as the world has not witnessed for some sixteen
centuries of recorded time.   Only those have any doubt of
this who do not know what is transpiring in the intellectual
world, and especially in the province of theology.

In almost every Christian sect there is to-day a not incon-
siderable body of men who have broken squarely with those
doctrines which less than fifty years ago were the staple of
all preaching, without believing which there could be no
salvation,—doctrines of Biblical infallibility, total depravity,
election, future punishment, and so on.   From the outspoken
utterances of these men a collection of disavowals could be
made which two centuries ago would have sentenced them
to prison or the stake, one century ago would have branded
them as atheists and infidels, and half a century ago would
have cost them all repute and standing in the more orthodox
churches.   Episcopalians and Congregationalists and Presbyterians vie with each other for the headship of the great
revolt.   Mr. Heber Newton remains and is likely to remain
unscathed while preaching doctrines which twenty years ago
were a little shocking in this church of ours, which has had
a radical tradition from the beginning ; and he welcomes to
his pulpit, on the most solemn day in the ecclesiastical year,

a troop of ministers of various denominations, all innocent of the regular "imposition" of Episcopal hands. Mr. Mac-Queary in the West, for preaching openly what hundreds of his fellow-clergymen believe, has been suspended for six months, but, objecting to such suspension, has cut himself down, and taken himself off in search of pastures new. Of the five clergymen who sat upon his case, two were for his expulsion from the ministry outright, two for his out-and-out acquittal. The fifth man, on the fence, the typical Episcopalian,— his church a compromise from the beginning,— determined the result, bringing the two who were in favor of expulsion about half-way round. In England there has emanated, as you know, from the High Church circle at Oxford a book, *Lux Mundi*, which explicitly and implicitly is far more destructive of traditional opinions than the Broad Church "Essays and Reviews" of thirty years ago. At the recent Convocation a venerable arch-deacon* anathematized it as containing "all the poison found in Tom Paine's 'Age of Reason,'" and moved a vote of censure, which was rejected by a large majority. Meanwhile the Rev. J. M. Wilson, one of the most straightforward of the liberal churchmen, yet recently made an arch-deacon, the next thing to a bishop, has been denounced as "one of the most heterodox of ministers outside a Unitarian pulpit." To which he answers that he is "entirely orthodox, in the ordinary sense of the term,— that is, he has with him, so far as he knows, every theologian of eminence in England at the present time." What Andover theology is you know; and what it lacks of absolute frankness is made up by Professor Schurman of Cornell University, an Andover lecturer on the Winkley foundation, which is hampered by no theological conditions. A few sentences will show the general drift of his discourse: "Modern science is not antagonistic to the religion of Christ, but it is fatal to those confessions of the Christian religion which have been embodied in an antiquated psychology, anthropology, cosmology, and history. The process

* Denison, the same that stirred up the opposition to the " Essays and Reviews."

of readjustment," he continues, " is going on; and it is much
more thorough in the actual beliefs of men than in the revised
creeds that are supposed to represent them. Even the new
Biblical criticism has won a victory almost as complete as
that of astronomy, geology, and zoölogy." Welcomed at
Andover, these words have great significance, but less than
certain utterances and events in Presbyterian circles. It is
not long since we imagined these impervious to liberal
thought. Suddenly there was in Scotland an outburst of
impassioned protest against the traditional creed, which
shook the English Presbyterians from their heavy sleep,
while their American co-religionists slept on and took their
rest as placidly as ever. Since then how much has come to
pass! In Scotland broadened terms of subscription, creed
revision, and rejection of offensive articles; in England a
new Confession, much softened from the old, which may last
a dozen years; in America the agitation for revision so
intelligent and resolute, so rich in personal ability, that it
were idle to imagine that it can be appeased with any miserable evasive shift, anything short of honest burying of "the
thing that dieth of itself." But most significant of all is the
appointment of Dr. Briggs, the most scholarly and liberal of
the revisionists, to a theological chair second to none in its
importance for the education of young men for the Presbyterian ministry. Here is a teacher bringing to the Bible
a more radical and reconstructive criticism than Theodore
Parker brought to it forty years ago. Here is a teacher who
advances Reason to an equal part in Revelation with the
Bible and the Church,— a temporary arrangement, seeing
that Bible and Church are both historical expressions of the
Reason of Mankind; but what a notable advance on the
position, not yet half a century back, that Revelation is in
defiance of all reason, or the expression of a truth which
reason cannot verify and to which it cannot attain!

These are but random snatches from an infinite multitude
and mass of public disavowals in the orthodox world of doctrines deemed essential by that world in its totality not long

ago. They might be multiplied a hundred-fold. Such an anthology were possible of rejections, qualifications, and admissions, touching the body of traditional belief, as might well make it seem a cause already lost. But the twilight of that belief does not declare itself so much in these outspoken phrases of a manly and unqualified dissent as in the *obscurantism* of the time,—the deliberate or spontaneous obscuration of the traditional doctrine, the maintenance of a show of venerable forms and phrases from which the original meaning has departed to return no more. But we must not be without discrimination in our judgments of this order of phenomena. It is the method of progress, the device of history, for softening the break between the old and new. The new wine is always being put into the old bottles, and the old labels are retained to recommend the vintage to the folk who think the old is better. The meaning of all language, and especially of all theological language, is a continual flux: it is always undergoing a subtile transformation. The atonement of Gregory of Nyssa was not the atonement of Anselm, nor the atonement of Anselm that of Bushnell. The literal fiery hell of Jonathan Edwards and the Westminster divines is for the orthodox theologian of the present time the anguish of unquenchable remorse, the imperishable recollection of a misused and irrevocable past. Especially have the followers of Hegel in philosophy a happy art by which every iron egg of ancient dogma discloses a golden yolk of rational idea. "It remains true, however," says Dr. Sterrett, an Hegelian teacher of theology to Episcopalian youth,— "it remains true that we can even thus only accept many traditional conceptions and dogmas in a Pickwickian sense." The children of this world have sometimes brought an accusation of such conduct against the children of light, but never before, to my knowledge, has the truth of it been cheerfully allowed. Yet not long ago we had proposals published for the absorption of the whole body of Unitarians in the Episcopal Church, without the change of one particular belief, even the most radical. Why not? The creeds and articles, the liturgical forms, are all so many hymns of which we enjoy the music — *i.e.*, the common worship — without thinking of the words.   When, using the Apostles' Creed, so called because it was not formulated till they had been some centuries dead, we say that Jesus was conceived of the Holy Ghost, born of the Virgin Mary, suffered under Pontius Pilate, was crucified, dead and buried; he descended into hell; the third day he arose from the dead, etc.,— when we make all these explicit statements, "we simply mean," we are assured, " to declare our belief in the *facts* of Jesus' history, *whatever they are.*"   In a like genial temper, an English clergyman, warmly approved by Canon Cheyne, "would venture to appropriate the results of present day Biblical work in the interests of a believing theology."   And he does appropriate them with no sparing hand; and, behold! the Bible is just as much inspired as ever, because, he says, "we mean by inspiration exactly those qualities and characteristics which are the qualities and characteristics of the Bible."   Here is indeed Mr. Gladstone's "impregnable rock of Holy Scripture."   Inspiration being just exactly what the Bible is, no matter what its critical transformation, the inspiration of the Bible is of course secure.   So in a thousand books and pulpits the old expressions, phrases, creeds, are kept along, but made the vehicles of doctrines and ideas which, as compared with those originally intended, are "as moonlight unto sunlight, or as water unto wine."   Even so, a pleasant consciousness of orthodoxy is retained, and the privilege is not forfeited by the people, if by the priest, of thinking contemptuously of those who have been pioneers in the great wilderness, and blazed the way or made the road for them to travel with a joyous heart.

But there is yet another way in which the Twilight of the Gods, the obscuration of the traditional theology, declares itself, which is the most significant of all.   Taxed at the custom-house for "unmentioned articles," Sydney Smith said promptly, "The Thirty-nine, I suppose."   Read his admirable sermons, and you will appreciate the aptness of his repartee. The thirty-nine were his *unmentioned articles* in sober fact. They were just this for many deans and canons, priests and deacons, of his day; they are for many more in ours. With the thirty-three of the Westminster Catechism it is not otherwise than with the thirty-nine of Anglican theology. In hundreds of pulpits they are allowed to sleep a sleep no preacher's voice disturbs. Not long ago the Devil was as conspicuous in sermon, hymn, and prayer as Father Son, or Holy Spirit, and now,—

> "Oh, no, we never mention him:
> His name is never heard."

It is not otherwise with doctrines of election and reprobation, vicarious atonement, eternal punishment, total depravity, and so on. Expressive silence meditates their former pride, their present low estate. It is this silence of the preachers, with their *unmentioned articles*, that, more than frank denial or mysterious transformation, marks the theological temper of the time and the contempt into which once venerable beliefs have fallen. And those of us who are Unitarians should be very careful about throwing stones at this glass House of Silence, lest we should be found pelting, with rude, irreverent hands, the house from which we ourselves came out. This policy of silence does not seem the manliest possible, but it is the policy which was adopted almost universally by the American Unitarians from the beginning of the century onward to the breaking out of the Unitarian Controversy in 1815,—silence as to things believed or doubted, with clearest affirmation of the things believed. It was the policy of our beloved Channing just as much as it is now the policy of Phillips Brooks, and even more. But mark you, friends, it was a policy which could not last,—a policy which found its term. And, as it was in 1815, so will it be in 1915, if not some years before. The difference will be — as there are a hundred silent ones to-day in orthodox pulpits where eighty years ago there was but one — that, when the silence is broken at last, the catastrophe and the reconstruction will be a hundred times more interesting and significant than it was then.

And, right here, we shall do well to pause for a few moments and consider our general attitude as Unitarians and liberals toward the stupendous changes that are going on around us and the men who are most affected by these changes. We are, I think, too prone to bitterness in our feeling about these things,— too prone to harshness in our judgment of the men who, thinking our thought, do not come over to our side. No matter now for those who think our thought, and, thinking it, go over *from* our side, to be with the majority, to hear the lovely music, and to offer premiums upon the bondage of the preachers who are struggling to get free. I mean that every liberal thinker who habitually attends a church traditionally bound makes it a little harder for the liberal-minded minister of such a church to do the perfectly sincere, straightforward thing. "Why should I go," he says, "when, if I stay, they come?" But let us not be harsh or hasty in our judgments of the men who, drawn to us or to our way by intellectual sympathies, still, somehow, find their feet so bound in one way or another that they cannot stir. The late Dean of St. Paul's, in his posthumous History of the Oxford Movement, has written words which we should diligently take to heart: "So subtle, so shifting, so impalpable, are the steps by which a faith is disintegrated; so evanescent and impossible to follow the shades by which one set of convictions pass into others; for it is not knowledge and intellect alone which come into play, but all the moral tastes and habits of the character, its likings and dislikings, its weakness and its strength, its triumphs and its vexations, its keenness and its insensibilities, which are in full action while the intellect alone seems to be busy with its problems." It does not follow, therefore, that the man who soonest acts upon the logical outcome of his thinking is always the best man. If a man were a mere logical machine, that would be a perfectly safe inference; but he is not that. To stay in the old church, when logic says, "Begone!" may mean less honesty,— it often does mean that; but it may also mean more poetry, imagination, heart. It is not a bad thing, it is a very sweet and noble thing, for a man to feel the hold of old associations, to love the venerable house his fathers built to God, and stay in it as long as possible, — till Conscience thunders "Elsewhither for a refuge, or die here." And then comes in the hope of widening the old church, so that the King of Glory, the new truth, may come in and be enthroned. "Come, let us be going," said one friend to another, standing transfixed before Rubens's "Crucifixion" or some other. "Not till they get him down," said he. "Not till they get him down," I seem to hear many a brave-hearted preacher say in churches where the Son of Man is crucified afresh by ignorant, foolish hands. But what is plainer, we are asked, than that, where there are definite ecclesiastical laws and regulations, a man should conform to them and obey them, or take himself off? But it depends. Suppose that he remains, hoping to break up the evil system, break down the obnoxious laws and regulations? And there are those who are staying in the dear old churches of their childhood and their youth, the churches that their parents loved, with this intent; and God forbid that we should do them wrong. The greatest thing in the world is not come-out-er-ism. "Wear it as long as thou canst," said Fox to Penn, wishing to know about his sword. There are those who would have a man cling to his political party, through thick and thin, and leave his ecclesiastical party, his Church, immediately he finds himself diverging ever so little from its creeds and forms. But the grand old Church quite as much as the grand old party has sacred memories, fond associations, binding cords of noble recollection, and high fellowship of souls. Wear it as long as thou canst *honestly*,— the church or party sword. Cleave to the old until there seems to be no hope of better things ; then, going forth, yearn for it ever after with unshamed affection, desiring for it every better thing. And, still, however earnest the appeal to us of such considerations, however helpful to our generosity and fairness they may be, for those entangled in the meshes of a questionable position forever sounds the memorable injunction of the modern seer : "What is incredible to thee thou shalt not, on thy soul's peril, attempt to believe. Go to perdition, if thou must; but not with a lie in thy mouth,— by thy Eternal Maker, no ! "

But in this connection let this, too, be noted carefully: that in the liberal and radical world there are various manifestations calculated to deter those whose allegiance to old things is shaken from breaking with them hastily. What is there in the mere zest of sneering and mocking at whatever is traditional that should attract any man of earnest heart? But such zest of sneering and mocking is pretty much the beginning and the end of a great deal of our modern liberalism which has wholly broken with the Church. Crass, ignorant, and brutal, its contempt for human nature is its most conspicuous trait,— a human nature which, it reckons, has concocted the vast unreality of religion or has had it foisted on it by sordid and designing priests and popes. For it is impossible to think well of human nature, if religion, on which it has lavished so much heart and life, is not of all things the most real. Moreover, the Church, which so often has been denounced as the Refuge of Superstition, may well seem to those within her gates, but not wholly satisfied with her walk and conversation, the appointed Refuge *from* Superstition for this vainglorious and blatant time. Not in the Church, but in the company of those who flout her superannuated claims, I seem to find the grossest superstition and credulity of the modern world. I could believe all the miracles of the Old Testament and New and all the miracles of the Roman Catholic saints more easily than some things which are solemnly put forth for our acceptance and swallowed "at one gulp, like a ripe strawberry,"* just because they are so different from anything which heretofore has been believed. A contemporary sermon on "The Split Mausoleum" is not by any means the most absurd deliverance I have seen of

* The phrase is Dr. Talmage's: he would have the Bible swallowed so.

late ; no, but the ponderous volume of some learned fool who argues that all Jewish and all Christian history for two thousand years as commonly received is but a fiction that was patched up a few centuries ago by wicked monks and Jews. Yet we have here only an aggravated specimen of a genus that has many sad examples in our time, men and women who will strain out a gnat of Christian miracle and swallow a camel of theosophy with a sweet and happy smile. It is less to be wondered at that many, whose position in the Church is far from satisfactory, are asking if something cannot yet be made of it, when we consider the enormous lack of intellectual seriousness and moral earnestness that is characteristic of the mighty and increasing mass of credulous incredulity and superstitious irreligion in our time.

But what have we in such credulous incredulity and such superstitious irreligion but other signs how deep the Twilight of the Gods has grown? At that period of mighty change when Paganism was dying out in Rome there came in a flood of worships and vagaries of all sorts ; and Christianity came also among them, and was accounted by the wise Senecas and Plinys not the least absurd. Such manifestations, now as then, are but the signs of change, the pangs of dissolution,— had we not better say of transformation ? — the travail of a new and higher birth. Shall we not find a happy omen in the sequel to that story of the Götterdämmerung with which we started forth ? It seems the great All-Father was not dead ; and Baldur, the good Baldur, kindest and best of all the gods in Asgard, he came back ; and in the dim half-light, beneath the moaning sea, a fair new world at length began to shape itself, and a new order, better than the old, began. And so for us, even if our twilight of religion should deepen to a night of starless gloom, that night would be the prelude to a new and better day. For the soul of man can no more endure without religion than his body without air and food and restful sleep. " When half-gods go, the gods arrive." And, I think, our twilight of religion will not be of long duration ; rather, like those of which we hear in northern lands, so short that almost before men can say, "The sun has set," it lifts itself again above the horizon's bar. Nay, better even than that,— sweet paradox!— before our sun has sunk, it rises without intervening night, with clearer, kindlier ray. The All-Father has not gone away from us. The good Baldur, the good Jesus, while not yet wholly vanished as a God, comes, as he came at first, a Man once more, with his great compassion, with his warm human sympathy, with his splendid hatred of iniquity and his devotion to all truth and good, to quicken us to ever holier things. There is no good thing of the past that shall not be better in the coming time. There shall be a Bible of completer inspiration, a Church whose ministers shall be all men and women qualified for mutual help, a Humanity of such exalted vision and such glorious hope that it shall seem less strange that Jesus was a man than that all men do not go about to do their Father's business with his zest and joy. O friends, may we so think and speak and act, so strive and so endure, that we may in no wise hinder any of these things from coming to their birth, but rather, albeit in some humblest fashion, speed their happy day.